Writing
for
Ourselves/
Writing
for
Others

Writing for Ourselves/Writing for Others

PATRICK DIAS,
ANN BEER,
JANE LEDWELL-BROWN,
ANTHONY PARÉ,
CAROLYN PITTENGER

Nelson Canada

© Nelson Canada,
A Division of Thomson Canada Limited, 1992
1120 Birchmount Road
Scarborough, Ontario
M1K 5G4

To show your appreciation for the time and effort that the author and publisher have invested in this book, please choose not to photocopy it. Choose instead to add it to your own personal library. The investment will be well worth it.

Every effort has been made to trace ownership of all copyrighted material and to secure permission from copyright holders. In the event of any question arising as to the use of any material, we will be pleased to make the necessary corrections in future printings.

Canadian Cataloguing in Publication Data

Main entry under title:

Writing for ourselves/writing for others

Includes bibliographical references and index.
ISBN 0-17-603507-9

1. English language - Rhetoric. I. Dias,
Patrick X. (Patrick Xavier), 1933-
PE1408.W75 1991   808'.042   C91-094898-4

Acquisitions Editor Allison Cameron
Production Editor Linda Collins
Cover Design John Robb
Text Design Janet Riopelle

Printed and bound in Canada
1 2 3 4   WC   95 94 93 92

In memory of
Professor John Harley,
writer, editor, mentor, and friend.

Bound to stay open

Table
of Contents

ào

Chapter One

Becoming a Writer 1

*Understanding writing and how you learn to write;
how you might use this book*

Chapter Two

Writing for Oneself
and Writing for Others 12

*Key notions about writing; discovering and recognizing
our resources as writers*

Chapter Three
The Writing Self   25

*Developing our personal resources as writers;
keeping a journal*

Chapter Four
Writing with Others   67

*The importance of collaboration in writing; strategies
for working together*

Chapter Five
Strategies for Effective Writing   89

*Ways of overcoming problems in writing:
ideas for discovering, generating, organizing,
revising, and testing your ideas*

Chapter Six
Forms and Forming   128

*Organization and structure in writing; generating forms and
shapes that help you communicate effectively*

Chapter Seven
Writing to be Read   165

Writers' responsibilities to readers and their needs

Chapter Eight
Looking at Language   187

What writers need to know about language and
present-day English in order to make appropriate
decisions while revising and editing

Chapter Nine

The Reflective Writer 228

*Reflecting on your writing and your development as a
writer, keeping a log, responding to writing*

Appendix

Writing with the Computer:
An Introduction 256

*Possibilities and limitations of the computer
as a writing tool*

ACKNOWLEDGMENTS

 è▲

This book is truly a collaborative effort. Named below are the large number of people who have contributed in various ways over the last dozen years to the development of Effective Written Communication, the course from which this book derives.

Helen Amoriggi, Audrey Berner, Cran Bockus, William Boswell, Christa Bartholl, Diane Bruman-Whyte, Jane Cooke, Linda Cooper, Monique D'Amour, Adelle Danovitch, Monique Demers, Anne Douglas, Juliet Dunphy, Robin Eley, Winston Emery, Merle Emms, Paula Engels, Karen Foley, Gerald Frank, Suzanne Frappier, Carolyn Gibson, Patricia Gordon, Sukumar Gowda, Frank Greene, John Harley, Nancy Hicks, Sean Huxley, Keith Johnson, Nancie Kahan, Diane Klempner-Russell, Andree Ippersiel, Elenitsa Kotoulas, Julie Lake, Sandra Langley, Glenna Loerrick, Donna Logsdon, Susan Mac-Donald, Mary Maguire, Jean Mason, Mary Mar, Diane McGee, Gisela McIvor, Kate McNeill, Maireva Mugore, Louise Murphy, Alison Newall, Barbara Newborn, J. Martin O'Hara, Mary O'Malley, Frances Phelan, Norma Prokopenko, Diane Rabey, Helen Raptis, James Rehrmann, Marilyn Rigelhof, Judith Ritter, Sharon Schwartz, Judith Slaughter, Elizabeth Sloat, Donna Lee Smith, Elizabeth Speyer, Ruth Stanton, Alayne Sullivan, Victor Swoboda, Wayne Tefs, Carole TenBrink, Sharron Wall, Janet Warne, Katherine Weary, Sylvia Wees, Claudia Weijers, Theresa Wilson, and Diana Wilson-Sirkovsky.

Most of those listed above are current and former colleagues. They have contributed, through their teaching and their participation in the weekly meetings and annual seminars, to key moments of discovery and gradual shifts in orientation. We have valued most the enjoyment and excitement they brought and continue to bring to inquiring and to teaching. We are deeply grateful.

Among those listed are members of the support staff at McGill University's Faculty of Education. We thank them for the graciousness with which they have responded to hundreds of student inquiries and our regular and frequent requests for assistance. We need especially to mention Louise Murphy, whose efficient handling of course-related work has afforded us some of the time required to write this text. As well, Louise has typed a considerable portion of this book.

Throughout this enterprise—both the course itself and the production of this text—we have enjoyed the strong backing of our senior administrators: former chairs Martin O'Hara, Winston Emery, and John Gradwell, current chair David Dillon, former dean George Flower, and our present dean David Smith.

We remain indebted as well to those who have visited the Centre for the Study and Teaching of Writing over the years and participated in our discussions; the speakers at our annual seminars; the key theorists and researchers referred to in this book; and, above all, the students, who have been our unacknowledged major partners in this effort and the encouraging and questioning recipients of our teaching.

For the opportunity to review their course materials, we thank Professors Mary Dean Lee, Ken Fraser, Eric Denman, Pierre Bisaillon, J.C. Osler, and Gerald Pollock. Our special thanks to Audrey Berner, Juliet Dunphy, Susan Macdonald, Donna Lee Smith, and Sharron Wall, who gave up considerable time to read and review the contents of this book. Their feedback has been invaluable.

Finally, we thank our colleagues, the teachers of Effective Written Communication, who have used the draft edition of this book and have suggested many useful revisions. They have also provided us with some very worthwhile feedback from their students. We thank Diane Klempner Russell for assembling and distributing this information.

We are very grateful to Mr. Milton Truesdell, who set the draft edition of this text, arranged for its printing, and was so patient with our last-minute changes. We thank the reviewers for their careful and intelligent reading of the manuscript: *Phyliss Artiss, Memorial University of Newfoundland; Andrew Seaman, Brian Bartlett, and Margaret Harry, St. Mary's University; Susan Hamilton, University of Alberta; Ritva Seppanen, Concordia University; and Hal Burnham, Algonquin College.* This final version of the book has gained much from their suggestions. Finally, we thank Allison Cameron of Nelson for urging us to write this book and for her continuing care and concern.

ANN BEER,
PATRICK DIAS,
JANE LEDWELL-BROWN,
ANTHONY PARÉ
AND CAROLYN PITTENGER

Introduction

ào

Writing for Ourselves/Writing for Others derives from a ten-year collaboration among teachers and students involved in a lively and successful writing course, Effective Written Communication, taught at McGill University. The book reproduces the assumptions that have directed this course and the procedures for teaching and learning to write that have evolved. In addition, the book describes the contexts within which the practices advocated are likely to be most productive.

Effective Written Communication grew directly from a question asked in a graduate education course on theory, research, and practice in the teaching of writing: How do we develop a writing course that takes account of what we now know about how people learn to write and develop as writers? The question was far more than a theoretical issue. The mid- to late-1970s had seen a virtual explosion in theory and research on writing, all pointing to a considerable shift in how writing ought to be taught at all levels of schooling. Most of the teachers in that course lived this question daily in their classrooms; however, the question took on reality and some urgency with a request from the Faculty of Management at McGill University to develop a one-semester writing course for their Master of Business Administration students and, later in the year, for their Bachelor of Commerce students.

These and additional requests led not only to the outline of a writing course but also to a process of continuing inquiry. Instructors and others interested in the teaching of writing met weekly to review students' responses and course procedures and to consider recent theoretical developments. They monitored each other's classes, and there were yearly course renewal seminars—all these activities driven by the need to keep the design of the course and teaching current and productive. This book is thus the result of ten years of discussion and reflection, a consolidation of developing theory and practice, and a staging point for further learning.

Writing for Ourselves/Writing for Others is addressed to writers at all levels: people who consider themselves novices as writers, people who believe they can write well but who sometimes feel inefficient as writers and frustrated by writing, experienced writers who would like to write more efficiently and effectively, and people who find themselves confounded by writing and see themselves as failures.

Because the book is based on an actual course given to a variety of students from different disciplines and levels of study, readers will find that the principles that direct this book and the procedures and practices they suggest are adaptable to a wide variety of needs, settings, and timetables.

The focus of this book is on learning to write, and in that sense teachers can serve their students and themselves best by being co-learners. Both students and teachers are admitted to these discussions about how we all keep learning to write. For that reason alone, this book should serve as a useful guide for those who are preparing to teach writing and who are looking for principles and practice based on current theory and research on writing.

This book differs from most other books on writing in that it deliberately de-emphasizes the role of the teacher; it insists that students assume responsibility for their own learning, that they look to their own resources and those of their peers. As students develop increasing independence as learners, they release teachers to far more productive activities: designing and managing the writing contexts that cultivate this growing independence, providing useful and critical feedback at the time when the writer most needs it, and recognizing and meeting the individual needs of students.

A Word to Teachers

We wrote this book knowing full well that there would not be a teacher's guide to accompany it. We have therefore worked to ensure that much of the information a teacher might require is included in the text. It is possible that we may not have been as explicit as we needed to be, and we would like to assure readers that we will respond to all queries and requests for advice and information. There are, however, certain guidelines that have emerged from our own use of this book and we are happy to pass these on:

The Role of the Textbook in a Writing Course

We use the textbook primarily as a substitute for the information and argument we formerly provided through lecture, discussion, and printed handouts. Assigning portions of the text to be read outside the classroom allows the teacher more time to answer students' questions about assigned readings and exercises, to respond to their writing, and to try out the writing activities that illustrate principles or strategies discussed in the text.

Sequence

The order of chapters is not meant to suggest a sequence for a course outline. In fact, topics treated in later chapters very often bear directly on the discussions that occur in earlier chapters. This is why teachers will find it necessary to read quickly through this textbook so that they can direct students to particular sections as the need arises. An early familiarity with the contents of this book will also enable teachers to plan a sequence of readings and writing exercises that match the needs of their students and what the course schedule allows.

At the same time, the chapter sequence is not arbitrary—it represents a movement from writing for oneself in a familiar context to writing for other readers within increasingly complex and demanding contexts. Most developing writers need to confirm themselves as writers and to discover their own resources as writers, even as they go on to try out and adopt strategies to deal with more difficult writing tasks.

Classroom Organization

Our classrooms operate as writing workshops. Our students often plan, write, and respond in groups. They write often, exchange their writing, and respond orally and in writing to each other's writing. Exercise 1 in Chapter Two provides an easy initiation to the classroom procedures this book advocates; many teachers, in fact, use that activity as their opening classroom exercise.

Using and Learning Writing Strategies

Teachers will probably find it necessary to refer students to sections of Chapter Five (strategies for effective writing), Chapter Eight (editing strategies), and Chapter Nine (keeping a log), as the need for information about particular strategies and practices becomes apparent. For those students who are not familiar with "brainstorming" and "freewriting," for instance, such direction may come very early in the course. As different strategies are introduced at appropriate times, students should adopt those they find most productive.

Reflecting on Your Writing

Although the topic of assessment and evaluation does not formally appear until Chapter Nine, discussions about this topic need to be initiated early in the course and returned to later.

Writing with Computers

Students who are new to writing with computers would benefit from reading the appendix first or very early in the course.

Usage, Grammar, and Conventions

We have not recommended a specific handbook, and suggest that teachers and students discuss which of the many available are appropriate for their needs.

Writing Exercises and Activities

Writing for Ourselves/Writing for Others demands regular and frequent writing from students. A large part of that writing happens through journals, logs, and freewriting and brainstorming activities in class. Exercises at the end of chapters provide a variety of writing tasks. Some demand writing at length over several days and require a variety of strategies. Others can be completed in one short sitting with the use of one main strategy. Teachers will need to decide which of the writing activities are central to the goals they have in mind and plan accordingly.

We recommend that students save all the written work that precedes the final draft. Such material is particularly useful at individual and group conferences between teacher and students, and can provide students with valuable insights into their own writing processes.

Teaching Together

Teachers of writing need to talk together about what they do and what happens in their classrooms. This text is a means of releasing us from our place at the front of the classroom so that we can observe at ground level what actually occurs in writing classes. It is these observations that will constantly send us back to our colleagues to question, wonder, and plan together and to share disappointments, discoveries, and successes.

Chapter One

Becoming a Writer

❧

So here I am ...
Trying to learn to use words, and every
*   attempt*
Is a wholly new start, and a different kind of
*   failure*
Because one has only learnt to get the better
*   of words*
For the thing one no longer has to say, or the
*   way in which*
One is no longer disposed to say it. And so
*   each venture*
Is a new beginning, a raid on the inarticu-
*   late ...*

T. S. ELIOT, *FOUR QUARTETS*

Many people come to writing with a deep-set belief that being able to write well is a knack—you either have it or you don't. This book works against that notion. Writing is not a single skill; nor is it a set of mechanical skills you acquire or are taught in the early years and retain for the rest of your life with little or no effort. To twist a common expression, writers are made, not born. We are all writers and, in a very real sense, we are all beginning writers. As

1

teachers and students of writing, we are all involved in the process of becoming writers. As long as we struggle to express meaning in writing, we continue to learn to write.

In the last twenty years there has evolved a considerable body of theory and research on writing to help explain how we develop as writers, what makes writing difficult, and what helps us become better writers. Such information makes clearer the relationships between thinking and writing, between speaking and writing, and between reading and writing, and how all these relations influence what and how we learn. We have also learned a great deal from the observations of successful writers and of those writers who experience difficulty. This book builds on this new knowledge and attempts to apply that knowledge to the teaching of writing.

This book contends that, although it is often difficult to write well, there are certain strategies we can apply in order to ease the passage to effective writing. Much of the difficulty we experience in writing arises from our efforts to get our thoughts down on paper—the "raids on the inarticulate," to recall our epigraph from Eliot. This book aims to provide you with the tools to help you conduct these "raids," to discover and develop your ideas, to form those ideas for yourself and other readers, and to make sure they follow the conventions we all recognize as readers and writers.

If you are to develop as a writer, you must understand that writing is not an isolated skill; your skill as a writer is tied in with your skill as a speaker and as a reader, and also with your knowledge of the things you choose to write about. There is a strong link between talking and writing—one that you should learn to exploit more fully. You will feel much more confident as a writer if you begin to see that writing can be as natural as talking, even though it may often require considerable work to achieve that naturalness.

An Overview of This Book

In Chapter Two you will acknowledge and examine your ability as a writer in modes that come closest to natural speech. In this chapter you will take stock of your writing habits—your strengths and weaknesses as a writer. You will write your own personal profile—your history as a writer—and consider the variety of situations in which you will be called on to write.

Chapter Three continues the exploration begun in Chapter Two as you come to realize the power of personal writing—the writing you do for yourself. You will discover a variety of ways in which you can develop your personal resources as a writer, with particular emphasis on the journal.

Chapter Four considers at some length the importance of collaboration in writing and the various ways in which you might try out this particularly productive strategy. We now know that in most business and professional areas, writing together is the norm rather than the exception.

Chapter Five explores a wide range of strategies for getting started in writing, developing ideas, and shaping your writing. This is a core chapter, one you will continue to refer to for a review of particular strategies and schemes.

Chapter Six explores the importance of form in writing—the ways in which you can generate the structures or shapes that help you communicate effectively, and the ways in which forms can either inhibit or free you to write. Can you use structure and form to ensure that readers receive your writing in the ways you intend? How do you exercise such control?

Chapter Seven picks up this discussion and provides exercises that will help you take account of and provide for readers when you write: who they are, what their needs are, and what they know and don't know. How can you assess what is acceptable in the different communities you write for?

Chapter Eight focuses on the English language as a tool, as a living and dynamic resource. This chapter should make you aware of the wonderful flexibility of written English, and the ways in which you can manipulate language for different purposes and situations.

Chapter Nine, which is a concluding chapter only in that it comes at the end of the book, is concerned with helping you become more reflective about your writing. As a writer, you must continually assess what you do: Does your writing do what you intended it to do? What is "good" writing for the purposes you have in mind, and does your writing meet those purposes? If you wish to develop as a writer, you must know what matters and doesn't matter in the choices you make. You will most likely need to refer to this chapter early in your reading for a discussion on keeping a log. Those who have begun to write with the word processor, or are planning to, will find it useful to consult the appendix, which considers the possibilities and limitations of the computer as a writing tool. With the growing use of computers as word processors, you should consider how you can use this powerful tool more productively in your writing.

As you survey the contents of these chapters, you should remember that the chapter divisions are artificial. Topics overlap, and considerations of readers, forms, goals, language, and personal voice enter consciously or unconsciously into every act of writing.

How to Read This Book

While this book can be read privately as part of your own personal education as a writer, we believe it is best read and discussed in community, whether the community be a class, a writing workshop, a computer-linked network, or a group meeting around a kitchen table. If this book is being used as part of a writing course at an educational institution, there will most likely be a teacher in your group. We see the teacher as a writer-learner—someone who is in a position to help you as a writer primarily because she or he is also learning to write. You will notice that many of the writing exercises we suggest assume that a teacher is present; if a teacher isn't present, you should adapt the instructions to fit your own situation. Like all worthwhile education, learning to write always brings us to the edges of what we cannot yet do well and what we still need to learn. If we sometimes speak of this book as a course, we emphasize that it is a course that is never fully run—one can always begin again at an even more demanding level.

Since this book will be used by many different people in many different situations, not everything we suggest will fit everyone's particular needs. In general, we have attempted to deal with the key issues that writers need to consider. While we have arranged the chapters in the sequence we find most practical for our own teaching situations, it is up to each writing group to order the material in this book to fit its needs. Generally, there is a movement, from chapter to chapter and within chapters, from writing for oneself to writing for others; from writing in a familiar and comfortable mode to writing in more formal situations for readers who are distant and public; from writing about straightforward topics to writing about more demanding and problematical issues. As we mentioned earlier, there is no fixed sequence of learning implied by the order of the chapters. The ideal movement is a back-and-forth movement. Where we can do so, we have indicated at several places in the book what pages or sections you might profitably turn to in order to deal with a particular problem or find additional information on a topic. The index will also help you follow up a particular topic. If you have a teacher, he or she will also be able to direct you to the relevant places in the text.

Writing Exercises

In order to help you better understand the writing strategies presented in this book, we have suggested a variety of individual and group writing exercises. These exercises are generally found at the end of each chapter. You need not complete all exercises or even follow them to the letter; your teacher may come up with other suggestions, or you may prefer to change the exercise to suit your own circumstances.

No writing exercise is tailored exclusively to the content of the particular section or chapter in which it is set. Thus you will often be drawing on strategies discussed earlier as well as anticipating strategies and approaches described in later chapters.

Knowledge about Writing

As you go through this book, you will realize that you are being reminded constantly to become more reflective about your writing, to re-examine your writing habits—even the ones you are most comfortable with—and to develop new ones. We want you to experiment, to stay with the experiment and not give up too soon, and to allow for some disturbances and disruptions in your ways of writing.

As you talk and write your way through this book, you will understand that becoming a writer is a process that is never finished. You will see that writing is not just a technique—it is a process that takes place in a social context: the assumptions of communities you write for, and the conventions of the discipline or field of inquiry you work in. This is why working with other writers is important—they make immediately available to you the community that enables you to negotiate and define what it is you need to know and do. It is you and your co-writers who will discover what matters most to you as a writer.

We mentioned earlier that a great deal of research on writing has helped make learning to write less of a mystery. It has helped to dispel the persistent myth that only gifted people can write. In fact, you can all learn to write clearly, effectively, and with imagination. And you need not be at the mercy of the muse, waiting patiently for inspiration. There are ways of tapping into your own creativity and using a wide variety of resources that are more accessible than you think. You just need to know what these ways are and learn how to access them.

If you are an experienced writer, you will find that this book will provide you with the opportunity to add new strategies to your repertoire, and to find new ways to evaluate your writing and the writing of others. These skills will be particularly useful to you in the workplace, where you may be expected to review the writing of others and suggest how that writing can be improved to meet the writer's objectives.

Although we advocate certain methods for learning to write, you shouldn't think of them as a set of inflexible rules. Learning to write is not primarily a matter of knowing some basic rules, a list of do's and don'ts. As philosopher Michael Polanyi has argued, someone performing a skilful act does observe a set of rules, but does not know them as a set of rules (49). Polanyi refers to this knowledge as *tacit* knowledge. In most of our everyday activities, we observe a complex set of rules. Adults, for instance, tend not to use the same language or tone in conversing with other adults as they do with children; customers at a fast-food counter order meals differently from the way they would at a table in an expensive restaurant; there are complex differences between the way people talk face-to-face and the way they talk on the telephone. In these different situations, people apply a set of rules, but do so without being aware of them as a set of rules. As users of language, and specifically as writers, you also unconsciously follow a complex set of rules. As you work through this book, you will become aware of your own set of rules about communication and writing, so that you can confirm those aspects of your repertoire that work well for you and add new strategies where you need to. You may also discover that you have been operating by some rules that are counterproductive and that inhibit expression. You will have a chance to reassess rules you have considered as fixed and inflexible, such as: "Do not begin sentences with 'and' or 'because,' " "Never end sentences with prepositions," and "Always think before you write."

A Writing Exercise

At this point in your reading, you may find it useful to think of your experience as a writer and write freely for no more than fifteen minutes about how you believe you learned to write (that is, learned to communicate as a writer). Who taught you and how? What did they teach you? Are there certain rules about writing that every writer ought to keep in mind? What are they?

If you are doing this exercise by yourself, save what you have written until you have a chance to talk to someone else about this topic and discuss with this person what you have written. Are this person's beliefs about writing the same as yours?

If you are working in a class, form groups of four and discuss for fifteen to twenty minutes what each of you has written. What experiences do you hold in common? What rules? How have these rules worked for you? At the end of your discussion, talk in your small group or in the class as a whole about what you believe you have learned from this exercise.

Working in Groups

As you go through the following chapters, you will discover the various ways in which a writing workshop can operate, and the kinds of writing activities you will be involved in. This book assumes that you will be writing as part of a group, with or without a teacher. Because you are writing in a group, you have at hand a vital resource—a bank of readers, a resource this book takes advantage of. One of the key principles that underlie this book is that we learn much about writing and about ourselves as writers from the responses of our readers. What makes this resource even more powerful is that you are all pursuing the same goal: becoming better writers. By responding to the writing of your co-writers, you not only provide immediate readership and useful feedback, you also learn for yourselves what works and does not work in the particular situation you are writing from.

You will also be writing a great deal in your writing groups. The ways you will be asked to write will not differ much from the circumstances you often find yourselves in as writers: starting off on a blank sheet of paper with a seemingly blank mind, exploring a new topic, searching for ideas, developing something you have already written, and revising on the basis of comments from readers. Your advantage is that you can learn not only from yourselves but from what others do as well.

The Role of Teachers

You may have noticed that we seem to be discounting the role of teachers. We would rather say that we have *redefined* the teacher's role as it applies to teaching writing. No teacher can hand over writing skills as though they were easily transferable items or bits of information that equip you as a writer. Each student must develop these skills by writing; the role of the teacher in this book, then, is to help create the strategic situations that will enable such learning to occur and to provide helpful feedback.

The writing situations will have to be sufficiently challenging if you are to learn anything worthwhile. You should be prepared to take risks—to entertain the possibility of failure. Thus, when you are designing topics to write about, you should allow for sufficient challenge with a necessary mix of prudence: think of your workload, resources of time, and available information, and set realistic goals. But always be sure to set goals that allow you to solve a difficult problem or gain new perspectives. Failure and error can be powerful occasions for learning—temporary setbacks but necessary steps to success. Your advantage, of course, is that you allow yourself several opportunities to learn from your "mistakes" and the "mistakes" of others. And for this you need to write often.

What about Models?

One of the major changes that has occurred in the teaching of writing has been a shift in focus from the end products of writing to the processes that lead to such writing. Over a decade ago, much teaching of writing worked by describing the features and qualities of particular genres—essays, reports, letters, and memoranda—and inviting writers to learn from models in order to produce similar products. Learning by imitation is a time-honoured tradition in education, but it is not a tradition that seems to work well for most people who want to learn to write. Models cannot represent to any useful extent the complexities of the situation that generated the writing. More often than not, beginning writers are reminded how short they fall from the ideal product, and wonder what they must do to arrive at such exemplary texts.

On the other hand, we could ask successful writers to answer questions such as, "What do successful writers do when they get down to writing something?" and "What strategies do they use to deal with writing problems?" Unfortunately, what most successful writers have said about their writing processes does not provide useful answers to these questions. There is, however, sufficient research on the writing processes of successful writers and beginning writers to provide comprehensive and useful pictures of what happens when people write. These pictures have been enhanced by knowledge derived from traditional and current rhetorical theory and from relevant work in cognitive psychology. It is these accounts that have guided the development of this book. This is why you will not find samples of expert writing offered here as models to imitate in your own writing. There will be samples of writing drawn from the work of both student and nonstudent writers, intended to illustrate how other writers have experimented with the strategies we describe.

At the same time, we are not saying you cannot learn from the work of expert writers. We would encourage you to read widely and often, to dwell in and become familiar with the language and forms of the disciplines you will be writing in. Find opportunities to talk about what you have read; it is a practical and effective way of acquiring the language of your discipline. As you read, you will begin to recognize the wide variety of ways in which writers and writing work—ways not intended for slavish imitation, but as useful reminders that each piece of writing is the product of a particular writer and a particular situation, of opportunities recognized and decisions made. You will learn much from reflecting on those situations and those decisions, but the solutions you arrive at for your own writing will be uniquely yours.

In trying to outline those aspects of the process of writing that will ease you into more productive ways of writing, we have not stressed products; nor have we emphasized formats, that is, agreed upon conventions for writing in particular fields and professions. You will discover and master these conventions as you write in various academic and professional contexts.

References And Further Reading

Eliot, T.S. *Four Quartets*. London: Faber and Faber, 1968. Reprinted by permission of Faber and Faber Ltd.

Polanyi, Michael. *Personal Knowledge*. New York: Harper and Row, 1964.

Smith, Frank. *Writing and the Writer*. New York: Holt, Rinehart and Winston, 1982.

Chapter Two

Writing for Oneself
and Writing for Others

࿐

*I like a room with a view, preferably a long
view. I dislike looking out on gardens. I prefer
looking at the sea, or ships, or anything
which has a vista to it.*

NORMAN MAILER

*I prefer small messy rooms that don't look out
on anything interesting. I wrote the last two
sections of* They Come Like Swallows *beside
a window looking out on a tin roof. It was
perfect. The roof was so boring it instantly
drove me back to my typewriter.*

WILLIAM MAXWELL

We all approach in different ways the complex intellectual
task of writing. This chapter asks you to look at your particular writing habits, the rules and rituals you follow—
sometimes unconsciously—as you write. It asks you to
examine your attitude toward writing and your perception
of what writing is for. In a very real sense, the basics of writing are not spelling and grammar but a clear understanding
of why one writes and how one turns data into information
and information into knowledge. To discover and recog-

nize your own resources as a writer and to develop these resources, you must examine the situations in which you write so that you can understand what aspects of your situation inhibit your writing, and so you can turn these situations to your advantage.

This chapter introduces some key notions about writing—notions that recur throughout the book and provide a vocabulary for thinking and talking about writing. Since this discussion is necessarily theoretical and philosophical in nature, and since it is always difficult to read about theory in the abstract, we ask you to do something concrete that will make the rest of the chapter easier to read and use. If your teacher has not already taken your class through Exercise 1 at the end of this chapter, stop and do the exercise now by yourself. It is designed to be done in a group, but it also works as an individual activity. Besides allowing you to make sense of the discussion that follows, this exercise introduces you to the workshop practices that are mentioned throughout the book: writing on request, exchanging your work with other writers, commenting on each other's writing, talking about your own writing, and reflecting on the writing process.

What you may have realized immediately after doing Exercise 1 is that your writing—how you write and with what degree of success—depends to a large extent on the situation in which you write. The topic you write on is important, but just as important are why you write and who your intended readers are. We will explore this subject at some length because it contains a key that will make writing a lot easier for you.

Writing for Ourselves

By "writing for ourselves," we refer to writing in which you are the primary if not the sole intended reader for what you write. In Exercise 1, some or even most of your class may have agreed that writing for yourself or someone close to you (the journal entry or personal letter) is far easier than writing for others (the letter of recommendation). For the first piece, you are not writing to meet the demands of someone you don't know. Moreover, you do not have to guess at what that unknown reader might really want to know about your topic. You can adopt a familiar voice, and you don't have to explain personal references. Writing for yourself is like talking to a close friend, where you can say things like "You know what I mean" and "You know who." In such cases, you usually feel free to take the conversation or the writing in whatever direction you wish. There is no one out there who needs to be informed by what you have written.

Then why bother to write at all? There is considerable satisfaction in using writing to discover what it is you actually think or feel about a particular issue. Graham Wallas in *The Art of Thought* writes of the little girl who, on being told to be sure of her meaning before she spoke, said, "How can I know what I think till I see what I say?" (Such an observation has been attributed to novelist E. M. Forster as well.) Writing to explore, discover, or recall is one of the most powerful aspects of writing, one we hope to further explore in this book.

Writing for Others

Some of you may have found the letter of recommendation easier to write. Is this because you are not used to writing for yourself and that most of your writing is intended for other readers? Could it also be that writing a letter of recommendation suggests a ready-made form to follow? Did writing the first piece make the second piece easier to write? Whatever the explanation, we are coming to understand that ease and difficulty in writing are very much related to the circumstances in which you write. Those who found the letter of recommendation more difficult to write may have come up with several reasons why this was so. As you wrote the second piece, you were probably aware that you were writing to get something done—that your writing would have consequences in the real world—whereas the first piece likely would not. You could not assume too much about what your intended reader knew about your subject, about you, and about your situation—certainly not as much as you did when you wrote for yourself. Your task as a writer was to decide what needed to be said and what could safely be left out. No such selecting was required when you wrote for yourself. You might also have decided to adopt a formal tone and style, and to ensure that your reader would understand exactly what you intended.

Transactional Writing

James Britton, a key theorist and researcher in the field of writing, uses the term **transactional writing** to refer to the writing you do in order to get things done. We encounter transactional writing most often in our working lives. It is writing that informs, explains, clarifies, instructs, and persuades. It is found in business reports, scientific papers, cookbooks, travel brochures, newspaper articles, political speeches, and in instruction manuals. As students, you encounter transactional writing in your textbooks, lab reports, term papers, memos and posted notices. In transactional writing, it is often hard to detect the personal voice of the writer.

Expressive Writing

The writing you do primarily for yourself—in diaries or journals, for instance—would be described by Britton as expressive writing. This writing is more personal and is closer to natural speech. The writer's voice is clearly evident; the writer's feelings and attitudes come through. Britton contends that when we speak, we do so most often in the expressive mode: it is the mode in which we clarify our ideas for ourselves and others. Expressive writing is most often tentative: it encourages us to express our feelings and explore new ideas. It is the writing of diaries and journals, of field notes, of initial observations and records. Britton argues that, since we do not have to do anything with expressive writing, we are free to explore and discover, to find the language that might surprise us, and to follow whatever line of inquiry our writing suggests.

Poetic Writing

Britton proposes a third mode of writing, the *poetic:* "Poetic writing uses language as an art medium. A piece of poetic writing is a verbal construct, an 'object' made out of language. The words themselves, and all they refer to, are selected to make an arrangement, a formal pattern" (90). Unlike transactional writing, poetic writing is not intended to get things done. Britton uses the term "poetic" to include stories as well as any writing where the delight in form and language takes precedence over the need to do something with the piece of writing.

We bring up Britton's distinctions simply because they provide a useful account of the different ways in which we use writing. Most of the writing you do in the academic world and in the world of work will be transactional; much of the writing you do for yourselves—the writing you do not present to others or publish—will be in the expressive mode. In some of that expressive writing you may see the beginnings of a poem or a story or a song. The lines between expressive, transactional, and poetic writing are not sharply drawn—they merge and overlap. What is important to remember is that in expressive writing you have the matrix, or the seedbed, as Britton puts it, from which the more demanding and finished transactional or poetic writing may evolve.

Here is a brief extract from writer Mark Abley's notebook as he travels north to Churchill, Manitoba:

> On the train north from Thompson, I had noticed that the telephone lines soon began to be supported by three poles, like a skeleton tepee, against the post. The train was about 1/3 full. Two Indian boys behind me impressed me by their quickness in spotting ducks and muskrats. They were roused in the middle of the night, a couple of hours beyond Gillam, and stepped off toward a few houses (one with a light on) that appeared to be utterly nowhere, but in all likelihood were at "Weir River"...

Notice how the writer's expressive writing (writing for oneself) moves toward the poetic as he shapes and forms it into a published account (writing for others):

A damp wilderness of shortening evergreens lay beyond
the town's prefabricated buildings and the line of telephone wires. I wondered how many demands, pleas or
loving reassurances were flitting past the stationary train.
In Manitoba's north, the wires are bolstered by a network of tripods, like skeleton tipis dividing up the land.
By balancing three short poles against each other, the
builders guarded against the ravages of permafrost ...

The darkness was intense when we deserted
Gillam, and the windows showed only a mirage of the
inner train. I accomplished the delicate task of removing
and storing my contact lenses at my seat. Sometime
around one we passed the invisible settlement of Bird.
An hour later, a jolt evicted me from a dream of gardens
and blossoming fruit trees: two Indian boys across the
aisle gathered armfuls of gear and stumbled out towards
a shimmer. I tried to find a name on a tripod. Failing,
bleary, I wondered at my need for names. (102–103)

In the following chapter, you will discover a variety of writing activities that show how useful and powerful the expressive mode can be as a means of discovering and finding a
shape for what you feel, recall, imagine, and think.

Writing and Readers

The expressive mode allows you to remain tentative and
exploratory—open to possibilities of meaning—because the
reader is not leaning over your shoulders demanding that
you make complete sense. James Moffett, another theorist
who has helped us understand writing and its variety of
functions, argues that the more our readers are removed
from us in space (they are not within familiar conversational
distance) and in time (they will read what we have written
weeks, months, or even years later), the more we need to
use the resources of the language to ensure that we will be
understood. We become more explicit, and work at finding
the words and structures that will convey exactly what we
wish to emphasize. We cannot rely on our readers to understand us, or expect them to know who we are and what we
mean. We communicate by inflection or gesture, or react

immediately to signs of misunderstanding and provide further explanation. As our demanding, questioning, more public audience comes increasingly into view, the focus of writing shifts from being exploratory and tentative to becoming precise and organized. Our writing now has to work for us across space and time. Moffett's account makes clearer the relationships between expressive and transactional writing. Why we are writing and who our readers are determine to a large extent what and how we write and to what effect.

From Writing for Ourselves to Writing for Others

You might want to think back now to the writing you did for Exercise 1 and reflect on how the theories of Britton and Moffett apply to what you wrote. You may, for instance, write about an interesting incident you witnessed recently, thinking of your best friend as your reader. Think then how that writing would have to be transformed if you had to prepare and sign a legal document concerning what you had witnessed. Think again of an interesting experiment or interview you conducted as part of a formal requirement for a course and how differently you would write about it in notes for yourself, in a letter to a friend, and in a formal report to your instructor. Do you think that doing the expressive writing first would make it easier for you to do the transactional writing?

Writer-based and Reader-based Writing

As you go about your writing, it is important to understand the differences between expressive writing and transactional writing. Linda Flower, whose research on writing has played an important part in the development of this writing course, makes another distinction that parallels the expressive/transactional differences but is not exactly the same. She distinguishes between **writer-based prose**, in which writers intend to write for someone else but are writing essentially to themselves and **reader-based prose**, in which writers deliberately take the reader into account. In expressive writing, writers are knowingly tentative and exploratory and consciously write for themselves or someone close to them. In writer-based prose, however, writers *intend* to write for a reader but seem oblivious to the reader's needs or concerns. A writer-based attitude is particularly apparent in some conversations, where speakers ignore questions and obvious signs of confusion, and continue along the trail of their own thinking.

Writer-based prose can result in some common problems in writing: The writing follows the structure of the writer's thinking, relating events or ideas in the order in which they occur to the writer. There may be an inner logic to the writing, but it is not necessarily apparent to the reader or particularly effective in presenting the details of a problem and its solution. Somehow, the writers must shift the focus of their attention from their own perception of the topic to the reader's goals and needs.

In Exercise 1, you recognized how writing for yourself enabled you to tap easily into what you knew. You may also have recognized how, in the second piece, you shifted your focus to attend to the needs of the reader and the goals your writing was supposed to accomplish. Your task as a writer will often be to transform your prose from writer-based to reader-based. To that end, you might turn to other readers, who will be able to point out some of the egocentric tendencies in your writing. As you grow in confidence as a writer, you will get better at maintaining a distance between yourself and your writing so that you will be able to put yourself in the place of your readers. The first drafts of much of your writing might often be writer-based prose. Because you are focused in those early stages on getting your ideas down on paper, you tend to keep your readers out of the picture. What is important is that you know the difference between such writer-based exploratory drafts and the reader-based final version you wish to produce.

Knowing Ourselves as Writers

We have discussed the theories of Britton, Moffett, and Flower because they help explain why we value writing for ourselves—value it not only for its own sake but also as a bridge toward defining and developing our ideas for other, more demanding readers and purposes.

When we speak of moving from writing for oneself to writing for others and of transforming writer-based prose to reader-based prose, we do not wish to create the impression that all expressive writing or writing for oneself needs to be revised to meet the needs of readers. When you write for yourself, you are often writing to discover, explore, and find a shape for what it is you know or are puzzled by or hoping to resolve and define. Such writing, as you may realize, can frequently be moving, amusing, and informative to readers other than the writers themselves. Think of published letters and journals you enjoy reading. You need only recall Anne Frank's *Diary* or Dorothy Wordsworth's *Journal* to realize that it is the quality of your engagement with what you write that makes your writing accessible to readers. Not all expressive writing, therefore, needs to be revised in order to accommodate the needs of the reader.

Our attention in this chapter continues to focus on the self as writer and reader, but now we need to remind you of the importance of knowing yourself as a writer. If you tried the writing exercise in Chapter One, you may have been surprised by the number of writing rules you either consciously or unconsciously follow when you write. If you are to develop as writers, you need to become aware of the principles, habits, and expectations that control how you write. Exercise 2 at the end of this chapter is designed to help you examine your beliefs about writing and your practices as a writer. You may wish to complete that exercise before continuing to read, or attempt it after you have finished reading this chapter.

Presenting Ourselves to Others

You have been concerned thus far to discover and acknowledge your own resources as a writer. You have drawn on what you know and kept the critical and unfamiliar reader at some distance. Because you are yourself a reader, you have most likely internalized the expectations you bring to writing done by people outside your own immediate situation. You can use your knowledge as a reader to make choices in what and how you write. Consider, for instance, some of the things you thought about your readers when you transformed what you had written for yourself (your journal entry, for instance) into a letter of recommendation intended for someone other than yourself:

- the identity of the person or persons who will most likely read your writing
- your assumptions about what your reader or readers already know about the topic of your writing
- the degree of interest or concern your reader(s) will have for the issue or person you were writing about

Depending on the particular situation, other considerations may enter into the decisions you make as a writer. The more the reader becomes visible to you, the more you need to take account of his or her needs and concerns, the more you need to select and leave out, the more you need to organize and arrange what you have written. You may have become conditioned to think of your reader primarily as someone in the role of a teacher. Most teachers of writing will tell you that you help yourself most when you write from an awareness of the particular goals you hope to achieve and the particular readers you have decided to address, and when you keep your teacher-reader very much in the background.

In subsequent chapters we will discuss readers at some length, but for now, you may wish to think about how you as a writer present yourself to readers: How will your readers regard you? Is that how you wish to be regarded? What do you want your readers to know about you? What don't you wish them to know about you? You may wish to generate other questions along these lines; in any case, look at something you have written recently, and in your group or by yourself try answering those questions. If you are working in a group, use your group to test whether your readers' version of you differs in any important ways from the one you intended. What changes can you make to clear up such discrepancies?

Thus far we have discussed writing that relies for its content on your own experience, and have shown how this writing can be adapted to meet the needs and expectations of your readers. In Chapter Three, we continue to explore how your own experience can be a rich source of inspiration for your writing, and how you can draw on this resource to develop as a writer. In the chapters that follow, we continue to move beyond drawing on comfortable and familiar knowledge toward organizing and presenting new knowledge. As learners in a variety of disciplines, you are constantly faced with the task of incorporating and shaping new knowledge to meet your own needs as well as the needs of readers, and considering ways in which you can draw on the variety of resources that are available to you as writers in our information-laden society

Exercises

Exercise 1: Explore Expressive and Transactional Writing

1. Think of someone with whom you have worked—someone who was particularly good or particularly bad at what they did. You may choose a co-worker or someone who was your subordinate. You may choose someone with whom you worked on a school project.

2. When you have a clear mental picture of this person, write approximately a page about him or her. Using only the person's first name (a pseudonym if you are working in class), write as though you were making an entry in your personal journal or writing a letter to a close, personal friend. Go quickly. Spend no more than five or ten minutes writing. Say whatever comes to mind. Describe the person; record your impressions.

3. When you have finished, think of a situation in which you are asked to write a letter of recommendation or evaluation for this person. (Remember that such letters can be negative or positive.) Think of who would request such a letter and why. When you have invented an appropriate situation, proceed as in part 1. Try to complete this letter in five or ten minutes.

4. When you finish these two short pieces of writing, read them over and make a note of which one you like best and why. Which did you find easier to write? Why?

5. If you are working in a writing group, exchange the pieces you have written. Discuss the characteristics of these pieces. Appoint a

recorder to report back to the class what you found distinctive about the two pieces and the experiences of writing them.

Whether you work with others or on your own, you will want to explore the difference between writing the journal description and the letter of recommendation. You should list several ways in which the two pieces are different even though they are both freewritten rough drafts. Look beyond their content at the style and tone of each piece. Look at the form and structure, and the mechanical aspects like spelling and punctuation.

When you have completed your list, you will be ready to participate in a large group discussion led by your teacher. Return to page 13 for an explanation of the two main factors that shape our writing: our purpose for writing and our intended readership.

Exercise 2: Create A Writing Inventory

A writing inventory is a detailed account of yourself as a writer: your writing history, your writing habits, what works and doesn't work for you as a writer, your aims as a writer, and so on. You may begin by brainstorming and/or freewriting (see Chapter Five) on this topic, using these points as a guide, and then organizing whatever you have written under descriptive headings.

Compare the headings you arrived at with those of other group members, considering what other points you might need to include in order to obtain a fuller picture of yourself as a writer.

You will find it interesting and useful to return to this inventory from time to time to consider whether your views of writing have changed and to what extent, and to add any new information to this inventory. You may draw on your observations in your journal (see Chapter Three) and in your writing log (see Chapter Nine).

One way of beginning your writing inventory is to prepare a list of the kinds of writing you do: personal, academic, or work-related.

The following questions will help you reflect on your writing habits:

Getting Started:
- Do I plan? How?
- Do I have any rituals before I get going and while I am writing?
- How do I generate ideas?
- Do I write ideas down or do I plan in my head?
- Do I read in preparation for writing? While I am writing?

- How much reading do I do in preparation for a paper or a report (in terms of time and number of pages read)?
- Do I discuss my topic or my writing with anyone else?

Writing:

- Do I edit as I write or do I postpone editing until after I have completed writing?
- Do I write at a stretch or do I allow myself planned breaks?
- Do I have certain habits that hinder rather than help me as a writer?
- How do I manage my time?
- How many drafts do I normally produce?
- When I revise, what do I choose to revise?
- Do I read my work aloud?
- Do I show my writing to anyone else for feedback?
- Do I think of my reader(s) as I write?
- Do I write best under pressure?
- Am I generally satisfied or dissatisfied with my writing?
- Does my writing usually do what I hope it will do?
- How do readers usually respond to my writing?
- What are my strengths as a writer?
- What works best for me as a writer?
- What do I find most difficult about writing?

References and Further Reading

Abley, Mark. *Beyond Forget: Rediscovering the Prairies.* London: Chatto & Windus, 1988.

Britton, James, et al. *The Development of Writing Abilities, 11–18.* London: Macmillan, 1975.

Flower, Linda. "Writer-Based Prose: A Cognitive Basis for Problems in Writing." *College English* 41 (1979): 19–37.

Mailer, Norman. Quoted in George Plimpton, ed. *The Writer's Chapbook.* New York: Viking, 1989. Used by permission of Penguin USA.

Maxwell, William. Quoted in Plimpton, *The Writer's Chapbook.* Used by permission of Penguin USA.

Moffett, James. *Teaching the Universe of Discourse.* Boston: Houghton Mifflin, 1968.

Wallas, Graham. *The Art of Thought.* London: C. A. Watts, 1926.

Chapter Three

The Writing Self

ફ**ર્**

Hey world! Come here! I wanna talk to ya!
ARTHUR BREMER, *AN ASSASSIN'S DIARY*

When we are free to select our own subjects for writing, we choose things we care about and want to make others care about. In developing a subject, we use many strategies—from intuition and general impulse to highly conscious and deliberate intellectual techniques like outlining key points or crafting topic sentences. Sometimes we write alone. Sometimes we write with others who help us generate and develop ideas, or realize the worth of our ideas and the effectiveness of our expression. Always we write with language, with words whose meanings we have absorbed from all the other language users around us. Because language is a social creation, even our most private uses of language have social dimensions; likewise, our most public uses of language reflect our individual thought and style.

This chapter is about the more private uses of language, about writing primarily for oneself, to make sense of one's world, to discover the meaning of things. It is based on the premise that reality is not only something we are given but also something we create by using language in public dialogues with others and in private dialogues we have with ourselves. As you read the chapter, keep in mind that writing is a complex activity, and it is probably impossible to completely separate the writing we do alone, for ourselves, from the writing we do with and for others. This chapter talks about one end of a continuum, one way to develop language and thinking skills.

The Journal Keepers

Scholars and poets, beggars and thieves, travellers and dreamers—all manner of people use journals to reflect on the relationship between themselves and the world, and to examine the implications of that relationship. The journal keeper knows that the chaos of life becomes meaningful as we reflect upon it, articulate and shape it with language, or interpret it through art. Indeed, so useful is this reflective writing and thinking, that teachers of all subjects at all levels increasingly recognize its value to themselves and their students. Today the journal is a popular assignment in the writing class. After introducing you to several remarkable people who used journals to develop their inner resources and gain a richer understanding of themselves and their world, this chapter looks at ways all of us—beginning and advanced writers—can use the personal expressive mode of the journal to increase our thinking and writing skills.

Although this kind of writing comes naturally to most of us, we can make it more enjoyable and rewarding if we understand how and why it works, set clear goals for ourselves, establish a writing routine, set up sharing networks, and pause occasionally to draw the value out of our efforts. Of course, writers who come from a culture that does not place strong emphasis on individual expression may find that journal writing is not at all natural. This chapter should help them bridge some of the ideological differences that may impede their ability to keep journals.

A journal—called by some writers a diary or merely a notebook—is a collection of personal observations and reflections, usually kept daily or at some regular interval and used for almost as many purposes as there are writers. Anne Frank's diary, perhaps the most famous journal of the twentieth century, sustained her hopes of freedom and acted as a sympathetic ear into which she could confide her sorrow, vent her frustrations, and dream her dreams. "The brightest spot of all is that I can write down my thoughts and feelings, otherwise I would be absolutely stifled" (159). And well she might feel stifled, locked in her secret annex with seven other people, all holding their breath and waiting for the sound of Nazi jackboots on the stairs. Without space or privacy, Anne created a wider world with her writing, a sanctuary that sheltered and nourished her as long as it could.

Believing that "paper is more patient than man" (2), she used her diary to work out normal adolescent anger, especially toward her mother and her sister: "I soothe my conscience now with the thought that it is better for hard words to be on paper than that Mummy should carry them in her heart." (115) Anne named her diary "Kitty" and considered it her friend, someone with whom she could be herself, with whom she could be completely at ease, completely honest. She used Kitty to help her sort out her feelings and her problems as she struggled to grow up in a frightening and claustrophobic world.

The space and freedom Anne was denied were the birthright of the nineteenth-century American philosopher, Henry David Thoreau, and he gloried in that freedom. Living on the edge of the unexplored American continent, shining and green, he kept journals in which his constant theme was nature, and his strongest belief that "in wildness is the preservation of the world." Although he wrote of many things—language, perception, and the senses, home and travel—the theme to which he returned again and again, and the theme for which most people remember him, was nature. Throughout a lifetime of journals, he never tired of describing nature's dress and moods or of drawing moral lessons from natural objects. A hundred years before it was fashionable to do so, he pleaded with the rest of us to respect the primeval forests:

NOVEMBER 1, 1853

Few come to the woods to see how the pine lives and grows and spires, lifting its evergreen arms to the light, to see its perfect success. Most are content to behold it in the shape of many broad boards brought to market, and deem that its true success. The pine is no more lumber than man is, and to be made into boards and houses is no more its true and highest use than the truest use of man is to be cut down and made into manure ... Is it the lumberman who is the friend and lover of the pine, stands nearest to it, and understands its nature best? ... No, no, it is the poet who makes the truest use of the pine, who does not fondle it with an axe, or tickle it with a saw, or stroke it with a plane. It is the poet who loves it as his own shadow in the air, and lets it stand. (192–93)

While a journal keeper like Thoreau is best known for his exploration of a single theme from many perspectives, others are remembered for their eclectic use of the journal. There is probably no better example of this than Leonardo da Vinci, master painter of the Italian Renaissance. In the notebooks he kept for over forty years, he speculated on every topic imaginable, sketched drawings, planned new engineering projects and artworks, recorded his dreams in minute detail, and copied out whole pages from books he had read. The thirty-one of Leonardo's notebooks that have survived over five centuries testify to his need to write down all his perceptions and observations. A small pad of paper hung from his belt so he could scribble notes on the spot when an idea struck. Later he sorted these little pages, grouped them thematically, and carefully copied them into his notebooks.

For reasons that remain a mystery, Leonardo, who could write perfectly normal script, chose to use mirror writing for all his notebooks. This unconventional script might have afforded him a measure of privacy, but it was hardly a secret handwriting. Reflected in a mirror, his reflective writing is clear and easy to read, and what a range of topics it reveals—anatomy and architecture, sculpture and painting and drawing, mechanics and engineering, literature, science, history, and philosophy. The drawings are equally varied—sketches of flowers and plants and people, along with technical designs for helicopters and parachutes. In the 1400s, when no one else even dreamed of such things, this man designed flying machines and deep-sea diving equipment. It is tempting to believe that the ideas of such a visionary appeared fully formed in his mind in some mysterious, miraculous way. By studying his notebooks, however, we discover that his ideas formed themselves much as ours do—slowly and with the aid of sketching, writing, and reflecting.

To see a single powerful idea growing slowly with the aid of writing and reflection, we have only to look at Charles Darwin's early journals, edited and published as *The Voyage of the Beagle*. One of the most revolutionary concepts of our time—the theory that all the species of animals alive today, including humans, evolved from earlier and simpler life forms—took shape in Darwin's notebooks over the five years he served as naturalist on HMS *Beagle*. From 1831 to 1836, he sailed the globe discovering an unsuspected world and recording in his journal all that he found. Enduring cramped quarters and constant seasickness, he sailed the southern waters to Tierra del Fuego, the Galapagos, Tahiti, and Australia. He made meticulous observations of the exotic plants, animals, and people he found in these remote parts of the world. His descriptions, like this one of the giant land lizard of the Galapagos, are concrete, sharp, and detailed:

> Like their brothers the sea-kind, they are ugly animals, of a yellowish orange beneath, and of a brownish red colour from above: from their low facial angle they have a singularly stupid appearance ...; several of them weighed between ten and fifteen pounds. In their movements they are lazy and half torpid. When not frightened, they slowly crawl along with their tails and bellies dragging on the ground. They often stop, and doze for a minute or two, with closed eyes and hind legs spread out on the parched soil. (335–36)

Darwin noted how these lizards scratch burrows out of the soft volcanic rock:

> I watched one for a long time, till half its body was buried; I then walked up and pulled it by the tail; at this it was greatly astonished, and soon shuffled up to see what was the matter; and then stared me in the face, as much as to say, "What made you pull my tail?" (336)

Naturally, Darwin used the journal for more than making observations; in it he speculated on the meaning of what he observed. In Patagonia, for example, he pondered the enigma of the ancient Megatherium, a creature whose fossil he had discovered, but whose presence on earth had long since vanished:

> It is impossible to reflect on the changed state of the American continent without the deepest astonishment. Formerly it must have swarmed with great monsters ... What, then, has exterminated so many species and whole genera? ... Did man, after his first inroad into South America, destroy, as has been suggested, the unwieldy Megatherium? What shall we say of the extinction of the horse? Did those plains fail of pasture, which have since been overrun by thousands and hundreds of thousands of the descendants of the stock introduced by the Spaniards? (149)

Darwin's careful observations and questions led him inevitably toward the notion of evolution. Of course he was not alone in developing this astounding idea, for no writer's thoughts are ever entirely self-generated. As novelist Virginia Woolf says, "masterpieces are not single and solitary births. They are the outcome of thinking by the body of the people, so that the experience of the mass is behind the single voice" (1929, 68–69). Darwin's masterpiece, *On the Origin of Species*, did not appear until twenty years after the voyage of *The Beagle*, years during which he read and considered the work of other thinkers like Jean-Baptiste Lamarck, the French biologist who believed that acquired traits can be inherited. One of the most powerful influences on Darwin was Thomas Malthus, the English demographer who had earlier claimed that human population will always expand beyond the food supply and had advocated stern limits on reproduction as the only way to improve the condition of humanity. As he read and wrote in his journal, Darwin worked to synthesize and integrate the ideas of other scientists with his own observations and hypotheses. Finally, in 1859, he published his theory, which created a sensation throughout the world and made his journals the most famous of the nineteenth century.

The prisoner and the philosopher, the artist and the scientist—these journal keepers found reflective writing emotionally and intellectually useful if not life-sustaining. But of all the men and women who scribble and jot and note their thoughts in journals, none seem to be more faithful at their task or more conscious of their efforts than the storytellers. Virginia Woolf is a classic example. In journal entries that capture life's outer trivia and inner turmoil, she worked off depression when her writing went badly, savoured childhood memories when she was lonely, and reflected on her own "queer use" of the journal to stave off madness. One day, before leaving her writing to prepare dinner, she noted wryly that "one gains a certain hold on sausage and haddock by writing them down." And, of course, like most storytellers, she used her journal to explore her emotions and find ways to use them in her novels.

Many authors use journals this way—to shape and create meaning, to get experiences to add up to an idea, and to savour emotions. The goal of this kind of writing is not mere release of feeling, but understanding and appreciation. As we remember our lives and reflect on them, something thinks itself in us. It is not so much that we see more clearly what has actually happened, but that, as we look again at what has happened, connections form and thoughts develop that were not part of the initial feeling or event. We need to do this kind of writing, because meaning and knowledge are never fixed once and for all. To reread a book from one's youth is to see it again with new eyes, to understand it in new ways. To write about events that happened yesterday is to approach them with today's emotions and perspectives:

> It seems, as one becomes older,
> That the past has another pattern ...
> We had the experience but missed the meaning,
> And approach to the meaning restores the
> experience
> In a different form ...
> T. S. Eliot, "The Dry Savages" (23–24).

When we are living through an experience—participating in it—we cannot easily stand back and observe ourselves, assess the meaning and value of the experience, and connect it to other experiences. To do this properly, we must stop participating, switch our mode of thinking, reconstruct the experience in our imagination and watch it happening, this time as a bystander or spectator who observes, reflects, and judges. Students on every level find this expressive writing valuable for creating and exploring the relationships between themselves and the world.

As explained in Chapter Two, this writing is characterized by a personal voice—the use of "I"—and by references to personal feelings and thoughts. The tone is casual, like a conversation with a friend, and the vocabulary is the comfortable vocabulary we use every day, including abbreviations, slang, and code words understood only by the writer or someone close to the writer. Expressive writing usually has an emotional component: both reason and feeling are used to make sense of information and assign value to it. Finally, there is an element of play, risk, or experimentation to expressive writing: it often contains imitations and parodies, drawings and doodles, puzzles and riddles, bits of stories and poems.

We can all use this kind of writing in our personal journals to forge a new consciousness for ourselves. Journals are not reserved for talented novelists or distinguished scientists—for those few people who lead unusual or exciting lives. Theirs are the journals we read, because they get edited and published. But we shouldn't be intimidated by these polished works. Our ordinary lives can supply us with a wealth of interesting topics. Think of what the novelist Eudora Welty wrote in her memoirs: "I am a writer who came of a sheltered life. A sheltered life can be a daring life as well. For all serious daring starts from within" (104).

Journals are for all of us who want to think about our world, sharpen our powers of observation and reflection, refine and confirm our values. Because of the ease with which we fall into them, journals help all of us to see ourselves as writers, increase our output and our confidence, find new topics, and hear the energy and authenticity of our natural voice on the page. All those who have problems to solve, feelings to ventilate, stories to tell, or dreams to dream can enrich their lives with journal writing. And journals are the perfect place for any writer to become more fluent in the language, more articulate, more comfortable putting thoughts and feelings into words.

Journals in the Classroom

In a writing class, a journal is a collection of the expressive writing you do regularly on topics of your own choosing. You share this writing selectively with readers who are interested, who can be trusted to listen sympathetically and respond helpfully to what you say. If a particular entry turns out to be extremely private, you can of course elect not to share it, but you should probably expect to produce at least one or two entries each week that can be shared. Try not to create a false dilemma by thinking you must choose either to be personal and private or to write about topics too trivial for anyone to care about. There is a middle ground—an enormous range of subjects you know about, care about, can be honest about, and can share with trusted readers.

These notions may already be familiar to you. Many students keep journals long before they sign up to take a writing class. Some write elegantly on fancy pages with printed borders; some secret their thoughts into locked diaries; others scrawl their messages in tattered notebooks. Whether they pen their lines with purple felt tips or click them out on laptop computers, they write at their own rhythm and pace, according to their own inspiration, and for their own reasons. If you are one of these writers, we encourage you to keep on with the methods you have found comfortable and useful, making only those adjustments needed to share a portion of your work with some trustworthy readers.

Of course, for every student who enters a writing class having had a happy experience in journal keeping, there are many others who have no background in this kind of writing, and even a few who have had negative experiences. Journal keepers must be free to write in ways that are comfortable to them, in their own time, and on themes drawn from their own storehouses of memory and experience. They must be free to decide how they will use their journal. Remember that Anne Frank saw her diary as a friend, Thoreau sometimes used his as a soapbox, and Darwin's was a laboratory notebook. Woolf used hers as a confessional and creative crucible; Leonardo's was a copy-book and sketchbook. Each writer must be free to shape the journal as he or she sees fit.

To ensure a positive experience with your classroom journal, establish your ownership rights from the beginning. Set your own goals and choose your own topics. Conduct your own experiments in the journal. Resist the temptation to ask the teacher what she wants you to write about. And take responsibility for your writing by selecting portions of it to share on a regular basis. Today most teachers who assign journals will show the way by sharing their expressive writing with you: by pinning a page on the bulletin board, by photocopying it and passing it around, or by reading it aloud. They will invite you to respond to this writing as you expect your own to be responded to, that is with thoughtful comments on the ideas expressed, not with corrections.

Many of us, when asked to look at someone's writing, immediately start rewriting it or thinking of ways to correct it. This is especially true in school settings. The urge to edit someone else's work is powerful, probably because this is what happened to our own work every time we shared it. But journals are not for editing; they are for reading and enjoying. The best way to break the correction habit is for you and your teacher to share selected portions of your journals on a regular basis. (Writers seem much more sensitive to each other's work when they are both in the same position.)

If you share journals this way, you will find that the real reward of expressive writing is not a grade, but an inner sense of achievement and growth, the pleasure of having receptive readers tell you what they enjoy and relate to in your work. Of course, even though we do not want our personal, tentative thinking slapped with a "79" or a "67," we all want, quite naturally, to receive credit for the assignments we do in school, including keeping a journal. Most writing teachers simply give you basic credit for keeping your journal as required.

Goals and Expectations

> JANUARY 24, 1856
>
> *A journal is a record of experiences and*
> *growth, not a preserve of things well done*
> *or said ... The charm of the journal must*
> *consist in a certain greenness, freshness,*
> *and not in maturity. Here I cannot afford*
> *[always] to be remembering what I said or*
> *did ... but what I am and aspire to become.*
> *(129)*
>
> HENRY DAVID THOREAU

Start by conceiving of the journal as your own thinking space—a sort of writing laboratory where you can experiment with ideas and language. Write freely every day about whatever you wish. No one will direct you to other topics or criticize what you say. Record the dialogues you are having with yourself in your personal and your academic life. Write about your memories—all the things you've heard and seen and read and felt that you can't forget. Speculate about your future, your hopes and fears, the things you'd like to change. Sort through the dilemmas and problems that challenge you. React to what you see on television and read in books. At the end of each story you tell, try to answer the question, "So what?" Don't reach for profundity, but do speculate on what it all means.

Ask yourself what you would like to accomplish with several months of expressive journal writing. Make your journal useful and valuable to you by setting your own goals. As you do, keep in mind the many traditional uses for this kind of personal writing. To begin, the journal is an opportunity for sustained practice in writing. Many of us find writing difficult because we lack practice. As school budgets tighten and class sizes expand, teachers are limited in the amount of writing they can assign and read and evaluate. In universities, some students, intimidated by the hard work and meagre rewards they find in writing, select their classes according to whether or not papers are required. They say it is even possible to get a degree in some fields without ever writing more than brief answers on their exams. The more practice they miss, the more they fear writing and avoid courses that require it, thus creating a vicious circle.

The larger community also offers us fewer and fewer opportunities to write. People who once kept in touch with each other by letters now use the telephone. Even personal notes or congratulations on special occasions are now the domain of commercial greeting card companies. The journal is an antidote to all this. It provides infrequent writers with a comfortable place to articulate thoughts and feelings on a regular basis.

Those who already do a lot of writing in school or on the job find in their journal a chance to enjoy the pleasures of writing under less pressure and without the need to edit for a critical reader. No matter on what level you operate, writing is always a struggle. No particular method or textbook can make you successful unless you have considerable practice. You need a place like the journal where you can work constantly at expressing yourself and developing a continuing and growing awareness of what you do as a writer.

The people we call authors—those who publish their work—practise constantly. They have writing routines. Whether they write standing up, like Ernest Hemingway, or with their toes, like Christy Brown, they write regularly. As the writer Flannery O'Connor said, "Every morning between 9 and 12 I go to my room and sit before a piece of paper. Many times I just sit there for three hours with no ideas coming to me. But I know one thing: if an idea does come between 9 and 12, I am ready for it." Set yourself a goal of daily writing and you'll find that, with time, more and more ideas come, and writing gets easier. Of course, writing never gets really easy and there are always dry periods, but with regular entries, your journal grows thicker and you prove to yourself that it can be done, you can write, you do have something to say. As one student explained at the end of her writer's journal, "I learned that even when my mind is blank, it really isn't—it is full with ideas and I need only a pen to write them down."

Besides establishing a habit of writing, regular expressive writing in your journal can help you develop two very desirable writing abilities: speed and fluency. When you write expressively, you are not worried about a critical reader, so you don't need to stop and edit for correctness and consequently lose your train of thought. Nor is there any need to stop and search outside yourself for things to say since you are drawing from your own pool of images, memories, and significant moments. Writing expressively without constant pauses to reread, reword, and edit the text produces its own fluency and coherence. As you concentrate on saying what you mean rather than worrying about the form of your text, you automatically write in ways that are familiar and easy to control—storytelling, listing, surveying, free associating. And by concentrating on meaning, you don't keep losing the threads of logic and emotion that lace your ideas together. As you pick up speed, you may make mechanical errors in spelling or punctuation, but your sentences will make sense, unlike the awkward or totally garbled sentences that sometimes show up in drafts. These truly incoherent sentences may be written by a writer who does not understand or is not interested in the ideas being expressed; but more likely the writer has simply stopped several times in mid-sentence to grope for more correct words or to criticize what has been written so far, and then started again, often with a different grammatical construction. After several start-stops, the writer finishes with a sentence that has lost its syntactic unity—its connecting, structural thread—and is actually several sentences spliced together.

As you pick up speed and fluency, you may learn another lesson: how to transfer this speed and power to the essays you write in school and the memos you write at work. Many writers claim that the most difficult part of writing these formal papers is getting started. Often they seek the perfect introduction or wait for some bolt of inspiration—techniques that lead only to frustration or procrastination. Yet these same writers, once they finally do get into the paper, find that the act of writing itself creates the ideas and the motivation they were seeking. Once they start making meaning, new possibilities emerge. They begin to discover what it is they really want to say. Journal writing can help all of us see that the traditional advice to plan what we are going to say before we say it doesn't always make sense. We can't always get our thoughts clear before writing. Indeed, often *it is only in expressing our thoughts that they actually become clear to us.*

Expressive writing can help us develop something else often missing in school or business writing: commitment to a topic. We all need time to work on things that interest us, to write about topics that will not be evaluated, corrected, or redirected by an authority figure. When we follow our own inclinations and include our own emotions, opinions, and personal values, we develop a sense of ownership in our writing. We see it as ours to shape and use, to give or not to give. Without such ownership, we just don't feel connected to what we write. Building such connections is a way to become enthusiastic about our work and determined to make it the best we can.

One of the qualities most important to any writer is confidence, yet university students and people who write regularly in their jobs routinely report that they lack this essential ingredient. To increase confidence, we all need to write more often and to share our work. When a sympathetic fellow writer reads our expressive pieces and is affected by them, we become confident that our ideas can affect others and are therefore worth sharing. We begin to want to affect others this way, to move them with our stories. Our confidence grows. It is this confidence, along with a strong desire to write and a lot of hard work, that will make us writers. Of course it is also important to master the conventions of standard English and to learn traditional ways to structure arguments and texts. But these alone cannot make anyone a writer. Writers need courage, confidence, and a desire to write as much as a fine sense of grammar and proper spelling.

Perhaps the number one reason most of us have difficulty developing our writing abilities is that we are not sure we have something worth saying, so we are reluctant to share our work with a reader. We hold back either from a lack of commitment or a feeling we won't be understood or appreciated. The journal, with its emphasis on personal topics and trusted readers, encourages us to let go, care, and give—all the things we have to do to develop our writing abilities.

Of course there are more practical goals you can set for your journal keeping. You can keep track of good ideas you may want to use later on as do all manner of professionals: scientists, managers, teachers, engineers, artists, and inventors. You may use your journal as a time organizer or as a calendar of important events. You may use it for brainstorming ideas or practising specific writing techniques. The practical uses of a journal are limited only by your imagination. In a recent writing class, one student used her journal to reflect on the job she was doing as a swimming coach. She planned her activities in the journal; after the lessons she recorded what had happened, evaluated the effectiveness of her coaching, and planned new activities. Another student used a large part of his journal to reflect on the lectures and readings he was assigned for a philosophy course he was taking during the same semester. Even though the philosophy course did not require any journal writing, he felt that writing freely about his reactions to the new ideas he was learning was a valuable way to make sense of the course and a good use of his writer's journal.

Along the same lines, a math student mixed logic problems and journal writing. *Skim* through the following entry from his journal and notice how he talks himself through an exercise, puts forth hypotheses ("I think ... Perhaps ..."), tests them out ("Now to see if my translation of this idea into symbols is also correct ..."), and reflects on the results. Toward the end, he also reflects on the act of journal writing and its value to him as a mathematician.

ECL JOURNAL   LOGIC EXERCISE   SAT. JAN. 20

This morning I am going to mix math homework
with my journal.
Two examples from logic notes:

1) NOBODY LOVES EVERYBODY _____ (A)
First I would think it best to clarify "NOBODY"
and "EVERYBODY". I would say that this statement means:

    THERE IS NO ONE WHO LOVES EVERYONE
_____ (A1) WHICH SEEMS SPECIFIC
ENOUGH.
$\forall x$ = all x , $\exists$ = there is an x (or there are)
L xy is the function which says   X loves Y

$\therefore$ My interpretation is

$$\neg \exists x \; \forall y \; L xy$$

(no X) there is not one   who loves everyone (all y)

EXAMPLE IN NOTES: $\forall x - \forall y \; L xy$ _____ (x)
which means (to me)   for all x (for not all y, x loves y)
         everybody loves not every body _____ (x1)
   or everybody doesn't love everybody _____ (x2)
which doesn't seem the same as
       Nobody loves everybody _____ (A)

x2) Meaning ambiguous perhaps. Everbody can
mean either a) everyone at the same time —
ie. the whole block of humanity or b) everyone
ie. each one and every one.

$\forall x$ is clear — for all x or everbody
$-\forall x$ is less clear — I would say that it means
    not everybody
$\exists x$ means someone, somebody
$-\exists x$ means nobody

Returning to first statement A) Nobody loves everybody
and interpretation of $\forall x - \forall y \; L xy$ _____ (x)
    everybody loves not everybody   (x1)

These two statements seem to be equivalent now,
if I think of the first everybody as meaning "each
and every one". But I think it easier (clearer)
to write nobody as $-\exists x$ ie. "not someone"
seems clearer than "everybody not".

So my interpretation $-\exists x\, \forall y\; Lxy$ should be
equivalent to $\qquad\forall x - \forall y\; Lxy$ if the notes
are correct and I properly understand the
statement.

Perhaps expanding this to the longer expression
will help. Setting universal set as set of people,
ie. Humans H.

$\forall x - \forall y\; Lxy$ becomes $\forall x \left[H(x) \Rightarrow -\forall y\, (H(y) \Rightarrow Lxy) \right]$

or for all x (there is a human x) there is not
everybody who is loved by x
or for all x not everybody is loved by x.
or everybody loves not everybody
ie.   nobody loves everybody

So I have finally convinced myself that the
interpretation of the example, and my interpretation
have the same meaning.
        ie. everybody loves not everybody $\equiv$ nobody
                loves everybody
Now to see if _my_ translation of ╱ into symbols
is also correct.

$$-\exists x\, \forall y\; Lxy$$
$$-\exists x \left[H(x) \wedge \forall y\, (H(y) \Rightarrow Lxy) \right]$$

ie. There is no human x, such that ~~every x is loved by all y~~
    x loves all y,
    nobody   _everybody_

$\therefore$ Nobody loves everybody.
Which seems more obvious to me.

So, what is the purpose of writing this all
down in my journal?

These simple problems have been bothering me
a lot. If it looks simple I expect to understand

it quickly. If it takes time I get anxious. When I am anxious, I lose my ability to proceed in an orderly way. Writing everything down seems to help to solve the problem.

WHY:
1) I can see where I have been and I don't have to repeat
2) Visual - turns problem into a more visual concept — I can "see" a direction - a train of logic
3) I can "see" where I have not been able to make certain (afterwards obvious) connections

for example, on page 1 I arrived at:
     Everybody doesn't love everybody _____(x2)
or even before   Everybody loves not everbody _____(x1)
which I said, doesn't seem to be the same as
     Nobody loves everybody _____ (A

On page 2, I arrived at (x1) and concluded (A

What happened in that interval.

A softening of a barrier.
I think that I was looking for falseness.
In going back through the analysis, *everything is correct, ie. both the example and my logic. Was I insisting before on finding one right and one wrong? It seems to be the only explanation - a resistance to seeing I might be right, and the teacher, at the same time.

Truth is, it just took a long time for me to understand that:
Nobody loves everybody $\equiv$ there is no one who loves everyone
and, Nobody loves everybody $\equiv$ everybody loves not everybody

$$\forall x - \forall y \; L_{xy} \equiv - \exists x \, \forall y \; L_{xy}$$

As someone keeps telling me CONCENTRATE!

I think that I will try organizing myself by writing my way through these problems. Seems too long, but I spent days trying to figure out the above simple example in my head – inconclusively. At least now, after a half hour of writing, I feel that I really understand it.

In the meantime, does nobody loves nobody mean everybody loves somebody? somebody loves everybody? there is no love? maybe nobody don't care.

If you find Neil's entry about the logic problem difficult to comprehend, remember that it wasn't written to be comprehensible to you, an outside reader. It was written to help the writer think his way through a problem, and like all first thinking, it is tentative—circular, digressive, and repetitive. The writer speaks in a sort of code as we all do when we think privately. When you write in your journal, you will discuss and explore topics that are significant to you—from Saturday morning cartoons to serial killers—and when you do, you will speak in your own code.

Here then are some of the goals you might aim for as you set out to keep your writer's journal:

- Seek insights into your own behaviour, solutions to personal problems, and challenging areas of your own life to explore.
- Get to know what you sound like on paper when you are not trying to satisfy a particular reader like your boss or your teacher.
- Practise articulating thoughts and feelings—finding words for what you want to say.
- Establish a habit of writing—a routine.
- Improve your image of yourself as a writer and develop confidence in your abilities.
- Develop speed and fluency.
- Take ownership of your writing and become committed to your topics.

- Learn how to court inspiration and motivate yourself to write.
- Enjoy writing.
- Share your writing and feel the reward.
- Learn how to use expressive writing to break through writer's block, to get started, and to generate ideas.
- Learn to discover new ideas and recover old ones from memory.
- Record good ideas.
- Track your progress as a writer.

Procedures

The artist Paul Gauguin began his private journal by writing, "This is not a book," a line he repeated frequently through-out the journal to remind himself that he was free to write what he chose as he chose, free to experiment and play, free to ignore the rules and conventions that dictate how books are composed. Gauguin was right: there is no correct way to keep a private journal, and no one to tell you whether to use pencil or pen, a leather-bound volume or a dime-store notebook. You choose your own materials and you design an approach that lets you achieve your own goals. If, for instance, you want to create a habit of writing, then you fix a regular time for making entries. If you want to make a record of your good ideas, then you carry your journal with you at all times so you can capture a good idea whether it occurs while you are flying along at 36 000 feet or waiting in line at the bank.

When journal writing becomes part of the assigned work in a writing class, however, your journal ceases to be entirely private, so you have to write in a way that allows you to share portions of your work. If you use a bound journal book, be prepared to photocopy some sections. If you use a loose-leaf notebook, you can occasionally remove pages easily for sharing. While a pencil allows you to make changes, ink is more permanent and easier for your reader to read. You may enjoy typing your thoughts directly onto a word processor and collecting the pages in a loose-leaf binder. If you write this way, be sure the printer gives you copies that are dark enough to be read easily. Whatever method you use, leave four or five blank lines after each journal entry so that, if you do decide to share it, a reader will have some space to write a response or a comment.

When keeping a journal as part of a writing class, you will want to make daily entries your goal. To improve your writing skills you must behave like a writer, and that means sitting down to write every day and writing more than a few lines. A full page is the minimum target you should aim at. Don't be content with short entries that merely record the events of your day. Each entry should be long enough to help you discover an idea, something you feel is worth saying. Push beyond observations to reflect on their significance: question and explore the facts you write about. Guess, wonder, argue, rant, cheer, justify—turn your observations into visions.

Use your journal to promote serendipity, that marvellous aptitude for making desirable discoveries by accident. Don't worry too much about appropriate topics. Use each entry as an opportunity to find something whose existence you can't even imagine when you first sit down to write. Dip into your stream of consciousness and net whatever floats to the surface. Concentrate on meaning as you write, not on form or mechanics. No one will be evaluating your spelling or punctuation, so try to turn off the editor in your head. Write quickly. Don't race, but don't stop frequently to reread or plan what to say next. Let your ideas lead you.

For most of us, this is a natural way to write; it comes easily. However, some of us have not really experienced the power of personal, expressive writing. This may be because we come from a culture that does not support individual expression. Or it may be because, all our lives, our writing has been directed and distorted by others, stretched out or chopped up, corrected or rejected. We have learned to write by rules imposed on us from outside rather than by releasing the energy and meaning within. Now we need to unlearn some of our habitual ways of approaching writing, or at least suspend them temporarily. The technique called **clustering**, developed by Gabriele Rico and described in her book, *Writing the Natural Way*, may help people who are not comfortable with free-fall writing, who want a sense of direction to get them started.

Clustering is a nonlinear form of brainstorming. The writer free-associates strings of words radiating outward from a key word or concept for a minute or two, then looks at the results, perceives a pattern or a sense of direction, and uses that insight to start a piece of expressive writing. Consider the following example of a student clustering exercise:

"Joy to the world, the Lord is come." Sounds of Christmas past echo in my brain. Silver bells and Rita's laughter, and carols sung in the old stone church by the river. At midnight mass candles glow on the altar, flames sway in the cold drafts. People cough and shuffle their feet as the priest chants the ancient Latin rite. Rita's eyes shine in the candlelight. She pulls her red shawl closer and takes Steve's hand. Later at home she holds the angel up to Steve standing on a ladder reaching for the top of the fat balsam. Laughing, she teases him about getting a Santa suit next year, getting ready for their first baby, already on the way. How could anyone know in a week she'd be gone? How could anyone prevent the drunk on New Year's Eve taking mother and child, and all the future Christmases, leaving silence and tears. The poet says, "He who kisses the joy as it flies will live in eternity's sunrise," and perhaps she does, but Christmas is not the same.

The cluster printed above contains a line from a carol, a piece of poetry, and a number of words that create images. The writing that follows the cluster is fragmentary, like poetry, and narrative, like a story. It is deeply emotional and personal. Most writers who use this technique claim that it helps them get beneath high-level abstractions and say things that really matter to them. It helps them write expressive pieces that resonate with strong feeling and vibrate with energy. The exercise at the end of the chapter will introduce you to the techniques of clustering.

Try this strategy by writing two short pieces. First write expressively for ten minutes about a specific emotion such as fear or love. Then choose another emotion. This time start with a cluster and follow it with the same ten minutes of expressive writing. When you've finished, compare the two pieces of writing. What differences do you notice? How do you explain these differences? If you do this exercise in class, you may wish to share your writing with others in your group and see if there is a general pattern of differences. Of course, if the writing is too personal to share, you should not feel obliged to do so.

Despite the ease of techniques like simple reflection and free association (clustering), some students report that after several weeks of writing in their journals, they run out of topics. If you have this problem, remember that no one can provide you with a personally meaningful list of topics or tell you what to *say* in your journal, but the following is a partial list of some things you can *do*. You are free to set your own goals; these are only suggestions.

Dump Your Feelings

When you are about to explode with anger or frustration, use your journal as a dumpsheet. Pour your feelings onto the page. Don't worry about being fair or even rational. Just write down your anxieties, your gripes, everything that is cluttering your mind. Go quickly and write for at least ten minutes. When you finish, looking at what you've written may help you evaluate the situation objectively and decide on an appropriate course of action.

Log Your Dreams

Record all you can remember of your dreams when you wake up in the morning. Or write about your daydreams. Elaborate on them and use them as prompts for stories. (A related activity is **guided imagery**. Daydream on paper by imagining yourself in your own beautiful, ideal location. Paint the scene vividly. Populate your scene with things you love, people who are special to you. Bring in a wise person or magician, someone real or imagined whom you want to talk to.)

Make Lists

Lists are a wonderful way to bring order out of confusion. You can make lists of all sorts of things: questions you need answered, fears, hopes, significant events in your life. You can list the things you'd like to change or the goals you hope to achieve. Lists can call up the times you'd like to relive or the unhappy experiences you'd change if you could. If it has been a while since your last journal entry, you could use a list to summarize what's happened since then. On a day when so many things have happened that you feel overwhelmed, a list can help you see the day more clearly and feel more organized and in control. Lists can suggest topics you want to explore.

Sketch a Portrait

Create a word-picture of someone you want to understand better. Try to capture not only this person's physical features, but the mental and emotional and spiritual aspects of the person. You can write about someone you like or someone you dislike, or even someone you only know through a book or a film. It might be an imaginary person.

Describe Something

Whether you choose a place, object, or event in your life, include as many concrete, vivid details as possible so you will really remember what is described ten years later when you are reading your journal.

Write an Unsent Letter

Use this technique for sensitive issues that you cannot actually bring yourself to discuss with your reader. Write to someone you know but cannot approach. You might write to someone in the future—perhaps to a son or daughter who is too young to understand you now—or someone in the past—someone who was important in your life but who is no longer around or close to you.

Create a Dialogue

The fun of this technique is that you get to provide the responses for both sides of a conversation. You can talk with someone or something: your body, aspects of your personality, or even your own **writer's block**. (Dialoguing with your internal critic when you are feeling blocked and can't write may help you to identify what's wrong, a first step toward fixing it.) This technique is a kind of role play that often produces surprising insights.

Shift Your Viewpoint

Write about yourself as "he" or "she." Write about someone else as "I." You can combine this technique with the dialogue or the unsent letter to help you see a situation from a sharp new perspective.

Respond to What You Are Learning

Use your journal to comment on your reading and lecture material. Provide your own examples of the concepts discussed in your classes. Connect the ideas you are learning with your own experiences. Such entries will move your journal in the direction of a learning log.

Explore Special Interests

We all have areas of expertise: hobbies, jobs, skills, arts or crafts, areas we've studied or read up on. Use your journal to record and guide your growth in one of these special areas. For example, you could keep an inventor's journal, a coach's planbook, or an artist's notebook.

Sharing

Since you keep a journal for your own pleasure, to record and validate your own experience, the primary reader of the journal is you. The expressive writing that fills its pages is rough, unedited thinking about issues you care about. Some of this writing is bound to be private and should be kept in a section of your journal that is not shared with other readers. This is easy to do if you keep your journal on loose-leaf paper in a ring binder.

Although you are your own first reader, you are not your only reader all the time. The act of writing is so intimately connected with reaching out to another person that it is difficult to write without addressing someone. But who is the reader? Or as Virginia Woolf asked, "Whom do I tell when I tell a blank page?"

One student who kept a journal in a recent writing course wrote several entries to her father who had died two years earlier. She was still angry with him for not taking better care of his health and for not being able to demonstrate his affection for his family. In some entries she carried on a dialogue with him by writing his parts: "I know what you're thinking..." "You believe that..." "You probably will say that...." Later she reported that these expressive dialogues had helped her clarify her thinking—that by imagining her father's words, she had come to see the situation through his eyes. But most of the time she addressed her instructor.

At the end of the semester she wrote, "It is funny how anxious I have become to get your comments on my journal entries. I am not sure if you and my journal are one and the same, but I always feel better, as if I have talked to a close friend, after writing in my journal."

The reader addressed by most journal keepers is someone who will understand and appreciate what is said. Perhaps the easiest audience to address is your future self. If you think of your reader as the person you will be many years from now, you'll be encouraged to capture as many details of your life as you can. As you record your experiences you will naturally include sights, sounds, tastes, smells, and physical sensations—for these above all things trigger the memory, to which nothing is ever really lost.

However, it can be difficult to move from an imaginary, ideal reader in your head (whether it is your future self or another sympathetic listener) to a real flesh-and-blood reader in the classroom. Some writers fear that sharing their expressive writing will inhibit them, that they will not feel as free to experiment and take risks and write about personal subjects if they know a reader will be looking at their words. But for most of us, the urge to write withers if there is never any sharing with a real person who responds to the thoughts and feelings we pour out on the page. Psychologists explain that if we do not get the appropriate response to our expression of emotions, we stop communicating and eventually lose interest in the world. What is true for personality development in general is also true for our development as writers. We need people to respond to our expressive writing, to encourage, sustain, and confirm us as writers. It requires courage, however, to share personal, tentative thoughts—courage and trust.

We have many reasons to be hesitant about sharing this writing. We know our thoughts were relevant and significant at the moment they flowed out onto the page, but now the words lie there, locked into print, incapable of change, while the mind whirls on, and its thoughts live and grow into new patterns of meaning. Then there is the problem posed by the emotional content of expressive writing, which makes us especially vulnerable to the responses of a reader. Just knowing there is to be a reader may cause us to lock on our psychological censors. Lastly, sharing expressive writing is problematic because of its unconventional form and unedited condition. When we wrote, we concentrated on meaning, not on form or mechanics like spelling and punctuation. Will a reader see through the externals of language to what we are trying to say? Will the reader sit in judgment?

Clearly, if we are to share expressive writing we need a special reader, someone we trust, someone who knows what expressive writing is, *someone who also writes and shares his or her expressive work*. Teachers who keep journals themselves and assign them to students take special pains to be this kind of reader. They invite you to share some of your entries at regular intervals and they respond to them in a positive and supportive fashion. They never correct your wording or your thinking. What's more, they model this form of response for you and your classmates so that you can learn to be supportive readers for each other. In an ideal situation where everyone in your writing group is doing expressive writing, you should be able to share your work with your fellow writers. Just select something you want to share and read it to your group. Tell them you want them to hear it and they need not worry about how to respond. Of course, you may read some response into the way they smile or don't smile, but that is not the point. The point is that you are heard. You take a chance, you take responsibility for your words, you give of yourself and your ideas.

After you are comfortable just sharing your work this way, try reading your expressive pieces to each other and providing only positive feedback, saying how the writing made you feel, what parts you liked best and why. To get a feel for the kinds of response that are appropriate for expressive writing, look through the following journal sampler. The entries collected here were written by students who shared portions of their journal with the instructor of their writing course.

Journal Sampler

夜行黄沙道中   辛弃疾

明月别枝惊鹊，   清风半夜鸣蝉
稻花香里说丰年，   听取蛙声一片

七八個々星天外，   两三点雨山前
舊時茅店社林边，   路转溪桥忽见

The translation of the above poem:

The moon's brightness permeates the branches and frightens
the birds.
Midnight, the chirps of cicadas accompanies the refreshing
breeze.
Fragrance of the blooming paddy tells the year's harvest.
The frogs' sounds are everywhere.
Seven or eight stars are in the far-away sky.
Two or three drops of the rain are in front of the mountain.
Long time ago, there was a thatched hut beside the forest.
At the turning of the road, a creek and a bridge would be seen.

I know that the above translation may not make sense to
most of the people. In fact, the Chinese one doesn't make sense
to me either when I went through it word by word. But to read
a Chinese poem is not a matter of how well you can understand
each word's meaning. The most important thing is if you can
get a picture and its significance in your mind. When you get a
whole picture in your mind, you can start appreciating the poet's wording.

The above poem can really give readers the picture of the countryside at mid-summer night. It talks about moon's brightness, cicadas' chirps, breeze, blooming paddy, frog sounds, stars, rain drops, thatched hut, creek, bridge, etc. All those things can give reader a vivid picture of the countryside.

The poem was written by a famous poet in ancient China. He was also a general. Most of his poems are full of patriotic spirit but he could also write an idyll. Like the one we have.

Thank you for sharing this poem with me. I feel enriched by it, which is surely part of the poet's intention. How often we need to refresh ourselves with such an idyll in the midst of urban ugliness and literal language.

She's sitting next to me on the couch. Maybe next isn't the right word—we are glued together watching whatever there is to watch on T.V. that night. I can feel the warmth of her body next to mine and the regular rhythm of her breathing. I look across at her once in a while and see the reflection of the television in her eyes. My lips make a smile, but she doesn't notice. I continue gazing at the tiny images on her eyes, and she realizes I've been looking at her. She smiles and I smile even more. I have a relaxed feeling in my body as my arms tighten around her waist and her head falls to my shoulder. I'm still smiling. When I think of her the feeling seems to come from my chest and not from where I know the thought is going on. There's something to the heart being able to feel emotions. How can centuries of writer-lovers be wrong? The warmth of her head against my neck reminds me of a fireplace with only glowing embers and a shag carpet that feels like a bearskin. My eyes close and I can see the future. Her face is a little older, her hair grey and in a ponytail. But I still see the same person I see now. Her radiance just as strong. She's looking at T.V. again, little Alpo cans flash on and flash off in her eyes. I'm grinning now. She turns to me again and she smiles, not just her mouth but her whole face. I feel a slight shiver and pull her closer once more.

WOW! I'M IMPRESSED with this WRITING and completely KNOCKED out by the fact that you decided to share it. Such a deeply PERSONAL piece usually ENDS up iN the pRivAte section OF the jouRNAl. I like the way you show RATheR than tell and the WAY you combine a gentle cadence with A strong message. These days one hears of so many problems between men and women -- abuse and ABANDONMENT. what a delight to hear of WARMTh and commitment instead! (who SAYS MEN CAN't EXpRESS their FEElings?)

Whew! What a day. I'm finally getting relaxed and ready to jump into bed. Today, I finally think I really, I mean really, found out what self-employed is all about.

First, I managed to sleep in late. When I finally did wake up, it took me forever to get ready. I rushed downtown, met Bette, had lunch, and attempted to finish my mock layout for Sun Life. I managed to get my proposal in shape, but the layout had a lot of work left in it. I started work at 2:00 and only finished at 7:00. But the end product was unblemished. I was satisfied with it and had no hesitations when I handed it to the security guard at the Sun Life front desk. What all this taught me was the responsibility of owning my own business. I really enjoyed running around today. If it was anything else, I don't think I would have even wanted to do it. Sure I was nervous and I panicked. Sure I was somewhat disorganized. Sure I cut it close to my deadline. And best of all sure I produced a professional attractive document which Sun Life Management will be sure to take a good hard look at.

All day these thoughts were running through my head like wildfire. Is the masthead right? Should I switch the typeface? Does the newsletter have the proper feel ... look ... taste? And I knew definitely that I had the perfect front cover.

I managed to get the pieces working together, instead of being individual parts just sitting side by side. The text and images flowed and pulled the reader's eyes across the pages.

The only problem is that I am up against two marketing/communications firms. Disadvantages: they have a name, they have more ideas. Advantages: I am more affordable, more personalized service. I think this is the first time in my life I have felt afraid in this way. I am scared of losing the contract. And I am scared of winning the contract. It would be my first real corporate contract with a major, established firm with real estate holdings reaching over the $2 billion mark. Yeah, I'm scared.

And once again everyone has been behind me all the way. Especially Bette. She had her own work to do today, yet at lunch and after work she helped me touch up the proposal. She really is one of a kind. She isn't at all selfish. She gives of herself and doesn't ask for anything in return. I guess that's why we are the best of friends. And I know she'll be there for me if I don't get the contract (knock wood!).

I am still young and I have many business years ahead of me. And even if I fail to succeed in my business, at least I tried. And I will have learned a great deal from the experience. As that old adage goes: "Man learns by his mistakes."

I can feel the adrenalin pumping through this page! Best of luck with the endeavour. And keep me posted about how things turn out.

It was raining and it was dark at the corner of Jean Talon and Outremont. There is hardly anyone around because it is dark, but the streets are full of water. There is too much water. My mother and brother want to cross the street from Dr. Tsouchas' office because Costa was sick. The cars are not passing, but all of a sudden, as my mother—who carries my brother in her arms—tries to cross, the car hits her. She is not moving. My brother falls on the windshield. The driver gets out and my father, waiting in his car, runs to see. It is so cold. It is a September night. My mother is just lying on the black pavement. I do not know what to do. I never thought an accident could happen in my family, to people I love. Yet it has happened. It is still raining. My father gives a black umbrella to a woman passing by and screams to someone to call an ambulance. My brother seems all right but he has scratches on his leg, on his forehead. His beige sweater is wet, dripping. My mother is unconscious, she does not speak. I do not know what to do. In the middle of Jean Talon Street where so many times we had walked and so many times we had shopped ... the ambulance is coming. I can hear it because of the siren. It is coming closer and the red lights are flickering. My brother's shoe is missing. His little white shoe is no longer on his foot. The ambulance driver and others try to put my mother on the stretcher. My mother is still unconscious. I do not know what to do. I cry, but nothing else. I remember seeing the ambulance drive away and hearing the siren ...

How did your mother come through this terrible accident? I hope she survived AND is well NOW. Your writing about this incident is powerful — disturbing as a dream, elegant as a scroll unwinding.

Today I got back the set of journal entries I gave you last week. I read the comments and could not believe that you liked them. It is wonderful to be praised for the work you do. I look forward to sharing more entries now. I particularly like the fact that you read them and respond to them ... In one entry I talked about the time an automobile hit my mother. Well, thank you for asking how she is. She is fine now, although she cannot work, she cannot lift heavy loads, and she cannot walk or sit for long periods of time. She needs to lie down often or else her leg hurts quite a bit. Her leg hurts most when the weather changes because she broke her pelvis in three different places in the accident. Her leg also gets swollen from time to time. I prayed she would come out of the hospital alive, and I did not care whether she walked again ....

I have a painting on my wall and it is very dear to me. It is painted on canvas and measures twenty-four inches by twelve inches. It is a painting of an Inuk woman with a baby on her back. You cannot see the baby—but you know she is there

I AM RELIEVED to LEARN your MOTHER SUR-
VIVED the ACCident, anD I hope she will
continue to get well. It is cleAR that you love
her very much.

sleeping. You can tell the sun is shining on her because you can really see some shadows of her hair on her face. The woman is smiling with her teeth showing. You can tell that this woman has done a lot of work with her teeth because it shows the flatness of them. Also it shows how she had used an old piece of cloth to tie her braids.

The painting means a lot to me because it used to belong to my cousin Akkittiq, who committed suicide two years ago. The painting is of his mother. One day he told me that he would always keep the painting even when his mother dies. In our culture, when a person dies, his or her photographs and belongings are destroyed. I knew how much the painting meant to him and how much he loved his mother.

When my daughter was born, I named her after him— Akkittiq. I used to wonder about the painting after he died— wonder whether it was destroyed or taken by someone who does not know the value of it. One day I asked about it. It just so happened that it was put away in storage. I wanted my daughter to have it because of her name.

When she is old enough to understand, I am going to explain the meaning of the painting to her. I have already taught her to say *anaana* (mother) when she looks at it. One day she will understand all about the painting, and I hope it will mean a lot to her—as much as Akkittiq meant to me.
I'm sitting in the library looking out at the football field. There's a game going on. The sun is setting. People are sitting around on the grass watching. The leaves are changing colour and some have fallen already. The McGill flag on top of the arts building is waving ever so slightly. I feel removed—watching it yet having no part of it. It looks like everything I thought university would be, yet everyday life here hasn't been like that—hasn't

Thank you for sharing this special and very personal piece of writing with me. It taught me much about your Inuit heritage and the spirit of your people. I especially enjoyed the rich feelings that vibrate through it - the pity and tolerance, the fidelity and love of children. And strangely I felt a kinship to the woman in the picture. Perhaps she is an archetypal mother to us all.

been what I expected it to be. Did it (they) let me down? There's an image of it that you see and feel before you get here—yet it wasn't quite like that for me. I'm not sure if they let me down or if I let myself down. Partly both, I guess.

Did I make the wrong choices, get involved in the wrong things? I know I didn't organize my time well enough, but does anybody? There's been so much guilt and worry. There have been funny kinds of social pressures—sometimes a pressure not to get work done. If your friends are behind, they don't want you getting ahead of them, and then again you don't really feel like doing it, so if you know that no one else (in your group of friends anyway) is going to do it, you don't feel bad if you don't get it done either. I wish I were more motivated to do it— to hell with them. I want to learn, but I don't have enough will power. The work is hard and I need help. Sometimes the professors and tutors are helpful, but sometimes not.

Opportunities I've missed. I always wanted to be on a team of some kind. Not being very athletic, I've had to rule out varsity and intermural teams, but the leagues that are organized for just anyone to sign up—I tried once, but even on these teams there's no tolerance for someone who's not good, so I gave up. We didn't practise enough, and there was no coach, so how could I learn and get better? Maybe the answer lies in just sticking with it anyway—but it wasn't any fun, and this *was* recreation—it was supposed to be fun. Hmmmm ... maybe after a while it would have become fun. Will life always be full of regrets or will it get easier? I mean do you learn not to regret, or do things happen in such a way that it leaves you with fewer things to regret?

Being able to do and choose the things that make you happy is a gift or a talent—I don't know which. Knowing what will make you happy is also a major achievement. Come to think of it, knowing when you are happy—at the time—is not always easy. I wish I could look back on my university days and say I was happy—and know it was true. I know I will look back and say I was, but I'll be influenced by nostalgia.

Sometimes I think I'm like a wet dishrag—no backbone—maybe that's what it takes—being smart enough to know what will make you happy and then having the determination to get it. Just think—it's as simple as knowing where to work and when to play and not letting anyone interfere with that. No more wishing—wishing you had done more work so you could go out—wishing you hadn't let yourself get so diverted and waste time and consequently no more sleepless nights of worry, no more guilt headaches. I feel like I've made a major discovery—but I know I've thought along these lines before. Maybe writing it down has helped.

I enjoyed your description of the campus and your graduation reflections. You made me wonder about my own definition of happiness. I guess for me it is a by-product, something I can't plan for, something that comes when I am pursuing other goals like drawing a picture or teaching a class or reading a journal entry like this one.

I wake up each morning tired, groggy and poorly rested. And each morning I swear I'll go to bed earlier from then on and get at least 7 hours of sleep. Undoubtedly, however, I'll end up going to bed late again the next night. I could never figure out why I tortured myself like that, but the cycle has continued since day one. Upon talking with other students in residence, I found they faced the same situation. No wonder everyone's always half attentive and falling asleep every class.

It wasn't until tonight that I realized why we persist in this sleep deprivation routine. There just aren't enough hours in the day to spend a third of it in an activity that appears very unproductive on the surface. Self-control is one of the main determinants of how early we go to sleep, but it is well known that university kids display the least amount of self-control of anyone. The main culprit in prohibiting sleep, however, is the classic university student debate on whatever issues might be brought up. Just tonight, some people on my floor were arguing for two hours on abortion. Once I entered, of course, I got hooked into the debate and of course had to stay long enough to get my ideas across clearly. I'd have been fine if I'd left after voicing my opinions, but when I thought about leaving, the topic changed to rape. Well, no doubt, I had to stay a little longer to get my two bits in there. The next thing you know, we were soon changing topics, from rape to religion, to the existence of God, to UFO's, to Ouija Boards, etc. etc. etc. Of course for each of these topics, I had to listen to what everyone else said, and had to state what was on my mind. This continued, and it wasn't until two and a half hours later that I figured that I had to leave. On top of the time lost while arguing, we still had schoolwork to work on. By the time all was said and done for the day, it's already the next day. This explains the late schedules that students follow, eventually producing a zombie-like pack of undead in class. So there ends up being sort of a tradeoff between learning schoolwork vs. learning outside of class, since the debates are great ways of learning things and expanding our minds.

So if you ever see a student asleep in class, please be understanding—he was probably just trying to learn something.

I love this explanation! Actually, I agree whole-heartedly about the value of such discussions (and for some reason they are best late at night, aren't they?). If university students can't do this, then who on earth can? It would be a sad day if studying and learning were only a matter of classes and exams.

• •
Playing with style in the manner of Queneau—

NARRATIVE: One sunny day, I was riding my bike to Montreal and it was very hot. So hot, so hot I couldn't believe it. I tried to go further to dry up with the wind, but it only got me sweating more. Then, looking to my right, I saw a banana tree sweeping by and understood why it was so hot: I had gone all the way down to Trinidad.

Of course, I had been dreaming the whole thing since I don't even own a bike ...

MATH: During a time interval (t = 0, t = 86400) sec, while a source located at infinity was emitting photons, my pointevise representation I was describing a parametric trajectory C towards point P (R, 90°, 45°) in spherical coordinates (origin at centre of earth sphere of radius R $\approx$ 6.37 x 10). The temperature function $T(\pi, o, \varepsilon)$ was very high, in the vicinity of T (R, 90°, 45°). My pointevise representation I converted potential energy into kinetic energy with the unexpected result of obtaining more calorific energy instead of causing an air-friction drying process. Then, directing a vision vector $\vec{\Pi} = \bar{T} +\langle 90°$ for T // C, I' I found myself located at the point of a large cylinder from which hung small yellow ellipsoids. This was the key element yielding a solution by inspection to the temperature function: I, instead of being I(R, 90°, 45°), was I(R ,85°, 5°), which explained the odd behaviour of T π, o, ε in this vicinity).

The solution, however, was unacceptable, for it was located in the imaginary part of the coordinate system.

NOTATION: In the summer. Myself, biking to Montreal. Way too hot. Tried to step on it. Didn't dry: sweated even more. To the right: a banana tree. Guess I overdid it. Went down to Trinidad. O.K. Just woke up. All a dream. No sense anyway: don't have a bike.

WORD COMPOSITION: I was Montreal-bike riding on an impossible-to-believe hot summer day. I tried to wind-refresh myself by fast-biking and ended up being tired-stinking-wet. Taking a right-look, I did a flash-idea-generated-understanding about the temperature because of the banana-tree-seeing revealing I was really Trinidad-riding.

My bikeunpossessing explained that I had been sleepgenerated-imagely misled.

· · · · · · · · · · · · · · · · · · · ·

your delightful parody of Queneau has shaken forever my image of engineering students as serious, dry, and conventional. I loved the neologisms, the Joycean wordplay and absurd story. Bravo!

Notice that the responses in the sampler are meaningful comments on the ideas expressed in the entries, not corrections or global remarks like "interesting" or "very good." In a brief sentence or two, they show that the reader has heard the message and shared the feelings—that's all. Notice also that these particular entries are easy to respond to because the writers are concentrating on saying something that really matters to them. Entries like Neil's logic exercise, printed earlier in this chapter, are less sharable, more coded, and harder to respond to even though they are perfectly valid entries.

Not all your expressive writing experiments will turn out like these. Some days you can go on for pages; other days you have trouble filling a single sheet. But as long as you focus on issues that are genuinely important to you, the journal will be valuable to you and interesting to those with whom you share it.

Evaluating the Journal

For many of us, the word "evaluation" is synonymous with testing and grading, but in truth "evaluate" simply means to draw the value out of something. Like all journal keepers, you should pause from time to time to do this kind of evaluation; that is, reflect on the writing you are doing in your journal and its value to you. You can do this informally by sitting with a group of fellow writers and discussing your journal achievements and problems. Such an exchange can renew your motivation, suggest solutions to problems you are encountering, confirm your discoveries, and expand your awareness of what is actually happening to you as a writer.

In a writing class, your evaluation may take the form of a summary you share with the instructor. Whether you are preparing for an informal discussion or getting ready to write a more formal summary, you can lay the groundwork by answering these questions:

- Now that you've kept a journal for some time, what do you think a good journal is in the context of a writing course?

- How satisfied are you with your journal? Is the experience what you expected it to be?

- What do you like most about keeping this journal? What do you like least?

- What problems have you encountered? How have you solved them? What problems remain?

- Are you meeting the goals you set for yourself when you began your journal?

- How often do you write? How much do you write each time? What do you use your journal for?

- Is expressive writing in the journal affecting your attitude toward writing or your writing ability?

- Can you think of ways to increase your enjoyment of journal writing or its usefulness to you?

But let us not end here—at the end. Let us return to the beginning, to the blank page that awaits. In June of 1942, Anne Frank looked at all the lovely blank pages in the new cardboard covered notebook she had received for her birthday and penned these lines:

> I haven't written for a few days, because I wanted first of all to think about my diary. It's an odd idea for someone like me to keep a diary; not only because I have

never done so before, but because it seems to me that neither I—nor for that matter anyone else—will be interested in the unbosomings of a thirteen-year-old school girl. Still, what does that matter? I want to write, but more than that I want to bring out all kinds of things that lie buried deep in my heart (2).

Anne speaks for all of us who would nourish the writer within. In spite of fears that our lives are not elegant or important, that no one will care to read what we write, or that our work won't measure up—in spite of all, we must tell the stories that lie buried in our hearts.

Exercise: Cluster and Freewrite

1. Put your key word in the middle of a page and draw a circle around it.
2. Instruct yourself to think of images (word pictures). Ask yourself what you see, hear, smell, and feel when you think of the key word. Be receptive to bits of songs, poetry, proverbs, jingles—anything concrete.
3. Now relax. Avoid consciously judging or choosing. Just let all the words that pop into your mind spill out on the page.
4. *Circle each one* and draw connecting lines between those that seem related. The strings of associations that cluster on the page may tumble out randomly, but a pattern will emerge when you stop and scan the cluster.
5. Suddenly you get a sense of what you want to say, where you should begin. If you try too hard, however, nothing will appear. Relax.
6. If you still see nothing, write a focusing statement that summarizes your cluster, and use that as a start.
7. Once you've got your sense of direction, write quickly and look back to the cluster only if you need more details. (Most writers leave the cluster behind entirely and just write.) Don't try to use everything in the cluster. Just use what feels comfortable, what fits.
8. As you get to the end of your writing, finish it off by repeating some aspect of your beginning—a word or phrase or idea or image. We know we have reached the end of a piece of writing when we find ourselves back at the beginning.

References and Further Reading

Bremer, Arthur. *An Assassin's Diary*. New York: Harper's Magazine Press, 1973.

Darwin, Charles. *The Voyage of the Beagle*. Toronto: Bantam Books, 1958.

Eliot, T.S. *Four Quartets*. New York: Harcourt, Brace and World, 1943. Reprinted by permission of Faber and Faber Ltd.

Frank, Anne. *The Diary of a Young Girl*. New York: Pocket Books/Washington Square Press, 1952. Reprinted by permission of DOUBLEDAY, a division of Bantam, Doubleday, Dell Publishing Group, Inc.

Mallon, Thomas. *A Book of One's Own: People and Their Diaries*. New York: Ticknow & Fields, 1984.

Murray, Donald. *A Writer Teaches Writing*. Boston: Houghton-Mifflin, 1968.

Rico, Gabriele. *Writing the Natural Way*. Los Angeles: J.P. Tarcher, 1983.

Thoreau, Henry David. *Journal*. Cited in Eliot Porter, *In Wilderness Is the Preservation of the World*. New York: Ballantine Books, 1967.

Welty, Eudora. *One Writer's Beginnings*. Cambridge: Harvard University Press, 1983.

Woolf, Virginia. *A Room of One's Own*. New York: Harcourt, Brace and World, 1929.

_____. *The Diary of Virginia Woolf*. 5 vols. Edited by Anne Olivier Bell. New York: Harcourt Brace Jovanovich, 1977.

Chapter Four

Writing
with Others

ॐ

It's difficult to work with others when you're omnipotent.

Q (ALL-POWERFUL MISCHIEF-MAKER FROM "STAR TREK")

In a writing workshop, participants read their work aloud, give and receive criticism, and collaborate on group papers. They work together to invent ideas, develop goals and plans for writing, draft, and—most of all—revise and edit their drafts. This struggle to negotiate meaning is never neat and tidy. While differences of opinion within the group challenge and stimulate writers, these disagreements also threaten them. Most of us recognize that we should welcome contrary ideas, for it is within the tensions produced by opposing views that learning happens; still, disagreement and confusion are always unsettling. To take full advantage of the opportunity writing groups offer us for fostering thinking and imagination, we need communication skills and specific strategies for monitoring the group process so that everyone receives a fair evaluation for the learning that takes place. This chapter discusses the growing trend toward group writing in all domains—in creative and literary as well as functional and technical subjects. It offers general advice on working with a writing group and specific strategies to help you communicate honestly with your group members and evaluate fairly the learning that happens in your group.

The Writer: A Romantic View

What do you see when you picture a writer? A Byronic poet alone in a garret scratching lines on parchment with a quill pen by flickering candlelight? Or something more modern— a bearded fellow in a flannel shirt, isolated in his mountain cabin, seated by the fireplace with only his computer keyboard and laser printer for company? These romantic, solitary, and predominantly male images of the writer are deeply ingrained in most of us. When asked to picture a writer, we don't usually see someone in a social setting. We don't see professional women and men—scientists, lawyers, teachers, engineers—working together, helping each other plan documents, invent ideas, word difficult passages, or edit manuscripts. We all know that these people, collaborating with their colleagues or working alone, write regularly to further the knowledge of their community and help it do its business. Yet these people are not what we think of as writers. The writer is someone we learned about in English class—the author of novels, short stories, and poems—someone apart from us, someone with more sensitivity and creativity, more insight and talent. This writer writes alone.

We all live in mythological frameworks without knowing that we do. This is what our image of the writer is—a romantic myth. Like all myths, it has some truth to it: novelists and poets do sometimes describe their writing situations as mysterious and themselves as isolated. For example, Yugoslavian novelist Negovan Rajic, a man who has lived in Canada for the last twenty years, claims that his quiet rural life so far from his homeland is ideal for writing: "To be a writer is already to be an exile. I am merely in a condition of double exile." While most writers don't go to such extremes, we can all appreciate a tranquil spot for writing, somewhere away from the noisy distractions of the world. But this aloneness is not all there is to writing. There is much that is false in the myth of the isolated, alienated soul observing humanity from afar and giving solitary birth to his masterpieces. Every writer collaborates with others, directly or indirectly.

The Writer: A Social View

According to James Reither and Douglas Vipond, there are three kinds of collaboration. In the first and most direct form, *co-authoring*, a team or group of writers produce a single work. Each author is acknowledged by having his or her name appear on the cover. In the second form, *workshopping*, individual authors share their works-in-progress with trusted and conscientious colleagues who act as readers and help them solve problems. These readers may help invent or clarify ideas, point out inconsistencies or gaps in information, suggest new sources of information, point out strengths on which to build, or correct grammar and mechanical errors. They give support and encouragement by expressing faith in the writer's ideas and abilities. The valuable assistance of these colleagues is recognized and credited in the writer's acknowledgment page. In the third and least direct form, *knowledge making*, authors write alone, but they collaborate with people they have never met—with all those in their field who have written and spoken before them. In each area of knowledge—literature, journalism, psychology, criticism, history—what has been written and spoken by others forms a sort of grand conversation that each new writer must fit into if she or he is to contribute to the knowledge making in this field. By reading widely and studying in one area, we learn what has been said, what needs to be said, and how to say it. We learn what can be taken as knowledge and what must be spelled out. We learn to recognize dominant metaphors and catch phrases, appropriate styles, acceptable ways to structure arguments and make citations. This long-distance collaboration may be difficult to acknowledge, but we do our best through quotations, allusions, footnotes, and bibliographies.

Given these three definitions of collaboration, let's look again at those writers of fiction who seem to be solo performers. Do they really work in a vacuum? Surely they read widely and draw from a common pool of stories and words.

Their work is shaped by all the writers they have read, by the cultural and linguistic forces that surround them, and (whether they admit it or not) by the reception they get from their readers. They have editors and publishers who work with them, friends who help them refine and shape their ideas, and families who sustain them. The novelist John Gardner, for example, acknowledges his wife's contribution to his writing: "If I have any doubts about what a character would say or what a room would look like, I ask my wife ... Perhaps I should have used 'John and Joan Gardner' on the titles all along: I may do this in the future." (222). Of course, he couldn't really do this because a co-authored novel is more likely to be greeted as an oddity than accepted as a genuinely artistic work. In the artistic world, it is acceptable to collaborate on a film script or record album or theatrical performance, but a co-authored poem or story would break with our modern, romantic belief in individual self-expression as the source of high Art.

In the realm of nonfiction, however, things are different. Here writers are more comfortable admitting the degree to which they collaborate with others. Essayists and critics, letter writers and report writers, journalists and researchers get help from colleagues; sometimes they co-author papers. For example, a team of scientists publishes a single article. (Just look at the work of medical researchers published in any recent issue of *The Journal of the American Medical Association.* Even the editorials are co-authored.) Government negotiators draft treaties together and spend long hours revising them to everyone's satisfaction. Teachers and school administrators collaborate to produce course outlines, calendar descriptions, committee reports, proposals, and policy statements.

This group writing in today's workplace is encouraged by a wide array of new technological tools: teleconferencing, electronic boardrooms, local area networks, and electronic bulletin boards and calendars. This new technology helps groups schedule activities, keep records, and communicate with each other; it even assists their decision-making. More exciting yet is the whole new class of software called groupware, which permits group outlining, drafting, revising, and editing. It is now possible for a management consulting team composed of specialists in marketing, information science, and economics to collaborate via computer on a single consulting report to a client. Likewise, an advertising firm can use groupware to let artists, copywriters, and sales people create a new ad together.

To learn just how much collaboration actually goes on among writers in the workplace, Andrea Lunsford and Lisa Ede recently surveyed seven professional organizations. When they published the results of their survey, they concluded that, although there is still a deeply held belief in our society that writing is an individual activity, in these professional associations collaborative writing is a fact of life. A full eighty-seven percent of the 530 people who responded to the survey reported that they sometimes write as members of a team or group. They brainstorm ideas together. They work together to plan their writing goals, analyze readers, research material, and share drafting responsibilities. They edit each other's work.

University Writing Groups

Recognizing the increasingly collaborative nature of writing in the workplace, some universities are designing more group writing projects for their students, offering them an opportunity to sharpen their group process skills, develop positive attitudes to group work, and learn strategies for writing in groups. For example, at UCLA, second-year MBA students work in groups to do a field study project that functions as the equivalent of a master's thesis. Their task is to write a twenty-five-page report that defines, analyzes, and solves a strategic problem for a sponsoring organization. (A strategic problem is one that affects the organization's goals.) The students control the entire project. They form their own groups, design the project, select the organization with which they will work, and choose the faculty members they want to act as their advisors and technical experts. They receive a common grade for their efforts.

At St. Thomas University, Professors James Reither and Douglas Vipond organize all their classes as collaborative investigations. There are no formal lectures or individual papers. Instead, each course sets a question that the students answer as part of a research team; their task is to divide the work, gather information (usually from the library), make sense of what they find out, write reports on their findings, and present these reports to the whole class. The course concludes with the publishing of a collaboratively written course book that contains each group's contribution to the subject. In this way, one of James Reither's English classes investigated how Lillian Hellman's work was shaped by the community of playwrights to which she belonged. Another class studied different ways of thinking about form and structure in two of Shakespeare's tragedies. Since there are no grades given to individual papers— indeed, there are no individual papers—the grade students receive for the course is determined partly by their effort and participation and partly by the value of their contribution to the learning of others. To determine this, all students in the course write a confidential assessment of the degree to which they have been helped by all the other students.

Co-authoring and other collaborative writing projects have even popped up in creative writing classes. At the University of Oregon, for example, author Ken Kesey (*One Flew Over the Cuckoo's Nest*) and a group of thirteen graduate students recently collaborated on a novel during a year-long writing class. The book they wrote, *Caverns*, was published by Viking Press in 1990 under the group name U.O. Levon.

Despite such moves to include collaborative assignments in the curriculum, however, competition is still the rule in most North American classrooms. As they write alone, competing for grades, students frequently learn to withhold information from fellow students and even tell outright lies to maintain a competitive edge. Whatever the benefits of such attitudes, they do not serve well the student of writing who needs social interaction to expand language skills. Authenticity, original thought, and personal responsibility develop best when writers collaborate with their peers—when they support and challenge each other in a workshop environment where they share research tasks, read each other's work, and even co-author papers. Writing with others, paradoxically, is the way one finds one's individuality. As writers test out ideas, they find resistance and differing perspectives. They are challenged to use the tensions of these conflicting viewpoints to create something new.

However, developing writers are understandably nervous when they find themselves in a workshop that requires group interaction. Suddenly, they have to present their writing to the group for judgment, and this can be a potentially threatening situation. To be helpful to their partners, they have to engage in a specific kind of reading, one that takes writing teachers themselves a long time to master. They have to take each other seriously and accept advice from each other as they would from their instructor. In some workshops students are further required to co-author papers for a common grade. This particular writing assignment raises more questions: Will this be an efficient way to write? Why bother doing this when I can do it faster on my own? How will I get credit for my share of the work? What will happen if someone in the group does not pull his or her weight? How much will I have to compromise? Will I be able to take criticism constructively?

Whether you are co-authoring or workshopping, you will find useful strategies and answers to your questions throughout this book. Chapter Five shows you ways you can work with others to locate a subject, generate ideas about it, determine an appropriate reader, and find developing patterns of ideas and supporting details. Chapters Seven and Eight discuss ways you can use the insight of your peer readers to help you revise and edit your papers. The remainder of this chapter looks at the benefits of collaborative writing, ways to set up groups and get started, strategies to support the group process, and ways to handle problems that might arise in group work.

Benefits of Writing with Others

A collaborative workshop setting offers you a number of rewards:

1. Improves Your Writing

Research shows that, for complex tasks that involve prob-lem-solving, **collaborative learning** results in higher-level reasoning, deeper understanding, and longer-lived reten-tion. By collaborating with other workshop participants, you can improve the quality of your papers; that is, you can gen-erate more ideas in the **synergy** of group brainstorming, develop your ideas more fully with the perspectives afforded by your peer readers, and improve the mechanical correctness of your texts with the help of peer editors. While you turn out a better product, you will be comparing your strategies with those of your fellow writers, gaining insight into your process and more control over it.

2. Increases Your Motivation

Group writing can help you discover new ideas, new capac-ities in yourself, new enthusiasms and interests. Writing teacher Peter Elbow explains: "When people ... find them-selves in a group where their words are heard and under-stood better than they usually are, they discover messages they want to send which they previously learned to ignore because it seemed impossible to get them heard" (123).

Group writing can help you see that writing is fun. If you have come to see it as a lonely, frustrating experience—perhaps even a punishment—the support of your writing group may free you to focus on the joys of writing and the range of small and large satisfactions it offers. With co-writ-ers or workshop colleagues, large tasks don't seem so large; ideas take shape quickly and are affirmed. Progress seems more immediate as your group members enjoy your works-in-progress—your new ideas, clever arrangements, and felicitous phrases. The sharing of works-in-progress also helps keep you on schedule and less likely to become impatient and frustrated.

3. Develops Critical Thinking Skills

Collaborative writing situations require you to formulate questions and solve problems. Through exploratory talk in a small group setting, you express and develop your ideas. Without a teacher present to make all the logical connec-tions, highlight the important points, and judge what is correct, you learn to listen to your colleagues—really listen—and then make your own decisions.

The collaborative approach is especially important to writers because writing is a process of constant decision-making: Will this opening sentence grab the reader? What's the best way to word this idea? How can I join these two paragraphs? Should there be a comma here? Is this what I really mean? Will this word offend my reader? Is this quotation too long? Do I need more proof? Answering these questions requires us to get outside ourselves and look at our words from the reader's point of view. We have to get beyond our own biases to see from someone else's perspective. The best way to develop skill in decision-making and judgment is to practise with colleagues, to help each other see things we would not see on our own.

4. Builds Confidence

Collaboration provides support for some of the most difficult aspects of writing. Sharing the tasks of generating and evaluating ideas and critiquing each other's papers builds confidence ("She's no better than me!"). One of the most common problems cited by student writers is a lack of confidence in their abilities, sometimes even a genuine depression over their hesitant command of language. The words and expressions they use never seem to match the elegant language they read in books and magazines. We all need to explore language with colleagues, to see the level of writing produced by our peers, and to realize how well we do in comparison.

5. Prepares You for the Future

As discussed in the earlier part of this chapter, the professional writing done in science, education, business, and industry is increasingly collaborative. Group writing in school can provide you with the skills you will need on the job.

Getting Started

There are several ways you can ease into group writing. For instance, your teacher may start by relating her own positive and negative experiences with collaborative writing. She may show a videotape of former students working together, or she may share with you a sample group paper and its group folder that describes the process the writers went through. If she then gives you a choice of people with whom to work, select those who share your interests and writing goals, those who want to write about topics that appeal to you. Working with friends is all right, *if* you can work and not socialize, and if they want to achieve the same writing goals.

When you do meet with your group members for the first time, make sure you introduce yourself and make a note of each person's name and telephone number. Then each person should take a few minutes to freewrite about his or her own feelings, fears, and previous experiences with group work. Share these pieces of freewriting and you will discover common problems, maybe even some solutions. Spend a few minutes discussing what you've learned from this sharing. List several ways you can make sure everyone in your group participates fully. Think of ways to encourage shy members of the group and ways to be sure no one person dominates your discussions.

Each time you meet your writing group, you will need to decide with your colleagues what the group's main function or goal is. You will also have to decide what role each person in the group will play. Writing groups can be formed for a number of purposes. You may have a research group seeking information and reporting on their findings, a role-play group staging a scenario to promote discussion and analysis of an issue, a regular discussion group, a brainstorming group, or a problem-solving group. Revision and editing groups that critique each other's papers are perhaps the most common type of writing groups.

The role each person plays within the group may change from meeting to meeting or as the function of the group changes. Many groups work smoothly with little or no leadership, but a discussion leader may help you get started, keep up the energy level, keep people on track, and encourage everyone's full participation. A recorder is nearly always necessary to keep track of ideas and make entries in the group folder that the instructor uses to evaluate your progress. Other roles you may wish to adopt include the devil's advocate, who challenges ideas; the speaker, who reports to the class on your group's progress; and the facilitator, who enters text into the word processor, tapes discussions, or photocopies material. It is best to decide on responsibilities for special jobs before you begin work, and to rotate responsibilities so that each person fills a number of roles during the semester.

The most important role you can play in your group, of course, is that of a fully active member who brings work in on time as agreed. Group work requires commitment and a respect for deadlines. Bringing "dead" writing—a draft you are not interested in improving and do not really want advice on—is a sure way to dampen everyone's spirits. When you submit your writing to your colleagues, you should be able to articulate your writing goals, tell them what you are experimenting with, and identify specific problems you would like them to help you solve. You should submit your work without apologies.

When you receive oral or written comments from your readers, remain open to what you hear. It is natural to get defensive and try to explain to the reader that he or she has missed something or misread something. Fight this urge to defend your draft. Instead, ask the reader to suggest ways to solve the problem that has been identified. After you have received advice from several readers, you will see where their suggestions match and where they don't. If several people identify the same problem, then you should begin to suspect that you probably do have that problem. It is up to you to reflect upon the advice you receive and decide which comments are helpful and which are not. In the end, you are responsible for your own writing.

Difficulties of Writing with Others

Despite our good intentions and a clear sense of purpose, we have all, at one time or another, had difficulties working with others to achieve a common goal. Most groups work productively, but a few do fall apart. The efficient and effective writing group is task-oriented, positive, democratic, and open. The members know that intellectual conflict is healthy but that emotional conflict is destructive. They recognize the various functions a group of writers may perform, and the roles individuals may adopt within the group. They see their members as authorities, as capable people who have valuable ideas and insights to contribute to any discussion. They see their instructor as a resource, not someone whose job is to supply them with definitive answers.

In contrast, the ineffective and inefficient writing group has difficulty setting goals, getting started, and staying on task. When asked to form a circle, they often move their chairs ever so slightly into a short row. One or two members may turn stubbornly away from the group. The negative attitude this immediately creates can manifest itself in a number of ways. Group members may read to themselves rather than exchange ideas; they may look to the instructor for direction or answers; or they may fall victim to one strong-willed person who passes judgment quickly or cuts off tentative commentary by others. Often this group merely goes through the motions; reading and responding to each other's papers in record time, offering each other only the most superficial comments.

All of us would prefer to belong to the effective group so we can achieve the benefits of collaborative writing outlined above, in particular, so we can learn to read and think critically as we improve the quality of our written work. To build such a group, you need a positive attitude and faith in the ability of your fellow students to assist you. Remember that peer collaboration works not because your group is made up of talented writers but because we are all better critics (readers) than writers, because teaching someone else is the best way to learn, and because group support builds the confidence we all need to develop our writing abilities.

Beware of some common misconceptions that can discourage people from working in groups and create a negative feeling about collaboration. First, students sometimes fear that the teacher will use the criticism of their peer readers against them, and that these criticisms will affect her evaluation of their work. This simply isn't true. Teachers who use a workshop approach evaluate you not on your peer readers' criticism, but on how you react to that criticism. They check to see whether you resist unhelpful advice while using insightful comments to strengthen your work. Another common fear students express is that working with others will destroy their individuality, will result in their giving away good ideas that might distinguish them from the others. Again, this fear is unfounded. What actually happens is that by taking advantage of differing perspectives, even the cleverest students find themselves with more ideas, and they develop those ideas more fully and creatively. A third misconception is that the group will slow the individual down needlessly. We have all heard someone moan, "I know I could do this faster on my own!" Yes, the group process does take time, but it generally results in an improved quality of thinking, more skilled writing, and a more conscious understanding of the concepts discussed. The extra time it takes is time spent learning, and one simply learns better by actively trying to find things out than by being told things.

Even if you know the benefits of group writing and approach it with a positive attitude, you can, of course, still find yourself working with people who create problems. Some may come late to meetings or leave early or skip them altogether. Nothing is more frustrating than arriving at a meeting only to discover that the others are missing or unprepared or not fully participating. A second category of problem people includes those who show up for meetings but bring with them negative attitudes. These sceptics belittle the process and constantly put down everything. Sometimes they actually launch verbal attacks on other group members, but more often they just shake their heads and let you know that whatever you're doing will never work. A last category of problem people includes those whose behaviour actually disrupts the meeting. For example, a loud, dominant individual may close off discussion by her or his very presence. Other disruptive behaviours include whispering, gossiping, or interrupting while others are speaking.

Any of these problem people can create emotional conflicts that will render your group dysfunctional. Remember that not all conflict is bad. You should expect intellectual disagreements; in fact, you should encourage them. Differences in ideas stimulate you and contribute to your creativity. The whole point of collaborative writing is to establish a climate in which differing opinions can be aired and constructive resolutions reached.

However, you will want to resolve any emotional conflicts that arise in your group and to solve any problems that prevent group members from learning from each other. Besides the problematic behaviour of others, there are two common difficulties that writers face when they work together. The first problem is that students have trouble reading each other's work helpfully. In peer revision groups, readers are often distracted by the topic of the essay they are reading, and they discuss that topic instead of the writer's handling of the topic. They do not look critically at how the writer presents his or her ideas. For example, if you are discussing someone's essay on hunting moose, you are not going to talk about moose or hunting but about how somebody *wrote about* moose hunting. The second problem is that even when there is a lively discussion focused on the writing and it seems to produce useful comments, writers sometimes leave the meeting room without a specific plan for revising or strengthening their work. Although peer review sheets, like those at the end of Chapter Nine, should suggest specific ways to improve the essay, they often contain only vague remarks: "Needs development," "Should be reorganized," "Very good work." All the clever ideas that emerged in the discussion disappear.

Strategies for Solving Group Communication Problems

To ensure that your collaborative work progresses smoothly, try some of the following strategies. Select those that are most appropriate to the type of group with whom you are working.

1. Keep a Group Folder

If you are co-authoring a paper or working in a writing group that will be meeting regularly throughout the semester, keep track of your attendance, progress, and problems in a group folder. Use an ordinary file folder and print the names of the group members prominently on the cover. Inside, make an attendance chart that the group recorder can fill in each time you meet. The recorder should also write a short, informal progress report to the instructor after each meeting. Put the date on it and explain what was accomplished, what problems occurred, what remains to be done, and what she can do to help. These will not be corrected in any way, but they will allow the teacher to monitor your progress and give you suggestions or help when necessary.

2. Log Your Group Process

Chapter Nine explains how you can use a log to chart your individual progress through a writing assignment. By recording what happened each step of the way and your reactions and comments, you become an observer of your own process. The log concludes with a self-evaluation of the paper and the process you used to write it, as well as any questions you want to ask your reader. In your writing group, set aside at least ten minutes at the end of each meeting for writing in your log. Using any notes you made during the meeting or any written comments you received on your writing, reflect on how the meeting went. Remark on any problems you encountered and explain how you solved them. Record carefully any revision suggestions you were given. React to those suggestions. Explain why you think they are valid or not, and how you plan to use them to help you revise your work. This log will be submitted to your instructor with the final copy of the paper you are working on; thus she can keep track of the strategies you and your group are using to keep the group functioning smoothly and solve your writing problems.

3. Tape-record Your Sessions

The tape allows you to perform, and then observe and critique your performance. Your instructor can collect one group's tape after each class meeting, listen to it, and record her responses. This is an excellent way to get the instructor's suggestions for strengthening your group work or solving any problems you are having. It has the added advantage of allowing you to recover specific material from group discussions. But perhaps the greatest benefit of taping your sessions is that when people hear themselves, they often adjust their behaviour without any outside help. (Just knowing the tape- recorder is operating may encourage problem group members to participate more effectively.)

4. Create an Acknowledgment Page

Along with your completed assignment, submit a page that names all the people who contributed to the paper and thanks them for the roles they played. This may include, for example, group members who read your draft and suggested changes, those who listened patiently as you voiced your opinions, those who gave emotional support when you became discouraged, and those who developed your thinking by what they said in class discussions. Of course, you can thank people who were not in your group: the instructor who conferenced with you about the paper and helped you narrow your topic, the roommate who did a final proofreading or spell-check; the people you interviewed to get data for the paper; or the writing centre tutor who guided you to choose appropriate time-management strategies. Along with your log, the acknowledgment page will make both you and your instructor aware of the sources you drew on to write your paper. Also, the recognition it gives to the other members of your group encourages them to be as helpful as they can.

5. Use Summaries and Questions

Group communication is greatly improved by the simple techniques of summarizing and asking specific questions to further the discussion. For example, an excellent way to obtain detailed, thoughtful reactions to your writing is to summarize your paper (explain what you believe you have said and the effect you are trying to achieve) and then ask

your peer-reader specific questions such as those listed
below. The more precise your questions, the more likely
you are to receive precise and helpful answers.

Weak questions:
- What do you think of my paper?
- How should I change my paper?

Strong questions:
- Does anyone know a better way to introduce my subject?
- Do I need all these examples? Which is the weakest?
- How can I convince my reader that I understand her or
  his point of view?

The "summarize the question" technique is equally useful in
dealing with people who do not participate fully in the
group or who display negative attitudes or behaviour.
Rather than ignoring those who have problems or create
problems, you can use one of the following approaches to
summarize what you see happening without passing judgment, to show that you understand their feelings, and to ask
how the group can change the situation.

- "You don't seem to be interested in doing this reading right
  now. Should we take a break or perhaps do something else
  first?"
- "This response has clearly discouraged you. I know it's
  hard to face a major revision. Shall we talk about the
  strengths of the paper so you'll know what to build on?"
- "You are having trouble bringing in drafts on the due
  dates. Do you think we should make a new schedule? Or
  is there something we can do to help you meet the deadlines as set?"
- "You obviously didn't like our response to your paper.
  Do you think we haven't read it carefully enough? Would
  you like another reading or can you suggest what we
  have missed?"

The five strategies described above will not solve every problem you have with group work, but they will help with many of them. If you should encounter an unsolvable problem, you can always ask your instructor for advice, or even ask her to step in and handle the problem directly. Fortunately, such serious problems are a rare occurrence in a well-run writing workshop, where everyone understands the benefits of collaborative work and feels that there is a fair evaluation system (group folders, logs, or tapes) that will let the instructor monitor and evaluate individual contributions.

If you would like to do a private evaluation of your peer review skills, you can use the following checklist.

When You Submit Your Writing for Peer Review:

- Do you meet your deadlines?
- Do you have a positive attitude about the process of peer review?
- Do you see your readers' suggestions as support rather than criticism?
- Do you refrain from apologizing for your rough drafts when you give them to your readers?
- Do you help your readers by articulating your writing goals and experiments, and by asking them specific questions to guide their reading?
- Do you respect your readers' abilities to give you useful advice?
- Are you open to the comments you receive?
- Do you ask for clarification of comments you do not understand?
- Can you reflect on advice given to you and use it selectively and judiciously?
- Have you developed sufficient confidence in your ideas and your writing to resist suggestions you feel are not helpful?
- Are you overly dependent on the teacher or the group to judge the value and quality of your writing?

When You Read and Evaluate Other People's Papers:

- Do you ask them first to articulate their goals and experiments so you will be able to judge how well they succeeded?
- Do you discuss the way the writer handles the topic and not get derailed into a discussion of the topic itself?
- Do you resist the temptation to rewrite a paper from your own perspective, choosing instead to help the writer see how to achieve her or his own goals more effectively?
- Do you point out to writers the strengths of their papers as well as the weaknesses?
- Do you offer advice in the form of suggestions rather than error corrections?
- Can you discuss the logic behind the changes you suggest?
- Do you offer specific solutions for the problems you see in someone else's writing?

Conclusion

This chapter has focused on ways to solve some of the communication and evaluation problems that can create disharmony in a writing group. We hope that you do not finish the chapter believing that writing groups are always problematic or difficult to manage. In truth, most students have fun collaborating with other writers in lively, active workshop sessions that make writing more challenging and less lonely. Students also find collaboration a realistic way to become members of the scholarly community where, as Hannah Arendt says, "For excellence, the presence of others is always required."

EXERCISES

Exercise 1: Instruct High School Students

A science teacher at a local high school has asked your class to prepare some materials for her science students in Grade 7. She is particularly interested in brief explanations of some relatively simple mechanical and electrical devices. This information will be used to teach the students.

Although the teacher may supplement what you give her with material of her own, it is best to assume that the information you supply will be all that these students will receive on the particular topic you choose.

Appropriate topics for this paper might include the following:

light bulb	**X-ray machine**	**hydraulic cylinder**
flashlight	**neon light**	**block and tackle**
thermostat	**battery**	**universal joint**

You will work in groups of four to complete this task. How your group co-operates is up to you. Keep a log that documents your activities, explains the strategies you try out, and shows how each member participated.

Suggestion: This project will come to life if you can locate a Grade 7 science teacher who will agree to distribute your papers and let students write back to you with their responses.

Variation: This writing assignment was designed for a class of engineering students. It can be altered to fit your particular interests. In other words, you can write about any subject in the high school curriculum that interests you and that high school students would like to know more about.

Exercise 2: Report on a Campus Problem

Write an analytical paper about a real issue on your campus. (See Chapter Five for problem-solving techniques). Follow the steps below, and keep a log as described in Exercise 1.

1. Working with the whole class in one large group, brainstorm problems particular to your situation in school, to your program or faculty. After you have thought of at least a dozen problems, select one that is challenging enough to involve everyone in a discussion of its causes and solutions. The definition of the problem and its solution should be of interest to those in a position to act on the problem.

2. In a group of four to six students, develop three or four specific questions that can be used in a survey of student opinion on the problem. These questions should solicit students' views on the specific nature of the problem, its importance and likely solutions. For instance, if you have chosen the problem of banning smoking in the school, you might want to know what percentage of students favour such legislation, whether smoking in school is enough of a nuisance to require a ban, and what particular moves students favour in implementing such a ban.

3. Working again with the whole class, each group should report its questions. The class should select from all the questions those that will make up a questionnaire. (There should be at least some open-ended questions that call for opinions, comments, and reflections; they should not all be questions answered by Yes or No.)

4. Produce and distribute enough questionnaires to the class so that each student can solicit the opinions of five other students from outside the class (representative of a particular level or program, if this is agreed on).

5. At the next class meeting work in your small group to pool the twenty to thirty responses you have collected. Your goal is to abstract from the data you've collected the information the authorities need in order to make informed decisions on the problem. Write up your analysis of the questionnaire and your conclusions as a preliminary report.

6. Each small group should now report to the whole class on the results of its preliminary analysis of the data.

7. Copies of the preliminary reports and questionnaire results are now made available to the other groups so that each group has access to the opinions of five to six times the number of people in class. The task of each group is now to analyze all the data and prepare a report for those who are in a position to act on it. This means that although each group will be using the same data, they will be trying to solve the problem in a different way. They may even be defining the problem differently or choosing different readers.

8. The reports written by each group are circulated to the other groups. After they are read, there should be a summary session in which the whole class considers similarities and variations among the group reports. In particular, you should note how the same data are interpreted in various ways and how such discrepancies could be overcome in a final class report. Discuss how such a report might be organized and presented to best effect.

Suggestion: As in Exercise 1, you may wish to submit the strongest report to the intended reader to see his or her response to your analysis and recommended solutions.

Exercise 3: Interpret a Dramatic Narrative

Select a fairly long narrative poem (one that contains elements of character, plot, and dialogue). You can find many such poems in the works of Robert Frost, including "The Death of the Hired Man" and "The Lovely

Shall Be Choosers." Or you can select a portion of a longer dramatic poem, for example, Michael Ondaatje's *The Collected Works of Billy the Kid.*

Work with at least one other person. (You may wish to have three or four people in your group if there are that many voices in the poem.) Keep a log throughout the project (see Chaper Nine).

Prepare the poem for oral presentation by assigning parts and reading it aloud several times. Discuss the poem's meaning and let that meaning guide your reading. Practise reading for emotional and dramatic power.

Present your poem to the class in a dramatic reading and lead a discussion of the poem with the whole class.

Write a paper that describes how you arrived at your interpretation (refer to your log for details) and then explain that interpretation in detail.

Exercise 4: Study the Group Writing Process

After you have worked in a group to complete one of the above exercises (or a similar group writing assignment), write a paper about the process of writing in a group. If your group encountered problems, you could focus on an analysis of your own group. As an alternative approach, you could gather data from the whole class by interviewing classmates and analyzing the material in their group folders or individual logs. Education students might want to create a curriculum package of materials for use in teaching younger writers about writing groups. Students with some background in psychology, sociology, or organizational behaviour might include material on group dynamics and communication theory.

References and Further Reading

Arendt, Hannah. *The Human Condition.* Chicago: University of Chicago Press, 1958.

Elbow, Peter. *Writing without Teachers.* New York: Oxford University Press, 1973.

Gardner, John. Cited in Tillie Olsen, *Silences.* New York: Delacorte Press/Seymour Lawrence, 1978.

Lunsford, Andrea, and Lisa Ede. *Singular Texts/Plural Authors.* Carbondale and Edwardsville: Southern Illinois University Press, 1990.

Reither, James A., and Douglas Vipond. "Writing as Collaboration." *College English* 51 (1989): 855–67.

Chapter Five

Strategies for Effective Writing

❧

A man's errors are his portals of discovery.

JAMES JOYCE

As you read through this chapter and try out some of the activities, you will become aware that there are many ways to approach writing. You will recognize some of your own approaches, but you will also discover some that are unfamiliar to you. Writing processes have been described in the work of researchers such as Linda Flower, John Hayes, Janet Emig, and Lee Odell; teachers such as Peter Elbow and Donald Murray have analyzed their own composing activities and written books about them; and we have added to this knowledge through our experiences as students and teachers. We hope that you will use this chapter to review your own ways of writing and to explore new ways.

Although we might label these approaches "techniques" or "methods," we prefer to call them "**strategies**" to avoid the suggestion that they are invariable, step-by-step procedures. The word "strategy" comes from the Greek *strategia*, which originally referred to the planning of military operations. Because we do not see writing as a military campaign, we prefer the modern usage, which extends this meaning to encompass plans for other kinds of endeavours

89

such as solving problems. In this book, we are using the term "strategies" to mean ways of overcoming writing problems, such as getting started, untangling complicated ideas, and developing meaning in written texts. For example, **brainstorming** and other free-association techniques are effective strategies for overcoming inertia and discovering ideas. Creating visual representations of ideas through sketches and diagrams is a strategy writers use to organize ideas. Asking a series of questions about a subject is a strategy that helps writers remember what they already know and to identify the information they lack about a subject. Thus, journalists often use the strategy of asking the "W5" questions (Who? What? Where? When? Why?) about their subject to help them develop a news story. Although the notion of strategy suggests a method or a plan, it also implies the trial and error of experimentation. Writing that matters very often demands a willingness to take a risk, try things out, and welcome the unexpected.

Over the years you have developed your own strategies for writing. This development has been shaped by your individual style and by your writing experiences at school, at work, and at home. In Chapter Two, you analyzed your strategies for writing and noted those that help or hinder your writing processes. You may have found that you are the type of person who likes to plan a piece of writing in your head before your pen touches the paper, or perhaps you are like many writers who write a rough draft before the real planning begins. Perhaps you have decided that your approach varies with the assignment, reader, or time available. Whatever you have concluded, you have probably noticed that you have a preference for certain ways of tackling a piece of writing, just as you have a preferred approach to any activity.

Your preferred approach may be spontaneous, intuitive, and impulsive; it may be reflective, analytical, and systematic. The strategies in this chapter use all these approaches—from the unstructured activities of freewriting and brainstorming to the systematic methods of structured analysis. While some of these approaches will readily suit your individual style, others will seem awkward or counterproductive at first. Through experience, we know that if you experiment with these strategies and learn how to use them, your writing will improve. As you increase your options as a writer, you become capable of handling a wide range of writing tasks.

The activities in this chapter follow a particular order for the sake of explanation; however, writing often happens not in orderly steps, but rather through a process of continuous revision, especially when the task is unfamiliar or complex. As ideas follow each other—in the writer's head or on paper—new connections are made, old ideas are rejected, and new ideas are explored. Thinking, writing, and rewriting activities occur as parts of a cyclical process that often begins with a wide circle of fuzzy ideas and narrows to a polished draft that expresses the writer's meaning and intention.

How to Use This Chapter

Before you try any of the suggested activities, we suggest you skim the chapter, rather than read it in detail, to get an idea of what it contains. Glance at the headings, read the beginning and end of the chapter, and try to acquire a mental map of the organization. Then begin with the strategies that seem most suitable for your immediate needs. You will find a range of activities in each section designed to help you understand the strategies and their potential applications in your writing. Given that there is no single most effective strategy or single correct writing process, we have provided a variety of writing strategies for you to explore. To help you read and understand this chapter, we have arranged it under the following headings: Understand Assignments, Unblock Writing, Explore Your Own Ideas, View Your Subject from Different Angles, Collect New Information, Find a Focus, and Test a Draft.

We suggest that you try the activities in the context of your own writing requirements. For example, if you are searching for ideas for a term paper, try some of the strategies in Explore Your Own Ideas. If you are faced with the task of organizing a large amount of information, try some of the strategies in Find a Focus. If you have just finished a report and are wondering how your intended readers may react to it, try some of the strategies in Test a Draft. You will find suggestions for assignments based on these strategies at the end of the chapter. In a writing class, your instructor may provide different assignments, or your writing group may find more suitable variations.

We encourage you to practise these writing strategies on the writing you do for other courses and in your work-related writing as well. If you practise them whenever you write, they will become almost automatic and, thus, available when you need them for a difficult or complex writing assignment. Once you feel comfortable with these approaches, experiment with them and shape them to suit your individual needs and specific writing activities. If you have a writing group, try doing some of the activities together to increase your understanding of a strategy and its variations. A journal or a log is a good place to record your own progress with the strategies and their effects on your writing. As you gain insights into your own writing processes, you will begin to recognize improvement in your writing.

Understand Assignments

Although we often write for the sheer pleasure of expressing our ideas and feelings or to make things happen, such as to obtain a scholarship or a bank loan, most of us have to write on demand as part of our academic or work responsibilities.

Read with a Purpose

In haste, writers often begin assignments without understanding what is needed. If you receive an assignment in written form, take time to read it carefully to get a general idea of what is required. Then reread the assignment for specific details. Make notes in the margins and underline key words such as *analyze, compare, contrast, identify, evaluate, recommend.* Restate the requirement in your own words. If the assignment is a case study, scan the case and the requirement, then read the questions before you reread the case more thoroughly. Look for the chronology of events and identify the key people who have a stake in the outcome. If you are asked to answer specific questions about a story or poem for a literature assignment, reread the text with the questions in mind. Note specific instructions about length and form. As you will discover in Chapter Six, specific forms may be expected in specific situations. For instance, some readers may expect a point-form summary, while others may expect complete sentences and paragraphs.

Interview the Intended Reader

Sometimes it may be possible to discuss the assignment with the intended reader. For instance, teachers, editors, and supervisors often welcome an early discussion to avoid misunderstandings. Whether or not you receive the assignment in written form, take along a written statement that reflects your understanding of the assignment as a starting point for your discussion. Ask the reader to suggest possible information sources; this will further clarify the reader's expectations and help you to set your own goals for the assignment.

Unblock Writing

Writers frequently have difficulty getting started. They sit before the blank paper or computer screen, give up, and resolve to try again later. This dilemma often results from a reluctance to put anything that seems less than perfect on paper: writers have strong internal monitors that censor ideas, word choices, and sentence structures. You may be familiar with the warning, "Think before you write." But writing assists thinking. The act of putting ideas down on paper or computer screen, without stopping to judge and select, helps you to see what you are thinking and provides an opportunity to explore and develop your thoughts. Instead of the paralysis that sometimes happens under the pressure to produce a completed draft, you have action that generates a wealth of ideas for further shaping. **Brainstorming**, **freewriting**, and **mapping** can help to unblock writing and get ideas flowing. These strategies require you to turn off the internal monitor and to "go with the flow."

Brainstorm

This strategy takes advantage of the ease of free association and is often used by creative thinkers, such as scriptwriters, scientists, managers, and planners, to generate many ideas quickly. You can often overcome a tendency to procrastinate by taking advantage of the time you spend waiting for a train or travelling on a bus to brainstorm a list of ideas for a difficult writing assignment.

Try this:

Concentrate on your subject, bring it into focus so that you have a mental image of it, and write down every idea that occurs to you. Don't stop to censor ideas; you want as long a list as possible, and "wild" ideas may prove valuable later on. This strategy works especially well in groups; good ideas often stem from the "chain reactions" developed during a brainstorming session as members add and combine ideas.

One student brainstormed the following list of ideas before writing an application letter for a summer job abroad.

- good at math
- 2 years university
- mother's business accounts
- camp experience
- storytelling
- English/French

- like travel
- trip-yugoslavia
- au pair - France
- work at children's hospital
- feeding sick children

Freewrite

Like brainstorming, freewriting also works through the free association of ideas, but extends the process to capture connections among them. Some groups, such as the Inkshed group of Canadian researchers and teachers of writing, use this strategy (which they have renamed "inkshedding") as an activity at their professional meetings. This rapid outpouring of ideas on paper helps meeting participants focus their opinions and questions in response to a discussion or presentation. Freewriting is a powerful means of overcoming writer's block because it does not require writers to select or revise ideas or words.

Try this:

Freewriting often works best if you put some pressure on yourself by setting a time limit. Try starting with three minutes and, instead of making a list of words, write your ideas in sentences as quickly as possible. Concentrate on your topic, put your pen to paper, begin to write, and don't lift the pen off the paper until your time is up. If you find yourself running out of ideas, repeat the last word a few times until your ideas begin to flow again, or try explaining why you have run out of ideas. You will be surprised at how easily this strategy unblocks the flow of ideas. Allow your ideas to go where they will; don't worry about straying from your subject. Don't stop to censor your ideas, correct your spelling, or form elegant sentences. You want to write quickly to capture ideas as they occur.

When the time is up, review what you have written. Underline or circle words that are repeated or that seem important in some way. Abstract words such as "freedom," "home," or "responsibility" can represent a whole complex of ideas relating to a writer's experience. Words like these can be expanded and developed to reveal a new web of ideas. Words that recur in your freewriting may reveal a key point you are trying to express. Try another brainstorm, freewrite again, create a map (described below), or use the clustering strategy described in Chapter Three to expand on these significant words. Ask a friend or someone in your writing group to circle words that may have multiple meanings. Computer specialists and city planners, for example, attach quite different meanings to the word "architecture." Read more about words and their potential meanings, especially "code words," in Chapter Eight.

The student who was preparing to write an application letter for a summer job abroad decided that her reader would want to know about her career goals. She used free-writing to help her explore the idea of her career:

> What am I really suited for in a career? Well I like children a lot especially since I had a chance to work with them for a month at the hospital last summer. But does that mean I should be a doctor or a nurse or a teacher? I'm good at math so maybe I'd get through medical school, but I think that's also a lot of memory work and I don't think I want to spend all that time studying and not doing anything. Do doctors <u>travel</u> a lot?—perhaps if they were missionaries or worked for the United Nations or <u>travelled</u> to exotic places to attend conferences. Perhaps I could help children by being a math teacher in a foreign country. I'm almost finished my B.A.—do I want to spend more time in school or am I ready to get a job and find out what life is really like? Maybe I don't have to decide on my final career now—I can finish my degree and get a job, make some money, and <u>travel</u> whenever I have a holiday. But what is my career goal? Holiday—holiday isn't exactly the same as <u>travel</u>. Now I'm stuck and don't know what to write—why? Holiday and <u>travel</u> seem to have different meanings in my mind—what do I really want to do? Can I combine them—can <u>travel</u> be a part of my career?

This writer studied her freewriting and discovered that travel appeared to be an important word because it was repeated and there seemed to be conflicting ideas about the concept of holiday travel and travel for work. To further explore this conflict, she tried the mapping described below.

Map Ideas

Donald Murray uses the term **mapping** to describe nonlinear brainstorming; he describes it as a way of "circling the subject and making unexpected leaps" (25). Mapping is somewhat like Gabrielle Rico's clustering strategy (described in Chapter Three) in that it creates a visual design to help the writer see patterns and connections among ideas. In

Chapter Three you used clustering as a way to begin a piece of expressive writing; you were urged to think in images and include fragments of songs and poems. In contrast, mapping depends less on images and more on bits of information that occur to you as you think of your subject.

Try this:

Choose a word associated with your subject and place it at the centre of the page (you might use a key word from your freewriting or a word that describes some aspect of your subject). Set a time limit and force yourself to concentrate on your word. Let yourself go, capture your associations, and jot them down on the paper in a line radiating from your central word. When you find yourself on a new tangent or a new aspect of your subject, begin a new string from the centre and carry it as far as you can. In ten or fifteen minutes you will have a web of associations—a graphic display of ideas surrounding your subject. When you have run out of ideas, study your map and look for ideas that seem to be connected. The search for patterns often results in a sudden recognition of the major point you want to make about your subject. This insight can be pushed for more ideas with another few minutes of freewriting.

The map on the next page is another strategy the summer job applicant used to explore her concept of travel. This map generated new ideas about travel, especially the consequences of being away from home and the possibilities for personal growth.

If you have tried all three strategies—brainstorming, freewriting, and mapping—you will have several pages of rather messy writing. Instead of twenty minutes spent staring at a blank page, you will have some of your ideas on paper where you can examine them. Study the results of your brainstorming, freewriting, and mapping to discover new insights into your subject. If possible, try these strategies with your writing group and discuss their applications. Writers find them useful not only for getting started, but also for extending ideas, finding an introductory or concluding statement, or reworking sections of a paper. Students find these strategies a great way to get started when they are overcome by panic in an examination.

TRAVEL

WAITING ~ lost luggage ~ airports ~ stories ~ ADVENTURE ~ STRANGERS ~ ROMANCE

SUN ~ WARM BEACHES ~ FUN ~ SHORT TIME

home ~ family ~ FRIENDS ~ FAMILIAR ~ boyfriend ~ FUTURE

EXOTIC PLACES ~ NEW FOOD ~ NEW CUSTOMS ~ NEW EXPERIENCE ~ GROWTH

CAMPING IN EUROPE ~ COLD ~ NO MONEY ~ ILLNESS ~ telephone calls

POVERTY ~ DISEASE ~ WAR ~ FAMINE ~ politics ~ cuso ~ aid

Explore Your Own Ideas

When you choose a topic to write about or when you receive a writing assignment, you need information. Before making plans to collect information, explore your own ideas, questions, and understandings of the subject. The following strategies will help to uncover what you know about a topic and indicate directions for further research.

Focus Your Freewriting

Like the freewriting described above, focused freewriting is a way of forcing yourself to concentrate on the subject so that you can get ideas down on paper quickly. Whereas ordinary freewriting may lead you from subject to subject, focused freewriting helps you stay with the subject and concentrate on a specific goal.

Try this:

Set a time limit, concentrate on your subject and purpose, and write as quickly as possible without stopping to reflect. If you notice yourself straying from your subject or losing your focus, reread what you have written and continue. If you find yourself stuck looking for just the right word, leave a blank space or empty parentheses to be filled in later. When the time is up, reread your freewriting and take note of areas where you know you will need more information. Look for *key words* (words that seem to describe an important aspect of your main point) and try to expand them. You can identify key words by imagining you are sending a telegram about your subject; only the most important words can be used (see more about key words in Chapter Eight). You may also discover that you know very little about this subject and may choose to write about something else or do some extensive research.

Sketch an Idea Tree

As the name suggests, an **idea tree** is an arrangement of ideas that reflects some kind of logical order, much as a genealogical chart portrays a family's history, or an

organigram chart represents the relationships among people and positions in a company. As an exploratory strategy,
try a quick sketch with paper and pencil to help you visualize your ideas, distinguish your major and minor points,
identify those that require more development, and experiment with possible arrangements. You might see it as a preliminary plan for your writing.

Try this:

One way to build an idea tree is to begin by brainstorming a
list of ideas about your topic. Study your list to determine
how it might be divided into categories of similar ideas.
Then give each category a heading that includes all the
ideas in that group. You will find that some ideas seem to
belong to more than one category or that some categories
have fewer ideas than others. This sketch helps you know
what decisions must be made about categories and which
ideas require more development. Experiment with your
tree and discuss it with a friend or your writing group.

Here is the way one writer used an idea tree to examine her
ideas. While writing a résumé for a job as a sales representative in a pharmaceutical company, she brainstormed the
following list:

- Bachelor of Science degree
- management course
- public speaking courses
- camp counsellor
- summer job in lab
- volunteer at hospital*
- summer job in store
- editor of biology
  newsletter*

The writer then scanned her list, grouped similar ideas,
formed the categories "Education" and "Work Experience,"
and sketched an idea tree (see following page).
The writer could see that the items marked with an
asterisk did not fit under the categories she had named. She
could have developed another category, perhaps "Interests,"
to account for her editing and volunteer work. Further study
of her idea tree revealed that management courses and
public speaking were not the same type of education as

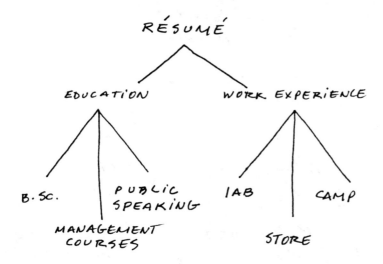

her completed science degree, so she went on to develop separate categories for degrees and for continuing education.

If you already know some of the main categories of your subject, you might begin your idea tree at the top level, with a general concept, and work your way downward to specific details. The tree on the next page illustrates one student's initial sketch for a term paper on F.R. Scott, a Canadian lawyer, politician, and poet.

The top level in this idea tree, "An outspoken Canadian," reveals the focus this writer plans for her paper—everything below should support this theme. Her second level of headings indicates the fields of F.R. Scott's contributions to Canadian life. In the third level, the writer indicates specific areas within the general fields. At this point, she had to decide which details would best support her argument that F.R. Scott was an outspoken Canadian. As she gathered more information, her idea tree grew (see page 103).

When this writer studied her new display of ideas, she realized that her tree revealed many contrasting ideas based on individual rights and society. This insight lead to her decision to change the top level of her idea tree to reflect her new focus on F.R. Scott's opposing interests.

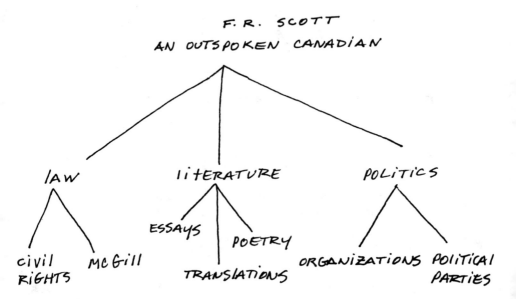

Another writer on the same topic might choose a very different organization, perhaps using specific writings of F.R. Scott to illustrate his social philosophy in the areas of literature, law, and politics—thus working from the specific to the general. A quick sketch in the form of an idea tree helps writers explore the many options available for the organization of ideas. See Chapter Six for additional suggestions for structuring ideas and Chapter Eight for a discussion of abstraction levels.

If you can, collaborate with your writing group to build an idea tree from a group brainstorming session and discover a variety of ways to create graphic displays of a subject. Compare your idea tree on a particular subject with those of others who are writing about the same subject, and then discuss the similarities and differences. Experiment with variations: write your ideas on slips of paper or index cards and move them around until you have a structure that reflects a logical arrangement for your subject. Ask a friend to comment on the logic of your arrangement. An added

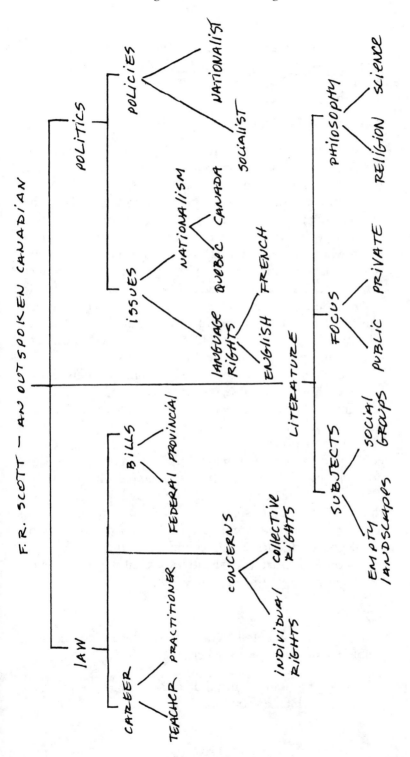

advantage of idea trees is that you can use them to capture main ideas and supporting ideas while taking notes during a lecture or studying for an examination.

Analyze a Problem

Viewing the subject as a problem is a strategy that helps writers explore what they already know and what they need to know about a subject. A problem exists when we feel or see a conflict. For example, a personal problem arises when you discover that you are in the wrong field after three years in your university program. A community problem exists when the only industry in town announces its closure. A workplace problem arises when a competitor announces a new and cheaper product. A political problem exists for certain countries when others reduce their foreign aid budgets. These examples describe problematic situations for which key issues can be identified and analyzed through the questioning procedure of **problem analysis**.

A problem also exists when something prevents us from achieving a goal. Suppose your goal is to improve your tennis game at the local tennis club on the weekends. But suppose the club has few members to play with, limited hours of play, and poor court surfaces. You might change your goal or find a new tennis club, but you might also decide to do some investigation and try to change the situation so that you have a tennis club close to home. By solving the tennis club's problems, you solve your own problem and perhaps the problem of other tennis players in your neighbourhood.

If you decide to do something about the problem, you must consider what you already know about the situation and what more you need to find out.

Try this:

You can adapt the following list of questions to analyze problems in almost any subject area:

• What are the issues surrounding the problem? (Which are facts and which are opinions?)

- What are the causes and what are the effects of the problem? (Are the poor surfaces and limited hours just symp-
  toms of a larger problem underlying the situation?)
- What is the real problem (the problem whose solution
  would solve all the subproblems)?
- Who is affected by the problem? Who will benefit from a
  solution?
- What are the alternatives or possible solutions to the
  problem?
- What constraints apply to a solution? (Are some solutions,
  such as higher fees, unacceptable to the club? to the members?)
- What is the best solution? Why?
- How can this solution be implemented?
- What will be the implications or effects of the chosen
  solution? (Will the courts be too crowded to play on the
  weekends?)

To answer these questions, you will need to seek information.

After discussions with the club manager, you decide
that the club's main problem is declining membership. At
this point, you can state the problem in the form of a question that will help to guide your investigation. Your question
might be: How can the tennis club increase its membership
so that it can repair its courts and stay open for longer periods? Further investigation reveals that the neighbourhood
population has changed and many of the former members
have moved away. After talking to some of the new people
in the neighbourhood, you discover that they don't know
much about the tennis club, but they would be interested in
learning about it. Now you can state the problem in the
form of a question that points to a solution. As Linda Flower
suggests, make your problem definition "operational" (89).
For example, you could say: How can we encourage the
new population to join the tennis club? Now you are in a
position to suggest alternatives for increasing the club membership. You will also have to consider the constraints on
your possible solutions. You may find, for instance, that the

club is unwilling to spend money for advertising. You will find that working with others provides the most effective and efficient way to collect information and generate solutions in problem analysis.

In some assignments, the problem will be clearly defined. For example, at work you might be assigned the task of finding reasons for a problem of increased absenteeism in your department. In an engineering course, you might be assigned the task of solving a design problem. In other assignments, your task is to identify a problem. In an anthropology course, for instance, you might be asked to read several works on the concept of culture and to identify a problem that explains the variety of conflicting opinions surrounding one of the issues. The final written communication that results from the problem analysis may be a letter, a report, an essay, or some other form appropriate to the situation and the reader.

View Your Subject from Different Angles

New ideas and fresh insights require writers to go beyond their usual ways of looking at a subject. Habit often blinds us to the possibilities for seeing in new ways. This section presents strategies that help writers stretch their imaginations in the search for new ideas and deeper understandings.

Create an Analogy

An **analogy** points out a comparison between two things or ideas that are not usually compared. Writers often use analogies to explore ideas, to create vivid images, and to explain abstract concepts in terms of concrete or familiar ideas. For example, James Jeans, a British physicist who wrote both scholarly publications and a number of popular scientific books, used an extended analogy to explain why the sky is blue:

> Imagine that we stand on any ordinary seaside pier,
> and watch the waves rolling in and striking against the
> iron columns of the pier. Large waves pay very little

attention to the columns—they divide right and left and re-unite after passing each column, much as a regiment of soldiers would if a tree stood in their road; it is almost as though the columns had not been there. But the short waves and ripples find the columns of the pier a much more formidable obstacle. When the short waves impinge on the columns, they are reflected back and spread as new ripples in all directions. To use the technical term, they are "scattered." The obstacle provided by the iron columns hardly affects the long waves at all, but scatters the short ripples.

We have been watching a sort of working model of the way in which sunlight struggles through the earth's atmosphere. Between us on earth and outer space the atmosphere interposes innumerable obstacles in the form of molecules of air, tiny droplets of water, and small particles of dust. These are represented by the columns of the pier.

The waves of the sea represent the sunlight. We know that sunlight is a blend of lights of many colours—as we can prove for ourselves by passing it through a prism, or even through a jug of water, or as Nature demonstrates to us when she passes it through the raindrops of a summer shower and produces a rainbow. We also know that light consists of waves, and the different colors of light are produced by waves of different lengths, red light by long waves and blue light by short waves. The mixture of waves which constitutes sunlight has to struggle through the obstacles it meets in the atmosphere, just as the mixture of waves at the seaside has to struggle past the columns of the pier. And these obstacles treat the light-waves much as the columns of the pier treat the sea-waves. The long waves which constitute red light are hardly affected, but the short waves which constitute blue light are scattered in all directions.

Thus, the different constituents of sunlight are treated in different ways as they struggle through the earth's atmosphere. A wave of blue light may be scattered by a dust particle, and turned out of its course. After a time a second dust particle again turns it out of its course, and so on, until finally it enters our eyes by a path as zigzag as that of a flash of lightning. Consequently the blue waves of the sunlight enter our eyes from all directions. And that is why the sky looks blue (25–27).

Try this:

Brainstorm a list of ways in which your subject might be similar to something else. Try for a comparison that seems unusual, and do some freewriting to find as many points of comparison as possible. Test your analogy with a friend or your writing group and ask for ideas.

Although you may choose not to include your analogy in a final paper or report, experimenting with analogies can help you become aware of different perspectives or relationships within your subject and can generate fresh words to describe it. Notice how others use analogies in books and conversations; write the particularly striking analogies in your journal for future reference.

Ask Questions

A series of questions often helps writers uncover new insights into their subject. A systematic inquiry guided by a set of questions about a subject is called a *heuristic* procedure (from the Greek word *heuriskein* meaning to discover or invent). As teacher and theorist Richard Coe explains, "A heuristic is merely a guide that increases the likelihood of your discovering the information you need and decreases the likelihood of your overlooking relevant material" (63). Asking the journalist's W5 questions (Who? What? Where? When? Why?) is a heuristic procedure. Another example of a heuristic procedure is a set of questions derived from those suggested by Alex Osborn in *Applied Imagination:*

- Put (the object, process) to other uses?—New ways to use as is?
- Adapt?—What else is this like? What other ideas does this suggest?
- Modify?—New twist? Change meaning, colour, motion, shape?
- Expand?—What to add? More time? Higher? Stronger?

- Reduce?—What to subtract? Smaller? Condensed? Lighter?
- Substitute?—What else instead? Who else instead? Other material?
- Rearrange?—Interchange components? Other sequence?
- Reverse?—Turn it backward, upside down?
- Combine?—How about a blend, an alloy? Combine units, purposes?

A group of engineers, charged with the task of creating a new design for the ordinary refrigerator, might begin to solve the problem by brainstorming answers to the above questions. Answers might include: (Modify) change it into a drying unit; (Substitute) replace it with a cold pantry; and (Combine) combine it with the household heating system to recycle the warm air exhaust. Although most of the answers will be unusable, even one creative possibility makes this exercise useful.

Consider how you might use these questions to develop a topic for a literature or history paper. For example, how would the topic change if events were reversed, if locations were changed, or main characters assumed larger or smaller roles? Try twisting these questions around until they fit your subject. Better still, create your own list of questions to help you see your subject from a variety of perspectives. Interview a friend or your writing group to help you generate a list of questions about your topic.

Explore Tagmemics

This term describes another heuristic procedure designed to help writers gain new understandings of their subject. The word "**tagmemics**" comes from the field of linguistics, where language is described in terms of systems that stay the same, change, and form parts of larger systems. We use the term here to describe the strategy of viewing a subject as a particle, a wave, and a field. To see a subject as a *particle* is to describe the characteristics of the subject itself. To see a subject as a *wave* is to see it changing over time or distance. To see the subject as a *field* is to view it in its context, as part of something larger. In other words, to develop your subject through tagmemics is to ask questions: What are the characteristics of my subject? (particle view); How does my subject change with time or situation? (wave view); and What is my subject a part of? (field view).

If, for example, your subject is aerobics, you might begin by describing it as a system of sustained exercises designed to strengthen the heart and lungs. To complete this particle view, you could describe the exercises that are particular to aerobics. Seen as a wave—something changing—aerobics can be seen as a form of exercise that has gained enormous popularity over the last decade and is now beginning to give way to body-building exercises. You can also see aerobics as a wave by describing the kinds of aerobic exercises designed for young people and old people. As a field, aerobics can be seen as part of a general move toward healthier lifestyles.

You can further analyze your subject by adding the concepts of *difference, variation*, and *distribution* to each view. For example, to explore the concept of *difference*, you could expand your description of aerobics as a PARTICLE by describing why it differs from other exercises such as golf and bowling, which are not considered aerobic exercises. The concept of *variation* can be developed by examining the different varieties of aerobic exercises such as high- and low-impact aerobics. Thinking about *distribution* could lead you to ideas about aerobics in such places as offices, schools, and health clubs.

You can generate even more ideas about your subject by applying the concepts of difference, variation, and distribution to your subject as a WAVE. As a wave, aerobics, viewed as losing ground to body-building in popularity, is *different* from hockey, which has always been a popular sport. *Variation* in this wave perspective might be that body-building exercises and aerobics are often combined as a fitness program. Thinking about *distribution* applied to the wave perspective might lead you to consider sports teams that have changed their traditional exercise programs.

You can also expand the FIELD perspective on your subject in this manner. For example, aerobics as part of a healthier lifestyle is *different* from a change in eating habits.

Variation in this field perspective might include other ways to increase health, such as through diet and work habits. The concept of *distribution* can be applied to the field perspective of aerobics as part of a healthy lifestyle to include a discussion of people who do or do not consider aerobics essential to their health.

In their book *Rhetoric: Discovery and Change*, Young, Becker, and Pike suggest a chart to help you outline these perspectives. The first part of the chart for the topic of aerobics might look something like this:

AEROBICS

	DIFFERENCE	VARIETY	DISTRIBUTION
PARTICLE SYSTEM OF EXERCISES TO INCREASE HEART/LUNG CAPACITY	• GOIF • bowling	• low-impact • high-impact	• health clubs • offices • schools
WAVE losing ground in favour of body-building exercises	• HOCKEY	• combination	• various sports teams
FIELD part of a move toward healthier lifestyle	• EATING HABITS	• DIET • work habits	• FOR AEROBICS • AGAINST AEROBICS

Try this:

Experiment with the strategy of tagmemics in a brainstorming session with your writing group or try it by yourself. There are no correct answers in this exercise; it is simply a systematic way to generate as many ideas as possible for your subject. Begin with the particle, wave, and field views, then try applying the notions of difference, variation, and distribution for each view. Choose an event, an object, or a concept and make a list of all the characteristics that define or describe the subject. Then think of the subject in terms of the way it changes over time. Finally, look at the subject in its context. How does your subject fit into a larger framework, system, or history? These strategies provide powerful ways of discovering what you know or don't know about a topic.

Collect New Information

Once you have explored your own knowledge, you will have a better idea of what further information you need. As the eighteenth-century English writer, Samuel Johnson, said, "The next best thing to knowing something is knowing where to find it."

Conduct Interviews

You may decide to collect information about your subject from interviews or personal observations. If you decide to interview people, take the time beforehand to learn something about your subject and the people you plan to interview so that you will be able to formulate your interview questions. Your questions will also depend on the purpose of your interview, which you should clearly define before the interview takes place. Although you may have specific interview goals, you may want to arrive at the interview with a list of topics to cover and then develop your specific questions as the interview progresses; this way you leave room for your interviewee to raise important subjects you may not have thought about. If you decide on a list of specific questions for your interview, be sure to leave time for discussion and clarifications. Test your questions with a friend to identify confusing or ambiguous questions.

Discover the Library

To discover what others have said about your subject, you will probably have to explore your library. When appropriate, ask your reader—your teacher or your employer—to suggest possible sources of information. If you are unfamiliar with your library, ask the reference librarian to show you how to use the library catalogue and where to find books, articles, and reports. If you know very little about your subject, the librarian may suggest you start with the encyclopedias or subject dictionaries and guides, which will give you some idea of the scope of the subject and the subject headings that will be useful in your search. These references will also indicate some of the major works in your subject area. Bibliographies at the end of articles and books will indicate further sources of specific information.

Current information usually appears in journals (often called periodicals) and can be found through the numerous indexes in the library. Ask the librarian how to use these periodical indexes. Many indexes can also be searched through the computer. Once you have scanned several types of information about your subject, choose the books or articles that seem most relevant, and read with a purpose. In other words, decide beforehand what you need to know and make a list of questions that will help to focus your attention while you read.

As you read, summarize the important points (you might try an idea tree as a summary), make a note of the questions that arise as you read, and copy a sentence or paragraph that seems to capture an idea in a particularly memorable way. When you finish reading, freewrite for a few minutes in response to what you have read. This writing will help you to make sense of what you have read and to integrate it with your own knowledge of the subject. These responses will also help you decide which materials are most important for your writing purposes.

Make a precise note of the title, author, date, and place of publication so that you will be able to document your information for readers who may wish to know more about your subject. Ask your librarian about style guides such as those described in Chapter Six. Devise a system to identify the ideas and words that must be attributed to the authors you have been reading. Your own ideas will come from the connections, insights, and conclusions you draw from the articles and books you read.

Even if you summarize, or *paraphrase*, an author's ideas in your own words, you must indicate this source in your paper. If you decide to illustrate a point with a quotation from a book, you must cite the pages where the quote can be found. Presenting borrowed ideas as your own (*plagiarism*) is neither honest nor acceptable; making careful notes during your reading will help you avoid this practice. Include people you interview in your sources of information as well. Professional writers also acknowledge those who have contributed ideas through informal discussion and reading of drafts.

Find a Focus

Writers often find themselves going off on tangents as they write a first draft. Sometimes the intended focus of a paper becomes buried in large amounts of information. The following strategies help writers to focus on the main point.

Decide Purpose and Goals

Whether you are writing a term paper, answering an examination question, or writing a report at work, your writing will benefit from a conscious decision about purpose and goals. The purpose of writing a term paper is usually to gain knowledge about a subject. When you are permitted to choose your own topic, the assignment becomes an opportunity to learn something about a topic you find particularly interesting. One of your goals will be to convince your reader that you have a good understanding of the topic. For example, if your assignment is to compare and contrast two forms of government in a twenty-page essay, you have a wide range of possible goals with which to shape your paper. From class discussions or your own reading, you may decide that you want to show that these two governments are essentially the same. Perhaps you want to convince the teacher that both forms of government can be appropriate in particular circumstances. You may want to demonstrate that a certain period of history most clearly illustrates the similarities between both types of government.

On another level, you may want to show the teacher that you are able to identify an important issue and argue your point. Your reader—the teacher—will also have expectations of your paper. The teacher will want to know what you have learned from the course and how well you can apply that learning. Decide where your goals overlap with those of your readers. Your paper will be most successful if it focuses on goals shared by both writer and reader.

Deciding purpose and goals is essential for all transactional writing. For example, if your manager has asked you to write a report justifying your request for new computer software, he may need your report to obtain the purchase order. Your manager may also want to use the information in your report to demonstrate his department's productivity to his manager. Although your immediate writing goal is to obtain the new software, the report will also help your manager achieve his goals as well.

Your goals for writing may change as you explore your ideas through writing or as you acquire new information. One way to focus on writing goals is to write out a *goal statement*. Your statement may be something like this: "I want to write to the bookstore to complain about the closing time." Your goal statement will be more helpful for guiding your writing if you expand it to include a reason and specific details: "I want to persuade the bookstore to stay open until six p.m. at least once a week because part-time students often can't get away from work in time to buy their books before the bookstore's closing time of five p.m." The difference between these two statements is that the first will result in a letter of complaint, whereas the second will request action for change and give a reason for the request. Remember that your intended reader will have goals too, and a shared goal provides a strong reason for the reader to read. In this case, if the bookstore remains open longer, the writer can buy his course textbooks and the reader can increase her profits by selling more books.

If you are writing an economics term paper on the effects of the free trade agreement between Canada and the United States, your goal statement may read like this: "I want to write about the effects of the free trade agreement on manufacturing in Canada." This goal statement suggests simply a list of effects and does not say what you are going to do with that list. An expanded goal statement would provide more direction for writing the paper and include the position you intend to take. For example, you might decide to set your goal like this: "I want to write about the effects of the free trade agreement on manufacturing because the experts do not agree on the effects and, after further reading and analysis of the various positions, I may be able to support a position for or against the agreement, or at least draw some conclusions."

Writing out a goal statement helps writers focus on what they want their writing to accomplish. Try explaining your writing goal to a friend, a teacher, or your writing group and ask for their suggestions. For example, the writers of the expanded goal statements above might ask for suggestions about solutions to the problem or further sources of information. Once you have decided what you want your writing to accomplish for you and your readers, make your goals operational. Brainstorm a list of all the possible ways to achieve your goals and then select the most feasible. Think of verbs: you want your writing to *do* something. Linda Flower offers the following example of an **operational goal** statement for a letter of application for a summer job: "I'll try to arouse the reader's interest enough so that he or she will read my résumé, will remember at least two things about me, and will then ask me for an interview" (89).

In your plan to persuade the bookstore to extend its hours, you might write a goal statement that includes the following subgoals:

- *Remind* them about the number of students inconvenienced by the present closing time
- *Suggest* extra staffing
- *Show* an understanding of the bookstore's position
- *Avoid* a focus on complaints
- *Keep* it short
- *Be* constructive.

One of your plans might be to do some research on alternatives. Included in your plans will be the form your writing should take. For example, your writing to the bookstore may take the form of problem identification, analysis, alternatives, and recommendation. You might also decide that a petition would be more effective than a single letter.

The writer of the paper about free trade might brainstorm a list of operational goals such as these:

- *explain* the free trade agreement
- *define* the manufacturing industry
- *compare* pre–free trade situations with present situations
- *quote* the experts
- *describe* the trends
- *use* statistics
- *describe* one or two cases to illustrate the effects.

Brainstorming a list of possibilities helps you see the choices available to you as a writer. Ask your writing group to add to your list, and explain your choices for the most effective ways of achieving your writing goals.

Try this:

The strategies of setting writing goals and making plans to achieve them can be practised with your writing group. As a group, choose a subject and a reader, or group of readers, who would be interested in your subject. Negotiate a writing goal with your group. To begin, you might all write out a goal statement for the chosen subject, read each aloud, and choose one of the statements. Once a goal has been chosen, the group can then brainstorm a list of ways to achieve the goal. The real discussion begins when the group starts selecting the best ways to achieve the writing goals.

If you are working alone, you can practise this strategy by sketching an idea tree with your goal at the top and the sub-goals as branches. Try one or two trees and study each one to decide which you think would be most appropriate for your purpose and your reader. As you begin to write about your subject, you will often discover new goals as your ideas become clearer and your reader comes into focus. As you read books and articles on the subject, notice the variety of ways writers achieve their goals.

Consider Your Readers

If you stop to think about your own reading process, you will recognize that you have particular goals and strategies for reading. As a reader, you read for a variety of reasons; depending on your purposes, you may read the entire text carefully, skim through it, or read only parts of it. The way you read a text and your understanding of it depend not only on your knowledge and experience, but also on your goals as a reader. Effective writers take into account readers' experience and expectations in their writing goals and plans.

You can make better decisions about how to achieve your writing goals if you consider who your readers are, what they know about your subject, and why they would read your writing. See Chapter Seven for more about the way readers read and the questions you can ask to help you know your readers.

Freewrite a Draft

Some writers find it profitable to put their notes away and freewrite a first draft.

Try this:

Concentrate on your writing goal and try to write as much as possible without stopping. Use brackets, underlining, or arrows to mark words or sentences you know will have to be changed. If you find yourself bogged down on the introduction, go on to the next section. This approach has the advantage of producing writing that is shaped by your own thinking rather than writing that is merely a collage of ideas from your information sources. You can add supporting information from your sources during revision. This freewritten draft often achieves a natural flow and a definite shape.

Peter Elbow describes this kind of freewriting as part of the "direct writing process," which consists of writing quickly and then revising (26). Elbow observes that, although this strategy may not always lead to the best writing, it is especially useful for writers who know a great deal about their subject or for writers who are in a hurry. The final form of your writing will be determined not only by your subject, but also by your writing goal and your reader's expectations.

Summarize

Another way to focus on your subject is to summarize your ideas.

Try this:

Imagine that you meet a friend who is in a hurry. Your friend wants to know what you are writing. Reread your paper, underline the main points, and then summarize your ideas in a few sentences, explaining your subject and answering the reader's main question, "So what?" Having to summarize your information in a nutshell forces you to make the relationships among your ideas explicit.

Try teaching your subject to a friend or to your writing group. Most teachers say they learn their subject best by teaching it. Be sure to take note of any confusion, disagreements, or questions.

Outline

Earlier in the chapter, we discussed idea trees as an exploratory strategy to help writers visualize their ideas. These sketches can easily be modified as new ideas and writing goals emerge through talking, reading, and trying various strategies. You can also use idea trees after you have written a draft of your paper to reveal the logic of your organization. You can create a more detailed picture of your organization by means of a sentence outline.

Try this:

Create a sentence outline by reviewing each section of your paper and, on a separate piece of paper, writing out the sentence that states the main idea for that section and the sentence(s) that support the main idea. This strategy will help you sharpen your focus by identifying (1) sections that seem out of order, (2) sentences or ideas that logically belong in a different section, and (3) main ideas without support. You might also ask someone else to review your outline for a logical order. Ask yourself questions like these:

- Are the main ideas clearly distinguished from the supporting ideas?
- Do some ideas appear in several sections?
- Could these ideas be combined into a single section?
- Does the arrangement support my writing goal, and will it meet my reader's expectations?

Test a Draft

After a great deal of thinking about a subject and long periods of writing, writers often lose the ability to judge the coherence of their writing. The following strategies help writers get an idea of how readers might respond to their writing.

Reread the Draft

When you read your own writing, you tend to read what you think you have said rather than what is on the page.

Try this:

To gain distance from your writing, leave your draft for a while before rereading it. Although a long period before rereading allows you to become a new reader of your writing, even a short period will help you to re-see your writing. Adopt the role of the intended reader, pose questions, and make comments as you read. Read your draft aloud to make it less familiar to you and thus increase your distance from it. This strategy works especially well if you tape-record your reading, because your voice will sound unfamiliar when you play the tape back.

Ask for Response

The most helpful way to gain a perspective on your writing is to have other people read the draft.

Try this:

Explain your subject and describe the intended reader of your paper before you ask a friend or someone in your writing group to read your draft. Ask someone to read your draft aloud so that you will hear your writing in a new way. Be alert to the reader's pauses and hesitations, which may signal confusing ideas or sentences. If you ask someone to read your writing aloud and make comments on tape, then you can replay it several times to catch the reader's comments.

Consider the type of feedback you want from your readers. Do you want a general impression or do you want specific comments on a particular idea or paragraph? You can help your readers by including a list of points you want them to consider. Your list might include the following:

- Is my main point clear?
- Is my analysis or argument convincing?
- Are my ideas connected to reveal a logical order?
- Does my tone seem appropriate for this reader and this situation?
- Have I made errors in grammar or spelling?

Donald Murray proposes three readings of a draft: first, for meaning (Is the writing understandable? Are readers' questions answered?); second, for order (Is each section of the writing developed and connected to the introduction and conclusion?); and third, for language (Is the language precise and appropriate?). Three readings may seem time-consuming, but the process becomes much easier and faster with practice. Murray also reminds us that positive feed-back helps writers to build on their strengths.

Make Comparisons

Match a reader's view of your draft against your own view. The following strategies can be explored with a friend or your writing group.

Try this:

1. Ask your reader to write a goal statement (see page 115) after reading your paper. Then compare the reader's statement with your own goal statement.
2. Make a short summary of your paper, but don't show it to your reader until she or he has also made a summary of your paper. Compare the two summaries and discuss the differences with your reader.
3. Make an idea tree of your draft, then ask your reader to do the same. Again compare the two idea trees and discuss the differences.
4. Try Kenneth Bruffee's **descriptive outline.** This strategy often results in surprises for writers because it demonstrates a reader's view of what a piece of writing *says* and what it *does*. To find out if you have written what you think you have written, begin with a brief statement of the main idea or key issue in your paper. Then, for each paragraph in your paper, make a summary statement of the main point and describe the function of the paragraph.

   Among the things a sentence or paragraph can *do* are *describe, explain, introduce, list, give examples, analyze, synthesize, compare, contrast, question, answer, defend, connect*, and *argue*. Observe how the paragraph functions in relation to the main point of the whole paper as well as the preceding and following paragraphs. If you find a paragraph that seems to function merely as a filler, use the phrase "fills up space" to describe it.

   Although the descriptive outline works well for writers in any situation, it can also be used to advantage in a writing group. Have a reader make a descriptive outline for your paper; then compare it with your own outline. You can organize your descriptive outline by numbering each paragraph and then listing the summary statements and functions on a separate piece of paper under the headings *Says* and *Does*. The following is an example of a first paragraph and its descriptive outline.

Reef-Building Sponges

A charming description of sponges reflecting once-held beliefs in spontaneous generation is given in Gerard's *Herball*, published in 1636: "There is a-growing upon the rockes near unto the sea a certain matter wrought together of the foame or frothe of the sea which we call spunges." Although we no longer entertain Gerard's romantic assertions, we still harbor our own odd twentieth-century conjectures about "spunges"—especially conjectures about fossil forms. Many fossil sponges lack close living relatives, so that paleontologists frequently have been obliged to base their biological theories upon reasoned conjecture using available analogues. In addition, environmental conditions have changed significantly during the earth's history, so we have no modern counterparts for many ancient environments and ecological habitats. Discoveries of new living sponges, therefore, represent important opportunities to extrapolate biological, ecological, and evolutionary inferences to related fossils. (Wood, 224–35)

Says: We do not know a great deal about sponges, especially fossil forms. Fossil sponges have few living relatives; therefore, we must make inferences about them and their environments from the discovery of new living sponges.

Does:

- *Captures* the reader's interest by quoting a fifteenth-century naturalist's description of sponges.
- *Introduces* the subject of sponges.
- *Compares* the state of current knowledge about sponges with that of the fifteenth century.

- *Argues* that we can learn about fossil sponges from a study of living sponges.

Your writing group is a good place to try these strategies, because each member can expect the same care and consideration in the review process. Once you have received feedback on your draft and discussed it with your readers, you will have to evaluate the feedback in light of your own writing goals and your knowledge about the intended reader of your writing.

If you have explored all the strategies in this chapter, you will have a good idea of the range of options available for improving your writing processes. You will have discovered that strategies, like almost anything else, are best learned through experimentation and adaptation and that, indeed, it is through our mistakes that we deepen our understandings. From discussions with friends or your writing group, you will have realized that in some situations and for some writers, certain strategies work better than others. A review of your journals and logs will reveal the many ways you have learned to adapt the strategies to your own needs. Continue to practise the strategies whenever you write so they become easily available to you for difficult or unfamiliar writing assignments. Knowing how to use a variety of strategies will help you write both effectively and efficiently.

Exercises

The following exercises will help you apply the strategies you have learned in this chapter to an extended piece of writing. We encourage you to write about subjects you are already familiar with or have the interest and time to learn about. We believe that good writing most often happens when you write with a sense that you are in a position to inform or persuade readers who want or need to know about a subject. Ideally, students write for readers both inside and outside the classroom. As well as writing for teachers, students write for interested members of the class, co-workers or managers at work, children in elementary and high schools, community leaders, and university administrators. Many students bring these readers' responses back for discussion in their writing groups.

When working on these exercises, use those strategies you believe will be most productive in light of the goals and readers you have in mind.

Exercise 1: Do A Problem-Solving Project

Note: Reread the discussion of problem analysis in this chapter before you begin. Be sure to discuss the following tasks with your writing group. Talk about the feasibility of your project and test your draft proposal and final report with your group members.

1. Identify a real problem that can be solved. Your first task is to identify a real problem that is causing real difficulties for real people. In other words, do not choose a hypothetical problem or a case study: the problem must be one you have worked with, been a part of, or have been affected by. The problem should not be a personal problem such as your own difficulties managing your time or getting along with a teacher or a boss. Nor should it be a large, vague problem such as war, racism, or pollution. The problem should be one that someone in a position to make decisions would want solved. Consider work, school, hobbies, or community activities as potential problem areas.

   The goal of this project is to define a specific problem, analyze why things go wrong, develop alternative solutions, and recommend the most feasible solution. Think of your reader(s) as a person or persons in a position to act on your report.

2. Write a proposal to study the problem. Once you have identified a problem area and made a preliminary analysis, write a brief proposal to the intended reader(s). This proposal should convince the reader(s) of the need to study the problem.

3. Communicate your analysis in a written report. Once you have completed your investigation and clearly defined the problem, design a report for your reader(s). Analyze your reader and develop a strategy for presenting your results.

Note: This problem-solving project can easily be adapted to the writing of term papers in specific subject areas. During your studies and your reading, take note of the issues and controversies that surround a subject. For example, in psychology you might look at some aspect of the conflict between the theories of Freud and Jung; in political science you might investigate some aspect of the conflict between society's needs and individual freedoms; in history you might choose issues surrounding the causes or effects of a particular event, such as the Riel Rebellion, in light of current events. Look for the problem areas in your subject and choose an issue that you can clearly identify and define. Your problem definition, analysis, and alternative solutions will come from class discussions and your understanding of the reading you do. Although you may not be able to recommend a solution, you will be able to reach some conclusions about the issue from your reading and writing. You can write your proposal to your teacher or your writing group. This proposal should identify the problem and explain how you know it is a problem. The remainder of your proposal should include your plans for investigating the problem, such as specific people you plan to interview and specific books, journals, and reports you plan to consult.

Exercise 2: Explore Nonacademic Writing

Because there are major differences between the writing done in school and the writing done in the workplace, writing researchers have begun to study the writing people do on the job. They study what people write, how they write, why they write, and the effects of their writing. The findings reveal a variety of complex writing purposes, processes, audiences, and documents.

Information about what is expected of writers at work will be a valuable resource for members of your writing group and for people who teach writing. Choose a field related to your career goals or your program of study. Interview someone who works in that field and who writes regularly as part of his or her job responsibilities. Write a report for the members of your writing group about one type of nonacademic writing. Think of your report as contributing to a bank of information about nonacademic writing.

Note: Exercise 10 in Chapter Six is a similar exercise that can be applied to a study of academic writing as well.

References And Further Reading

Bruffee, Kenneth. *A Short Course in Writing*. Boston: Little, Brown and Company, 1980.

Coe, Richard. *Form and Substance: An Advanced Rhetoric*. New York: John Wiley and Sons, 1981.

Elbow, Peter. *Writing with Power*. New York: Oxford University Press, 1981.

Flower, Linda. Excerpt from *Problem-Solving Strategies for Writing*, Third Edition by Linda Flower, copyright © 1989 by Harcourt Brace Jovanovich, Inc., reprinted by permission of the publisher.

Jeans, James. *The Stars in Their Courses*. Cambridge: Cambridge University Press, 1948.

Murray, Donald. Excerpt from *Write to Learn* by Donald M. Murray, copyright © 1984 by Holt, Rinehart and Winston, Inc., reprinted by permission of the publisher.

Osborn, A.F. *Applied Imagination*. New York: Scribners, 1956. Reprinted with permission from the copyright holder, Creative Education Foundation, Buffalo, N.Y.

Wood, Rachel. "Reef-Building Sponges." *American Scientist* 78 (May/June 1990): 224–35. Reprinted by permission of *American Scientist*, Journal of Sigma Xi, The Scientific Research Society.

Young Richard E., Alton L. Becker, and Kenneth L. Pike. *Rhetoric: Discovery and Change*. New York: Harcourt Brace Jovanovich, Inc., 1970.

Chapter Six

Forms
and Forming

ঽ৶

The thought behind I strove to join
Unto the thought before
But sequence ravelled out of reach
Like balls upon the floor.

EMILY DICKINSON

What is form? In this chapter, and throughout this book, we use the word "form" in two ways. First, we use it as a verb meaning to shape, mould, order, or arrange. This chapter provides experiments in forming. Second, we use the word "form" as a noun meaning the pattern or structure of finished written **texts**. In this usage, "form" is synonymous with **format**, organization, or arrangement. In the pages that follow, you will find examples of some of the forms used in and outside of school.

As you read, you will find invitations to try the exercises at the end of the chapter. These exercises are examples only; if you wish to extend, adapt, or alter them, by all means do. However, we strongly encourage you to attempt some version of the exercises, because they will help you understand and experience variations in forming and form. For example, Exercises 1 and 2 provide an introduction to the chapter, and we invite you to try them before continuing. Finally, we recommend that you do the exercises with others, because group work will increase not only your enjoyment but the effectiveness of the tasks as well.

Forming

> Thinking is a matter of seeing relationships—relationships of parts to wholes, of items in a sequence, of causes and effects; composition is a matter of seeing and naming relationships, of putting relationships together, ordering them.
>
> ANN E. BERTHOFF

Forming, or giving shape to experience, begins with perception. We make sense of the chaos we see by discerning shapes, colours, contours. We distinguish foreground from background, we focus and select, we see where one thing begins and another ends. We are able to do this because we recognize repetitions and patterns and form them into categories. At first, however, everything is a blur. For instance, very young infants cannot distinguish individual shapes; after a while, they form the category of "face" and can see their parents in the swirl of colour and movement around them.

Beyond perception, at the more abstract level of ideas, we make sense of our world by establishing links and relationships; we form meaning by building conceptual structures, by relating one thing to another. We move from the concrete to the abstract, we generalize, hypothesize, and theorize. We see similarities and differences; we classify and categorize; we recognize causality, sequence, contrast, variation. When we think, we are forming.

Writing—all language, in fact—is simply another manifestation of the human habit of forming. When we use language, we name, and naming creates individual cases, categories, and groups. To say "Fido is a dog, and dogs are animals" is to separate Fido from all dogs, dogs from all other creatures and, at the very same time, to bring them all together. When we use language we collect and connect, we reflect and remember, we link old ideas, and we create new ones. The activity of writing is aptly called the "composing process": when we compose, we shape and structure. That is why writing is such a powerful way to explore and discover.

However—and here is the heart of the matter—*we do not all create identical forms* when we see, think, speak, or write. We do not experience the world in exactly the same ways. One person sees the forest as part of a delicate ecological balance; another sees it as so many board feet of lumber. As a result of upbringing, culture, ideology, and many other factors, we view the world differently. When we write, we are asking our readers to see the world, or some part of it, as we do. In this sense, *all* writing is persuasive: we want others to understand, and perhaps agree with, our perceptions and beliefs. Forming and form are inextricably linked to this effort.

From Forming to Form

Throughout this book, we encourage you to exploit the forming power of language. By brainstorming, freewriting, or simply talking with a colleague or friend, you can begin to collect and connect ideas and to consider the most appropriate sequence for those ideas. This freedom to experience writing as a process often has an immediate and dramatic effect on people. By initially ignoring such secondary concerns as spelling, punctuation, and grammar, writers can focus on the making of meaning. This leads to an often messy but usually rewarding process of exploration and discovery.

Unfortunately, writers occasionally abandon the rich findings of the writing process when they move to the actual drafting of a text. Then, perhaps from force of habit, they return to the standard formats, opinions, or arguments they have used in the past. It is as if, after assembling and preparing the ingredients for a lavish and elaborate meal, the cook popped a TV dinner into the oven. This split between process and product is a split between forming and form and is indicative of a very real problem: how can we move from creative freethinking, which some of the strategies in Chapter Five promote, to the constraints of written formats? How can we move from the often personal and idiosyncratic structures found in freewriting, clustering, and mapping to the formats readers expect and need? How can ideas be arranged to suit the topic, the writer, and the readers? Exercise 3 at the end of the chapter will help you address some of these questions.

Generally, when moving from the forming process to the formal product, writers are faced with two broad arrangement options: they can create the form of their texts or follow the forms set out by the discipline, organization, supervisor, or teacher for whom they write. Between these poles of creation and compliance, however, is a vast range of choices. And in either case, the form of a text is not something imposed on ideas but, rather, a shape inseparable from those ideas. Even within such apparently rigid forms as lab reports, letters of recommendation, or book reports, considerable leeway exists for the writer to order ideas in a pattern suited to his or her intentions and the context in which the text will be read.

Ideally, as you talk, think, and write about a topic, the shape of the finished text will grow naturally. It may be that there is a form inherent to the topic. For example, certain processes and procedures follow a chronological order and can be described within the framework of time. When chronology cannot help, some other logical structure will be necessary. Perhaps you can present arguments for and against a position, or outline issues in declining order of importance, or give examples leading to a conclusion. Most topics of any complexity can be arranged in a variety of different forms, and although one overriding structure may govern a text, there will almost certainly be a variety of substructures within the larger form. The strategies presented in chapter five provide the writer with deliberate and systematic methods of experimenting with form.

As we move through the process of forming to the form of the final product, we are moving toward greater and greater clarity, both for ourselves and for our readers. Clarity is achieved, in part, by creating a distinct shape or structure in our texts, a structure that consists of separate elements and the connections among them. To create this structure, we need to consider three things: the size of ideas, their relationships, and their sequence.

Size

The "size" of an idea refers to its level or degree of abstraction (see Chapter Eight for a discussion of levels of abstraction in language). The movement from abstract to concrete is usually a movement from a concept to a relatively specific instance of that concept. For example, *furniture* is a more abstract idea than *chair*. Likewise, *pollution* is the abstract term, and the *acid rain* that is killing maple trees in Quebec is a concrete example. Even when words or ideas are not related, it is often possible to rank them by "size." Which is the "larger" (more abstract) term, *peace* or *wallpaper? literature* or *home run? international trade* or *mountain climbing?* What makes something more or less abstract than something else? Every idea lies somewhere on a continuum from abstract to concrete. Like those Russian dolls that fit one inside another, ideas are "smaller" or "larger" than other ideas. For example, try ranking the items in the following list from 10 (most abstract) to 1 (most concrete) and compare your ranking with others.

means of conveyance

technology

fuel burning machine

Honda

privately owned vehicle

compact car

motor driven transportation

Accord

my rusty 1982 car

automobile

Exercise 4 at the end of the chapter offers more opportunities to experiment with the "size" of ideas.

Relationships

In terms of relationships, there are three patterns to consider: superordination, coordination, and subordination. To return to a previous example, *furniture* is superordinate to *chairs* (and, of course, *chairs* are subordinate to *furniture*), while *chairs* and *tables* are coordinate—they are on the same level of generality. The same relationships hold true for abstract topics; for instance, *emotion* is the superordinate to which *anger* is the subordinate, with *fear* as a coordinate of anger. The following figure shows these relationships in graphic form:

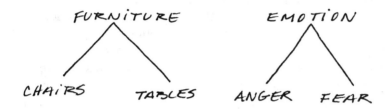

These patterns of relationship are the basis for many of the forming strategies introduced in Chapter Five, particularly the idea tree. When you provide an example in writing or speech, you are relying on this link between ideas: the more abstract (superordinate) idea is illustrated by the concrete (subordinate) instance. Definitions, too, move between levels of abstraction, although usually in the reverse direction: when you say that unequal pay for equal work is sexual discrimination, you are defining the concrete by reference to the more abstract. And much writing is structured so that points of view or ideas of approximately equal (coordinate) abstraction are compared. For example, in an essay on censorship, you might contrast an individual's freedom of expression with his or her responsibility to society. Or, in a paper on investment, you might compare real estate with savings bonds. In either case, you are comparing ideas of approximately equal, or coordinate, abstraction. Exercise 5 explores relationships of superordination, coordination, and subordination.

Sequence

Finally, form consists of the sequence or order of ideas in a text. Rarely do we find ideas linked in simple patterns, from smallest to largest or from concrete to abstract. Usually, the writer strings ideas together in a sequence appropriate to the topic, her or his goals, and the needs of the reader. For example, many documents begin with a summary of the entire text, often called an "abstract." Necessarily, this capsule version of the document will be more general than the text proper, which includes details and elaboration. The goal of the summary writer is to provide an overview of the text, a synopsis that allows the busy reader a quick sense of the whole document. Similarly, an effective argument will be arranged so as to have the greatest chance of persuading readers. There is no one way of forming *the* successful argument. Perhaps the writer will choose not to mention the conclusion until the very end, for fear of prejudicing the reader before the full argument is made. The writer may decide to present various views on an issue ("On the one hand ...on the other hand ..."), or state a case and then critique or qualify it ("However, ..."). The sentences in Exercise 6 at the end of the chapter are out of order; rearranging them will help you understand the idea of sequence in texts.

As you shape your ideas through writing, you will be moving from abstract to concrete (and vice versa), you will be creating relationships, and you will be arranging ideas in a sequence. What was a confused jumble of impressions and information will take shape. You will see the beginning and end of concepts and their connections to other ideas; you will see the parts as well as the whole. For that arrangement to be clear to your reader, you must carefully link the separate parts of your text—the forms within the form.

Forms within Forms

Although an effective text has an overall, cohesive structure, that large form consists of many smaller forms. From short passages to the full document, a text is an intricate design of ideas, a pattern of forms within forms. Paragraphs, sections, chapters—even sentences—have some arrangement. (Chapter Eight looks at syntax and sentence structure.) When we move beyond the sentence to the next formal element of text, the paragraph, the possibilities for structure multiply.

Strangely, though paragraphs are common to most texts, there is no general agreement on what they are. They have traditionally been described out of context, without reference to readers or purposes, as units of thought larger than a sentence. That vague definition led to the belief that paragraphs should have a single main idea announced in a "topic" sentence. Although some paragraphs do have such a clearly identifiable structure, most teachers and textbooks nowadays concede greater variety in paragraph organization. Some paragraphs are organized around issues, opinions, items, or ideas. Others present a series of events or steps in chronological sequence. Occasionally, they state a problem and offer a solution, or begin with an abstract concept and move on to concrete details. Following a less linear pattern, a paragraph may take the form of an image or metaphor. Even concerns about layout can determine paragraphs: large blocks of text intimidate readers, and indentations and other white spaces make a page more readable. They give the reader a break.

Despite the great diversity in their structure, it is safe to say that effective paragraphs, like other aspects of form, are not randomly constructed. They are shaped by the topic, readers, and purpose of the overall text. Exercise 7 at the end of this chapter provides an opportunity for examining paragraphs and other units of text.

Forms

We are all familiar with hundreds of formal or structural features in spoken and written discourse. In stories, we know the forms of beginning ("Once upon a time ...") and ending ("And so they lived happily ever after ..."), and many other elements of narrative structure we may not even be conscious of knowing. In daily speech we follow tacit rules of form in everything from answering the telephone to ordering food in restaurants. According to linguists who study such things, even so-called "informal" conversations are shaped by complex rules of structure and procedure. We know a considerable amount about the form of jokes, excuses, apologies, requests, questions, arguments, and

other kinds of language. And we know, too, about the form
of plays, movies, television shows, and commercials. (Try
Exercise 8 to discover how much you already know about
form in language.)

Perhaps the most natural and easily followed form is the
narrative. It is usually structured by chronology, although
flashbacks and other devices are sometimes used to vary the
form. As listeners and readers, we know how confusing a
story can get if the arrangement of events falls out of time
without explanation. Similarly, certain descriptions of process are chronological, such as instructions for assembling a
bicycle or a furniture kit. The predictability of these and
other forms benefits both writer and reader. The form helps
the writer select the relevant ideas and information; that is,
it acts as a heuristic, shaping and directing the writer's
thoughts and helping the writer choose what *should* be said
from all that *could* be said. And form helps the reader anticipate and comprehend—it directs the reader's attention and
forms the reader's understanding.

Underlying our simplest documents is a pattern of logic,
an arrangement of ideas; even a grocery list will be organized according to some sequence of thought. Perhaps the
food is listed in the order in which it ran out, or grouped
according to type or location in the store (fruits and vegeta-
bles, meats, dairy products, and so on). Other lists might
reveal classification by meal: breakfast foods, material for
lunches, quick and nutritious suppers. At the very least, the
list-maker's memory of what was needed would determine
the sequence.

Occasionally, paragraphs or whole texts are structured
around a metaphor. Exercise 1 at the end of Chapter Four,
in which experienced students write to younger students
about technical topics, frequently results in texts that have
metaphors underlying their form. For example, electricity
may be compared to water, and thus the movement of electricity through a circuit may be described using an image of
water and hoses. The analogy strategy in Chapter Five may
help you find an image around which to arrange a text.

We invite you to try Exercise 9 at the end of the chapter.
The texts listed in that exercise have no standard pattern of
organization, but you will have no trouble identifying

potential sections and possible arrangements for each of them. For example, letters home are usually written sponta-neously and may not be arranged in any deliberate or con-scious fashion, but they still have a form; like all texts, they follow some sequence or pattern. Perhaps the letter describes aspects of the writer's life: school, work, extracur-ricular activities, finances, health, recent books or movies. Or maybe it is arranged like a history or narrative, reporting events that have occurred since the writer last wrote.

The point is that forms are created by the thinking that produced them; indeed, the thinking and the forms are inseparable. If you examine closely the formats used by a particular group of people—scientists—for instance, you can learn much about the ways they think. Such analysis can also help you discover how writers or practitioners in a given field believe others should think. If you are intent on entering a certain profession or discipline—engineering, commerce, education, journalism, or social work, for exam-ple—a close reading of the academic and nonacademic texts in those fields will be of great value to you.

Forms and Forming in School

Students face a bewildering variety of often conflicting writ-ing demands. From one course to another much can change: formats, reasons for writing, implied readers, topics, referencing methods, and so on. One teacher wants rich descriptions full of narrative, personal observations, and speculation; another wants only the pertinent facts in pre-cisely the right order. Some instructors give only the vaguest indication of their requirements for papers and reports, while others provide detailed explanations. This variation is due partly to the fact that conventions change from one field to another. What counts as reasonable argument in English Literature may be considered hopelessly "subjective" in Economics. But even within a single discipline the stan-dards vary from teacher to teacher.

Unfortunately, most people have had limited opportuni-ties to think about or experiment with the arrangement of ideas in writing, simply because forms are often perceived as inflexible. One popular arrangement is the three-part structure frequently proposed for school papers: introduction, body, conclusion. A slightly more elaborate version of this form calls for division of the body into three to create the much-taught five-paragraph essay. The major problem with this arrangement is that it is usually presented without reference to actual writing situations, as if form could exist in a vacuum. However, form can hinder rather than help communication if it is not organic, that is, if it does not fit the topic, the writer's intentions, and the reader's needs. If the five paragraphs are merely a concession to prescribed form, they will be an empty structure.

In school, as elsewhere, writers face a range of choices concerning form—from self-created forms to the standardized forms typical of certain disciplines. In all cases, however, writers must make the form work for them; they must ensure that the form is in harmony with their topic, goals, and reader's needs. In the following pages, we will examine two different writing assignments and the problems of form they present.

The first assignment comes from a university writing course. It grants the writer full autonomy over topic, audience, form, and intention. In other words, the students can write about anything they want, to whomever they want, for any reason, and in any format. We will follow one student's attempts to find form for this assignment by tracking the process through her log and rough work to her final written product.

The writer, Anna, decided to write on the topic of women and science. Following her initial brainstorm, Anna made this entry in her writer's log:

- Brought out some ideas I would like to research.
- Haven't done any research—not too sure about things yet.
- Very broad areas—I'm going to have to cut a lot of these ideas and narrow in topic.

After some research and some more brainstorming, Anna wrote this in her log: "Will definitely narrow topic down to just reasons why girls opt out of sciences at high-school level." She then tried to arrange her ideas in a rough tree form; in her log, she responded to that attempt:

- Oh dear! Just couldn't do one!
- Going to have to go through notes and structure—make a plan on paper.

Anna went through her pages and pages of notes and began to freewrite under the following headings:

- Women in workforce
- Women in engineering (physical sciences)
- Early conditioning and genetics
- Dropouts
- Stereotypes
- Major forces creating problems for women

In her log, she commented about the freewriting:

- Put together some good sections from my notes.
- Starting to give me structure ideas.
- A lot of ideas, but not organized properly yet.
- Good start in thinking things through.

Anna then wrote a first draft and made a rough outline based on that draft. Her log comments indicate that her understanding of the topic, her own goals as a writer, and her emerging sense of readers are helping her find the form for her paper:

- Added new sections from freewriting.
- Sectioned things off with titles.
- Set up an outline to work with for second draft.
- I now have a pretty good idea of my structure.
- I went through all my notes and numbered parts according to which section to put them in—this seems to have worked as a method of organization to make sure everything I have is included.
- I still don't have a specific audience but think it'll work to make this a paper to make people aware of social differences and what can be done.

Before beginning a second draft, Anna also sketched the following tree.

Finally, after two more drafts and the addition of an introduction and conclusion, Anna's paper had three major headings: Sex Differences, Environmental and Social Differences, and What Can Be Done. Her original goal had been to explain "why girls opt out of sciences at high-school level"; during the writing, she decided she wanted to address, in her words, "anyone who would want to argue that men are smarter than women." In the end, however, Anna decided to assume that readers would not need to be convinced of intellectual equality between the sexes and, instead, she focused on the reasons there is a shortage of women in science and on solutions to that problem. Her knowledge of her topic, her goals as a writer, and consideration of her readers had allowed her to find a suitable form.

Anna's assignment represents one end of a spectrum that describes the degree of control students have over the form of their academic papers. Whereas Anna had almost complete autonomy, the writers of the next assignment we will examine have next to no control of arrangement at all. The assignment is a technical paper in a university engineering course. Fortunately, the course handout has many clues, and many outright instructions, concerning the form of the final paper. The first indication can be found in the opening sentence of the course description: "The ability to write clear, concise, and accurate technical reports is one of the most important skills that an engineer needs to develop." Since form makes an important contribution to how clear, concise, and accurate a text will be, it can safely be assumed that structure and order are valued in this course. The handout goes on to give valuable insights into what an effective technical report should consist of:

> *Title*—should be chosen with care to indicate as specifically as possible the content of the paper. Keep it short.
>
> *Abstract*—a capsule version of your paper, stating objectives, methods of solution, conclusions, and recommendations as concisely as possible (50–150 words).
>
> *Acknowledgments*—should briefly indicate if this work was the result of a summer job. Who helped you with the material?

Table of contents—should list the major headings and subheadings with page numbers. Avoid too extensive a breakdown.

List of illustrations

Introduction— must include a clear statement of the problem as well as the objectives of the paper. It may also include an outline of relevant background pertinent to the specific topic.

Background—a separate background section may be used but only if preliminary information is included that is essential to understanding the paper. If you are uncertain whether the reader will understand your background information and want to write more explanatory or descriptive material, this should be placed in an appendix.

Discussion—must present a logical progression of analysis to lead the reader from the problem statement to the conclusion. This section should be subdivided into the appropriate headings: Method of Analysis, Criteria of Selection, Alternatives Studied, Results, Discussion, Assumptions Made (and their limitations), and so on.

Conclusions and recommendations—must present an answer to the problem stated in the Introduction. Together, the Introduction and Conclusion should make sense without the rest of the paper.

References

Figures and tables—should be used when they will help to clarify, illustrate, or summarize pertinent information. All figures and tables must be specifically referred to and fully discussed in your text.

Appendices—should be used sparingly, and only if needed.

As mentioned above, it is important to note the links between readers and form. Although most university papers may not appear to have an authentic reader (that is, one in real need of the information supplied), it helps to imagine how such a reader might approach and read your text. Consider these comments about the reader from the engineering course handout:

> To help you organize your presentation, it may be useful to pretend you are trying to convince your superior, who is an over-worked executive, to act on your recommendations. You should take into consideration how your reader will read your paper. Generally, he or she will read it at three levels:
>
> **1.** the abstract
> **2.** the introduction, conclusions, and recommendations
> **3.** the whole paper
>
> You must write your paper in such a manner as to entice your supervisor to read the paper at all three levels. This is not done by building up suspense about the purpose of your paper (the mystery novel approach). On the contrary, you should be as informative as possible about the objectives, conclusions, and recommendations of your paper at all levels, varying only the detail of reporting from a very concise synopsis in the abstract to a full discussion of all relevant material in the body of the report.

Elsewhere in the handout, a further clue is provided: "The technical report should be written to convince the reader that there is a situation that requires attention, to develop for the reader some ways to deal with the situation, and to recommend solutions." These three major goals create the foundation upon which the report is constructed.

Unfortunately, not all teachers are as explicit about their organizational preferences as was the professor of that engineering course. In fact, although some teachers say very little about the features they favour in the texts they assign, they evaluate the final product as if they had. Such teachers may assume that everyone knows what they want, or they may believe they have made their demands clearly known; in either case, the student is left in a difficult position. If you have ever been uncertain about the form required for a written assignment, Exercise 10 will help you develop strategies for finding the structure implied by the description of the assignment.

Sometimes the best method of discovering appropriate form in academic writing is simply to ask the teacher some or all of the following questions:

- Is there a standard format for this assignment?
- May I develop my own form?
- What elements (or features or sections) do you expect?
- Is there a style guide or handbook that describes appropriate organizational patterns in this field of study?
- Can you recommend a professional journal that contains models of the kind of writing you expect?

Although students may fear that asking these kinds of questions will display their ignorance, this is rarely, if ever, the case. Your questions might help the teacher articulate what he or she expects but has not explained. Do not be afraid to ask for elaboration on an assignment; it is your right to know. See Chapter Five for ideas about what to ask when interviewing readers.

Forms and Forming Outside School

> We need to study form—and forming—much more carefully and in many more contexts than we have: form as organic, as construct; as flexible, as rigid; as generative, as constraint; as an instrument of creation and meaning; as the social penetrating the personal.
>
> RICHARD M. COE

In the past decade or so, people interested in the theory and practice of writing have become increasingly curious about the way writing occurs within disciplines and organizations. Much of the research in this area has helped us understand that there are many differences in writing between one field and another. It is not simply that language itself changes, although all fields have some specialized terminology. What seems more remarkable is the range of other variations: the implicit and explicit rules and reasons for writing, the roles and relationships for writers and readers, and the many documents and formats; all these change depending on the group with whom and for whom one writes.

In fact, the nature and use of writing (and speaking) so clearly distinguish one group from another that the term **discourse community** was coined to describe a group of people whose common pursuits and interests are discussed in ways particular to that group. For example, the writing that electrical engineers do is different from the writing that other people do, including other types of engineers. The language they use, the assumptions they share, the topics they write about, the formats they use, the reasons they write—all this and more makes the writing of electrical engineers distinct and qualifies them as a discourse community.

However, discourse communities, and membership in them, are rarely clearly defined; the boundaries are blurry. For instance, there are similarities between some communities, and individuals do move back and forth between them: a progress report from an electrical engineering laboratory may share many features with a progress report from a mechanical engineering lab. And within one community finer distinctions can be made, so that it is possible to distinguish between economists within the academic community and economists within the business community, for example. The economists may share a broad, specialized discourse, but each group will also have its own reasons and rules for writing. In our academic and professional lives, we all write and read within a variety of communities. Learning a new school subject or a new job is in large part a process of learning to read and write the discourse of a new community.

A major distinction among communities is the forms they use, especially the clearly regulated or standard forms. Standard forms—those governed by a community's guidelines—are a way of ensuring that writers in the community produce reader-based prose. Just as the structure of assignments in school must conform to the topic, the writer's goals, and the reader's needs, so too must the forms specific

to a discipline or organization. In addition, by joining a particular discourse community, the writer takes on the topics
and writing goals of that community. The *Publication Manual* of the American Psychological Association (APA)
explains it this way:

> Rules for the preparation of manuscripts should contrib-
> ute to clear communication ... These rules introduce the
> uniformity necessary to convert manuscripts written in
> many styles to printed pages edited in one consistent
> style. This spares readers from a distracting variety of
> forms throughout a work and permits readers to give full
> attention to content. (11)

In the case of standard arrangements, the forms form us:
they cause us to think about our topics in certain prescribed
ways. In other words, standardized forms represent the
ways in which a community or discipline thinks, and the
ways in which it wants its writers to think. We are con-
strained by these forms—restricted in what we can say, in
how we can say it, and in the order of its saying. On the
other hand, as the APA *Manual* points out, "Consistency of
presentation and format ... enables authors to present material systematically" (18). While forms can inhibit, they can
also liberate; they can be beneficial or detrimental. Simple
fill-in-the-blank forms, like application and tax forms, ask
for certain information and provide space for it. Such a
structure frees the form-filler from having to make decisions about what information to put first, what second, and
so on. However, there is often little or no room for additional information. We have all tried to cram too many
words into the cramped little boxes on those forms.

An examination of texts and guidelines can help you
discover the logic in a community's systematic presentation
of material. Some groups are more explicit than others
when it comes to form. There is little public agreement, for
instance, on the shape or structure of an essay in political
science or English literature. On the other hand, the writers
of many scientific and technical documents are frequently
directed by exact guidelines. In the following pages, we will

examine the form of three different types of text: the experimental research report, the newspaper article, and a social work assessment.

The structure of reports on experimental results, although not inflexible, remains similar across and within many disciplines. The following description of that structure, adapted from a biology laboratory's guidelines, clearly indicates the influence of the topic, the writer's goals, and the reader's needs on the form of the report.

Introduction: Explanation of the research problem and statement of the purpose or goal of the study.

Readers' questions:

- Why has the experiment been performed?
- What makes the experiment interesting or important?
- How does it relate to previous, similar experiments?
- What questions were asked?

Methods: Description of the method(s) used in the study.

Readers' questions:

- How was the experiment performed?
- What materials were employed?
- How can others repeat the experiment?

Results: Report of the findings or results of the research.

Readers' questions:

- What happened when the methods were applied?
- What changes were observed?
- Which information is worth noting?

Discussion: Elaboration and discussion of the findings; interpretation of results.

Readers' questions:

- What do the results mean?
- What is most significant?
- How do the results relate to other results?
- How do the results affect theory and practice?

Our second example—the newspaper article—usually has a typical structure, sometimes described as a pyramid or triangle. *The Canadian Press Stylebook* gives the following explanation for this form:

> Most hard-news stories are constructed in a way that presents facts in descending order of importance. This gives the reader on the run the most interesting information right away. And it provides newspapers with a story that is easily chopped to fit the space available.
>
> For an action story—a plane crash, for example—put the most dramatic elements in the lead paragraphs, then go back to the beginning of the action and narrate it as it happened. Finally, round off the story with background and assessment, which can be trimmed easily.
>
> For statement and opinion stories—a politician's speech, for instance—cover the key points in the lead paragraphs, then present the rest in descending order of importance, being careful not to bury prime facts, color or quotations. (283)

As you can see once again, the topic, the writer's goal, and the reader's need determine this form. The most interesting or important information goes first so that the newspaper writer's goal—getting information to the reader—can be achieved. Newspaper readers tend to skim, looking for the main facts and issues; if important information is included at the end of the article, the readers may never reach it. In addition, when newspaper editors have space restrictions, they begin to cut articles from the bottom up.

The fact that readers move quickly through a newspaper results in another important feature of form: the "lead," or opening, paragraph(s) of an article. "The lead should arouse readers' interest by featuring the most important and most interesting points of the story as a summary, one or more paragraphs long" (Canadian Press, 283). The paragraphs in a newspaper article are short—one to three sentences long—and packed with information. Many newspapers and magazines have in-house style guides that help newcomers learn the forms they need to master.

Our third example is a document with a very different form. The predisposition report is an advisory report that social workers write for judges in the youth court system in Quebec. This report provides details of the life of an adolescent found guilty of a criminal offence. Judges use the report to determine the most appropriate sentence for the adolescent. Although there are minor variations from worker to worker in the form of the report, the document is generally structured in this way:

Face Sheet: a covering sheet with facts and figures, such as names, addresses, dates of birth, etc.

Basis of report: list of the sources of information used to write the report.

Summary of offence: the official description of the charge against the adolescent and versions of the offence supplied by the adolescent, his or her parents, and the victim (if there was one).

Official antecedents/prior alternative measures: information about previous offences (for which the adolescent was found guilty) and the sentences resulting from those offences.

Assessment of adolescent: evaluation of the youth, including comments about personality, aggressivity, maturity, presence or absence of remorse for the offence, etc.

Assessment of adolescent's social situation: evaluation of the adolescent's behaviours at school, work, and among friends.

Family assessment: evaluation of the adolescent's family and its ability to provide support and guidance to the youth.

Summary: a brief synopsis of the main points in the report.

Recommendations: the social worker's suggestions to the judge concerning the sentencing of the adolescent.

Again, consideration of the context for this document sheds light on the logic underlying the form. The predisposition report is read by the judge, the defence lawyer, the Crown prosecutor, and the youth and his or her family; it is entered as evidence at the adolescent's sentencing hearing. Its purpose is to convince everyone that the recommended sentence is fair (given the youth's offence) and appropriate (given the youth's circumstances). The context for reading is naturally controversial, since one of the lawyers is likely to disagree with the recommendation, and the family is certain to be upset. In recognition of this, the form allows the social worker to build a case by accumulating detail leading up to a recommendation. Unlike some of the other reports we examined above, this report's recommendation comes at the very end of the document and no hint of it is given earlier. This form is typical of persuasive texts, when knowing the conclusion in advance might prejudice the reader's attention to the argument.

Close inspection of the writing done in any field will reveal much about the thinking of the writers and readers involved and the contexts in which they operate. Conversely, examining the circumstances within which a particular type of writing occurs will often explain the forms and functions of that writing. Exercise 11 outlines a procedure for an inquiry into writing. It suggests sources of information about writers and writing and some of the questions you might consider asking in your investigation.

Form Warnings and Final Words

Before leaving this discussion of form, we would like to sound a note of caution—two notes, actually. The first encourages you to be sceptical and critical about form, to resist the inappropriate imposition of structure, to question the validity of certain common forms, and to examine closely the standard forms you may be required to use, both in and out of school. The second encourages you to draw form out from your topic, your purpose, and a consideration of your readers, but to beware of the obvious or seemingly "natural" form that may first occur to you; you must be ready to revise form.

Resisting Form

The question of form brings out some extreme positions in discussions of writing. The reason may be found in the history of writing instruction, which for centuries has focused primarily on the formal features of completed texts. Unfortunately, this focus often ignores the messy but productive process of writing, when form is discovered and developed. One result of this is that many people were taught to make an outline before doing any writing—a practice that privileges form over exploration.

Underlying this approach is a common, yet faulty, metaphor that separates form from content. Form is *not* an empty container into which ideas are poured. Although standard formats do exist, the relationship between the shape and substance of texts is far more complex than the relationship between, for example, a glass and water. Perhaps a better metaphor, though still unsatisfactory, would compare form to a balloon, which both shapes and is shaped by its content. In other words, there is a reciprocal and dynamic relationship between form and content.

The important point to remember is that form does not merely carry or contain meaning, it *is* meaning. When you select the order in which your information will be arranged, when you group concepts or topics together, when you present ideas in a list rather than in a paragraph, you are making decisions that will affect the form and, therefore, the meaning of your text. And even when you work within the apparent confines of a standardized format, the decisions you make about organization will help determine your meaning. Although the outer form of two documents might be nearly identical—that is, they may look the same—their deeper structure, the arrangement of their ideas and the relationships among those ideas, might be dramatically different.

We all carry with us rules about form, as you may have discovered by completing the writing exercise in Chapter One. Many of those rules make sense; some of them, however, may not be appropriate. It helps to become more conscious of the rules we write by, in order to assess their effectiveness and to adapt or reject them if necessary.

Likewise, some of the standard forms we encounter in and out of school should be carefully considered. Why are they the shape they are? What features of the writing context explain the form? In other words, what is it about the writer, topic, purpose, and readers of the text that cause it to be structured the way it is? Does the form continue to fulfil its original purpose? What changes might make the text more effective? By understanding the logic behind a form, we can become more adept at using it. In addition, familiarity with form allows us to change or alter the standardized documents we must use. Companies, institutions, communities, even entire disciplines revise the shape of their texts from time to time.

Simply fulfilling the requirements of form is not enough. Effective writers take full advantage of the arrangement options open to them. Even within the confines of standard forms, you have considerable control over the sequence of ideas and the relationships among them. However, you must understand the forms you work with—both those you develop yourself and those that are imposed on you.

Revising Form

Throughout this book we have encouraged you to use writing to discover your meaning. If you follow that advice, you will also be discovering form. As you develop a piece of writing, as your goals evolve and your meaning becomes clearer, you will also be changing the structure of your text. However, conscious attention to form too early in the writing process can be counterproductive. There is not much point in worrying about structure when your ideas are still in flux, when they are still being collected, connected, and clarified. On the other hand, failure to pay deliberate attention to the form of your text may also lead to difficulties, especially because the structure of first drafts tends to reflect the order in which ideas occurred to you, which may not be the most effective order for presentation.

As we have suggested elsewhere, one solution to this problem is to ignore the form of your text during freewriting and initial drafting. Allow the ideas to emerge, be open to new perspectives, accidental discoveries, and unexpected connections. Then, once you have a reasonable draft, turn your attention to the form of your text. In order to begin the process of revision, it helps to know that initial drafts frequently suffer from one of three organizational problems: *narrative, survey,* or *idiosyncratic* structure.

The Narrative Structure

A narrative structure follows a sequence of events or stages in a process: it tells a story. Perhaps because of its logical simplicity, narrative seems a natural and appropriate form. Also, we are all familiar with narrative, since it is probably the most common structure in conversation and in much of our reading. However, it is often not the best way to arrange information. For one thing, a narrative structure may bury key points and obscure the links between ideas, since the pattern of time may overwhelm other relationships. In addition, readers can become frustrated if they do not see the point of the narrative; almost inevitably, a story makes full sense only at the end. Although freewriting and initial drafts quite often follow a chronological sequence, and despite the effectiveness of this arrangement for certain texts, you should use narrative structure with care.

The Survey Structure

Similarly, a survey or encyclopedic structure, though natural for drafts, may not be the most appropriate form for finished texts. Such a structure lists all there is to say on a topic, often without indicating the relative importance of ideas or their relationships. It is often the underlying structure of brainstorming and freewriting, when you are first exploring a topic. Initially, you strive to find all that *might* be said, but eventually you have to choose what *should* be said. That choice is based on your goals and your readers, and it can be made by answering such questions as these: Which ideas are most important? How can I best bring my readers' attention to those ideas? How should they be arranged and linked? Which ideas can be minimized, which discarded? Our experience in school often leads us to believe that good texts are crammed full of information, but a well-formed text is preferable to an overly full text. Readers often find a survey structure boring or confusing, since it simply lists ideas without connections or apparent reason. Although it is difficult to throw out ideas once you have generated them, or to reorganize a text that seemed to flow so naturally when first written, it is advisable to avoid a survey structure.

The Idiosyncratic Structure

Another common structural problem concerns overly personal, or idiosyncratic, arrangements. Such arrangements reflect the writer's own thinking or experience, and though the writer may find the text clear, readers may not understand the logic of the piece. We have referred to such writing in other parts of this book as "writer-based" prose. Part of the problem with writer-based prose is that the form suits the writer more than it does the reader. Again, as with narrative and survey structure, it is quite natural for an initial draft to follow closely the contours or patterns of the writer's thinking, but for writing to be successful the draft must be transformed. Some of the exercises in Chapter Five can help you create "reader-based" prose by testing and revising the form of your rough drafts.

Another invaluable aid in the development of effective form is the computer. Since computers allow you to move small or large sections of text easily and quickly, they encourage the kind of deep revising needed to turn early drafts into reader-based final drafts. With very little effort, you can delete, add, substitute, reorder, and otherwise shape texts. You can experiment with various layouts and designs, adjust the location and size of headings and subheadings, and test the effect of underlining, boldface, italics, and other graphics. You can print and compare two (or more) different draft versions of the same document. See the appendix for suggestions on the most productive use of computers for writing.

Form is a complex topic, worthy of its own book. However, for a writer, it is more beneficial to experiment with form than it is to read about it. This chapter can help you begin that experiment, but you must move beyond these pages to your own texts, to the texts you find around you, to the texts you write and read in school and on the job. An understanding of form and its relationship to your topic, your goals, and your readers will make you a better writer. That understanding comes from awareness and experience.

Exercises

Exercise 1: Brainstorm and Chunk Information

Communication is possible only because human beings see and experience things in similar ways. However, since we are not identical, our differences make communication necessary, exciting, and often difficult. By taking advantage of our similarities and being sensitive to our differences, we can become more effective writers. The following exercise will help you experience first-hand the similarities and differences in the ways we see and understand.

1. As a group, brainstorm aloud on a broad topic, such as the environment, winter, money, technology, or school.
2. Fill the blackboard with the words and phrases of the brainstorm, but write them down in random order, not in a list.
3. Individually, place the words into four, five, or six different lists; don't worry about naming or titling the lists until after you have put them together.
4. In small groups or as a full class, compare lists. Explain to each other the logic or rationale behind your list.

The act of creating the lists was an act of forming. Most likely, many lists will be similar, and some may even be identical. Even when lists vary, we will often understand why someone else has grouped items in a different pattern. Why? How is it that we can agree that some things belong together while others do not? How can we understand another's list even when it differs from our own? As a variation on this exercise, you may wish to create lists in small groups, once the whole group has brain stormed a blackboard full of words. When the small groups have completed their lists, each group can present and explain its arrangement. Again, these questions arise: How can we agree on categories? How can we explain differences? How can we understand another's arrangement?

Exercise 2: Create Lists

The following exercise is a variation on Exercise 1. It will involve you in a number of attempts to find form. You may wish to try them all at once, or select just a few. Whether you do them individually or in small groups, it will be worthwhile to compare and discuss the results with others after you have attempted them.

1. List the events of your day so far.
2. In order of importance, describe the qualities necessary for success in university.
3. Briefly note the arguments for and against capital punishment.
4. Place the following words into four different categories:

love	colour	science
theatre	relationships	men
talent	money	ideas
beauty	morals	pleasure
religion	food	truth
home	anger	children
literacy	passion	women

5. Aside from the obvious biological ways, how do men and women differ?
6. List the features, stages, or parts of the following: a hockey game, a symphony, a detective novel, a good party, making a salad, painting a room.

Obviously, there are no correct answers here; however, as with Exercise 1, you will note differences and similarities in the ways in which people select and arrange ideas. And you will also notice again that people will generally understand each other's lists, even when they differ. When you have completed the exercise, consider what logic or structure governs the result. Why are there differences between lists? Can you understand the rationale behind another's list? Why, or why not? Have such factors as personality, training, or culture helped determine the lists?

Exercise 3: Explore the Form of Freewriting

Choose one of the following topics and freewrite for fifteen to twenty minutes.

- a special place
- an old friend
- a favourite pastime
- a life-changing event
- an accident
- a parent or sibling
- a triumph

When you have finished, read over what you have written. You will have mentioned some things about your topic and not others. Also, there will be some sequence or order to your freewriting. Ask yourself these questions:

- What is the logic or pattern in my freewriting?
- Could a reader follow the pattern?
- How are my ideas linked?
- How could I use form (sequence, arrangement) to help a reader understand or appreciate what I have written?

Reflect on your own writing process. Considering all you *might* have written about the topic, can you explain why you wrote what you did? What process of selection was at work as you wrote? How has your piece of freewriting been arranged?

Exercise 4: Create a Hierarchy

When we group ideas together and rank them, we are forming a *taxonomy*, which is simply a hierarchy of classes and subclasses. Biologists use the following taxonomy to categorize living creatures: kingdom, phylum, class, order, family, genus, species, breed. Create a hierarchy for each of the following words: book, cheese, kindness, interest rates, welfare, racial prejudice, the government. For example, a hierarchy including the word *cheese* might look like this: food, dairy product, cheese, cheddar, Kraft slices.

Exercise 5: Create an Idea Tree

Using the tree form described in Chapter Five, arrange the following terms by superordination, coordination, and subordination. As you arrange the words, add your own; you may need to use some words more than once. Try this exercise alone, in pairs, or in small groups.

shoulder pads	**equipment**	**skiing**
sports	**gloves**	**mountains**
swimming	**racquet sports**	**diamond**
location	**gridiron**	**bird**
gymnasium	**goggles**	**poles**
water	**cleats**	**team sport**
individual sports	**outdoors**	**baseball**
court	**football**	**net**
badminton	**racquet**	**tennis**

There are many variations on this exercise. Ideally, this type of forming exercise is done with your own ideas—from a brainstorm, for example.

Exercise 6: Reorder Sentences

The sentences from a paragraph have been rearranged below out of order; reorder them in the sequence that makes the most sense to you by numbering them from 1 to 11.

Finally, when the sap reaches the sugar camp, it must be gradually fed into large, specially made pans for boiling.

People who make maple syrup must work very hard for a brief period of time each spring.

However, it takes approximately 45 litres of sap and plenty of work to make a single litre of syrup.

When night-time temperatures drop below freezing and day-time temperatures rise above 4°C, then the sweet sap-water runs.

First, the trees must be tapped.

As a result, the fire must be kept extremely hot and the workers must be constantly alert.

Syrup-making is not for everyone; the days are long and the work is hard and hot.

That period is determined by weather conditions.

On the other hand, those who do it find their efforts richly and sweetly rewarded.

The best syrup is made when sap is boiled down quickly and removed from the heat at precisely the right moment.

Second, the sap must be collected, either in individual buckets attached to each tree or, more often nowadays, by plastic piping.

Once you have completed this exercise, ask yourself or your group members the following questions:

1. How did you decide the best order of sentences?
2. Are some ideas "bigger" than others?
3. Is there a hierarchy of ideas?
4. Can you identify and name the links or relationships that allowed you to rearrange the paragraph?
5. Can the sentences be ordered in more than one way?

Exercise 7: Compare Forms of Different Texts

By comparing two or more texts, you will get a sense of the diversity of form and the relationship between form and meaning. Sample texts might include a newspaper article, a novel, a textbook, an instruction manual, a cookbook, an academic journal, and so on. You could also compare two chapters of this book. Start with the following questions, but feel free to develop your own:

1. Is there a difference in the length of paragraphs?
2. How are individual paragraphs ordered? What is their logic?
3. What other units of text are indicated?
4. Are separate sections of the texts clear to you?
5. What is the logic behind the sequence of paragraphs and other units?
6. Are there transitions between sections?
7. Have the authors used headings, underlining, boldface, or other types of graphic clues?

Exercise 8: Test Your Tacit Knowledge of Form

Working in groups will increase the enjoyment and effectiveness of this exercise.

1. Write the monologue a student might produce in asking a teacher for an extension on a paper or project.
2. Write a fill-in-the-blank thank-you letter you could use for several occasions and/or a variety of gifts.

3. Make an outline for a spy movie.

4. Imagine you have just met a friend you have not seen for quite a while. Write out your first few lines of your conversation with each other.

5. Write a scene outline for a television soap opera.

Once you have finished and shared your writing, analyze it. What typical features or elements did you draw on to create what you produced? Are there other features that you might have used? Is there a particular sequence or order to the elements? Could they be reordered? Have other groups identified the same elements and structures?

Exercise 9: Examine Forms of Everyday Writing

How might the following texts be structured? What might be the cause for the structure? In other words, what logic might affect the writer's selection and arrangement of ideas?

• a letter home to your parents
• lecture notes
• a personal diary
• a list of weekend activities
• a book report

What separate sections or parts might the above texts contain? Is there a particular sequence or order these parts might be arranged in? This exercise will be most helpful if you can examine some actual texts. With lengthy documents, such as textbooks, a close inspection of the table of contents can tell you much about form. Why has the writer chosen to address these issues in this sequence?

Exercise 10: Analyze Form Requirements in Course Assignments

The following assignments come from two quite different university courses. The first assignment is typical of those found in undergraduate English classes.

The purpose of this assignment is to help you develop your own theory of tragedy. Begin with Aristotle's definition of tragedy and use it to compare Shakespeare's *King Lear* and Miller's *Death of a Salesman*. Pay particular attention to the ways in which the two plays support and/or contradict Aristotle's definition. In addition, note how the two plays suggest quite different beliefs about the nature and dramatic portrayal of tragedy. How has the tragic hero changed over time? What elements of tragedy seem to have remained consistent, from Aristotle to Shakespeare to Miller? Finally, with reference to Aristotle's explicit definition and the definitions implied by the two plays, explain your own concept of tragedy.

Even without having read the plays or Aristotle's discussion of tragedy, you can anticipate the possible structure of this paper. What separate sections might there be? How might ideas be sequenced? Individually, or with others, create a graphic representation (tree, rough outline) of a potential structure; compare the result with others. How much flexibility in form is granted the writer?

Now consider the following assignment from a university management course (it follows a brief case description):

> Write a 5–8 page consulting report giving the client your diagnosis of the problems in his company and recommending a program of action for improving the situation. You can suggest actions for him, for others on his staff, and also actions involving your firm's consulting services. Most important, recommend a process of problem solving that will have long-term payoff in the general effectiveness of the company. In your report, draw on your understanding of how a manager can best initiate change in an organization. Give the client clear advice. Don't be afraid to do some straightforward teaching; the client is impressed by academic expertise. Furthermore, he will want a clear rationale for your recommendations.

Again, although you do not know the details of this case study, you can infer a considerable amount about the content and structure of the report from the assignment description alone. Try the following:

• Make a list of everything the client wants or needs.

• Briefly state your goals as the writer of the report. In other words, what do you hope to achieve with the report?

• Create a tree, chart, or outline that sketches a possible structure for the completed report. Be as specific as you can; identify topics and subtopics, or headings and subheadings.

Once you have completed these tasks, try a similar analysis of one of your own course assignments. If you are working with a group, it would be best if you examined a variety of assignment descriptions from as many different disciplines as possible.

Exercise 11: Do an In-depth Study of Form

One way of beginning this exercise would be to brainstorm a list of different contexts for writing and various documents, genres, or formats. The list might include writing in business, writing in the arts, writing in engineering, writing with computers, writing in groups, or any of a wide variety of texts such as proposals, reviews, reports, articles, essays, and so on. It should be possible to make finer distinctions within each context or type of text; for instance, there are many kinds of reports. You may use this list or choose a discourse community that you hope to join or a type of writing that interests you. If you are a student, you may wish to investigate the writing done in your chosen field, or if you have often wondered about journalism, you might want to look at writing for magazines.

If possible, conduct this inquiry with others; multiple investigators will allow you to cover far more ground. When you have determined the focus of your research and some of the questions that interest you, consider the following sources of information:

- **Published accounts of writing by writers.** For example, Annie Dillard's book, *The Writing Life,* provides a fascinating look into a professional writer's process, and the *Paris Review* interviews do the same thing for a wide variety of poets, novelists, and essayists. If you have some favourite writers, you might check to see if they have written autobiographies, or have had biographies written about them; in either case, there is bound to be considerable comment on writing.

- **Style sheets.** Many disciplines and professional organizations have guidelines for writing. We have mentioned the *Publication Manual* of the American Psychological Association and *The Canadian Press Stylebook,* but there are many others. One widely used manual is the *Handbook* of the Modern Language Association. Such guides generally explain the rationale behind certain writing conventions or standard features in a discipline or profession.

- **Professional journals.** There are journals that specialize in written and spoken communication. Some of these have quite a broad focus, such as *College Composition and Communication,* while others emphasize particular types of writing, such as the *Journal of Technical Writing and Communication.* In addition, professional journals in most fields publish occasional articles or special issues on writing.

- **Observation.** If you are involved with an organization that produces many texts, you are in a position to observe and record the creation and use of those texts. (We advise you to alert people to this type of inquiry, especially if you are planning to report your observations to others or to make the organization's documents public.)

- **Interviews.** Many people write at work. You can discover much about writing in different fields by interviewing a parent, friend, or neighbour. It helps to prepare your questions in advance.
- **Text collection.** We all handle hundreds of different texts at work, at school, and at home: letters, memos, reports, textbooks, course handouts, and junk mail by the ton.

There is no end to the questions you might ask in your investigation. The following questions are suggestions only and focus primarily on forming and form.

1. What techniques do people use to help themselves form or structure their texts? Do people take notes, make plans, use graphic representations (idea trees, outlines), follow guidelines? Why do they use these methods? How did they learn them?

2. What typical forms do people follow? Are these forms idiosyncratic or are they determined by a group or organization? How much flexibility is there in the standard forms people use? In other words, how much can writers deviate from the standard?

3. Do people consider form important? What do they know and say about form? Are they aware of their own struggles with form?

4. What justification is there for the forms people use? What is the logic behind the relationships and sequence of a form? What separate sections of a text are identifiable? What is the reason for each section?

5. How does the form of a text affect its readers? Conversely, how do the readers' needs determine the form of the text? What is the relationship between the purpose of a text and its form?

References and Further Reading

American Psychological Association. Excerpt from "Introduction" of the *Publication Manual of the American Psychological Association*. 3d ed. Washington: American Psychological Association, 1983. Reprinted with permission.

Bazerman, Charles. *Shaping Written Knowledge: The Genre and Activity of the Experimental Article in Science*. Madison: University of Wisconsin Press, 1988. Reprinted with permission.

Berthoff, Ann E., and James Stephens. *Forming/Thinking/Writing*. 2d ed. Portsmouth, N.H.: Boynton/Cook, 1988. Reproduced with permission of the publisher.

Canadian Press. *The Canadian Press Stylebook*. Toronto: The Canadian Press, 1983.

Coe, Richard M. *Toward a Grammar of Passages*. Carbondale: Southern Illinois University Press, 1988.

_____. "An Apology for Form; or, Who Took the Form Out of the Process?" *College English* 49 (1987): 13–28.

Cowley, Malcolm, ed. *Writers at Work: The "Paris Review" Interviews*. 1st series. New York: Viking Press, 1958.

Dickinson, Emily. "I felt a cleavage in my mind." In Martha Dickinson Bianchi and Alfred Leete Hampson, eds. *The Poems of Emily Dickinson*. Boston: Little, Brown and Company, 1944.

Dillard, Annie. *The Writing Life*. New York: Harper and Row, 1989.

Gibaldi, Joseph. *MLA Handbook*. 3d ed. New York: Modern Language Association of America, 1988.

Plimpton, George, ed. *Writers at Work: The "Paris Review" Interviews*. 2d series. New York: Viking Press, 1963.

_____. ed. *Writers at Work: The "Paris Review" Interviews*. 3d series. New York: Viking Press, 1967.

Chapter Seven

Writing
to be Read

ༀ

*In my view the great weakness of written lan-
guage is that it can never be sure of saying
what is meant. Writers are always tempted to
think that their text is transparent, because
they are the ones who know what they wanted
to say. They are not only denied the recipi-
ent's perspective, they lose control of the text
the moment it is read.*

FRANK SMITH

Reading and writing have for a long time been considered
as though they are isolated, independent processes; however, it should be clear from what you have read so far that
readers are never far from the writer's mind. Even when you
are writing for yourself, you are responding all along as a
reader. The strategies described in Chapter Five and the discussion of form in Chapter Six are concerned not only with
ways of discovering, generating, and shaping your thoughts
and feelings; they also represent a regard for the needs of
the reader. Readers have figured prominently in these chapters simply because, whether we are writing for ourselves or
for others, our "audiences" do influence what and how we

write. This chapter focuses on how you can incorporate into your writing process a fuller awareness of readers and their needs.

We speak of "readers" rather than of "audiences" because the word "audience," though it is commonly used in books about writing, conveys the impression of the writer as a performer and the audience (readers) as passive spectators, unable to change or influence what is happening on "stage." Moreover, "audience" suggests a group that responds together to the same text in more or less the same way. In fact, current understandings of the reading process present a different view of the role of readers and what is involved in the act of reading.

There is, for instance, a common assumption that the meanings we derive from written material are delivered entirely by the text, as though the text transmits those meanings and the eye and brain passively receive them. But words on a page do not communicate on their own; they are no more than black marks on paper until a person reads them. And it is the person who reads them and the **context** in which they are read that contribute substantially to what that person understands. For instance, the words, "Save at regular intervals and avoid disaster!" have one meaning for a customer in a bank but a very different meaning for a student at a keyboard in a computer lab. The meaning is not contained entirely in the words on that notice; it depends as well on the location of the notice and the intentions of its readers. Increasingly, those who study writing are attending to the dynamic relationship that exists among writers, readers, and contexts—a relationship that is not represented entirely in the words on the page. It is not surprising then that disputes regarding wills, past judicial decisions, and even carefully framed constitutional documents centre on how certain key phrases were intended to be understood by the writers of those documents. To guard against multiple interpretations, some writers, especially writers of legal contracts, use very specific language in the texts they write, thus hoping to avert the effects of the varying expectations, needs, and experiences the readers of those documents are likely to bring to them. Likewise, some manufacturers of consumer goods go to considerable effort to ensure that information that they believe is of importance to their customers is presented directly and without ambiguity.

Clearly, readers are not to be perceived as passive receptors of meaning. Their intentions and expectations affect both their approaches to the text and what they understand. To test this notion, read the following passage either by yourself or in a group and, after you finish reading it, write down your first three impressions.

RECYCLING: AN ENVIRONMENTAL IDEA THAT MAKES GOOD BUSINESS SENSE

It is not only with virgin fibre that Canada's papermakers do their work. More than 40 of Canada's 145 pulp, paper, and paper board mills recycle waste papers for all or part of their raw material needs. Some have been doing so for more than 50 years.

The pulp and paper industry welcomes additional supplies of high-quality waste papers to meet its fibre needs. In fact, the quantity of recyclable papers has been increasing steadily: in 1980, 1,200,000 tonnes of waste paper were used; in 1990, that figure will exceed 1.9 million tonnes.

GROWTH OF WASTE RECOVERY

Nearly 25 percent of the paper and paperboard used in Canada is collected for recycling. Recovering papers from a variety of sources, once the province of small entrepreneurs, community groups, and service clubs, has also become the domain of businesses of significant size.

Market forces and environmental considerations will continue to shape the recycling business. For one thing, people are asking for recycled content in the products they buy. For another, landfill sites are becoming more difficult to find. Recycling enables the industry to respond to the recycling ethic and to ease the environmental burden created by increasing municipal solid waste.

INDUSTRY RESEARCH

As research solves the technological problems that today constitute barriers; as supplies of recyclable papers become reliable; **and as more markets open for recycled papers, Canadian mills use greater quantities of waste paper.**

In keeping with the spirit of its **Environmental Statement,** the pulp and paper industry is resolved to strike a balance between its business opportunities and its responsibilities to the environment.

Recycling is an expression of that resolve.

Consider your response to this passage. Does your response have anything to do with your knowledge of the subject or your own personal experiences? Is your response generally positive or negative? What aspect of the text are you responding to: format? content? style? If you read this passage in a group, discuss how your responses differ and why you think they do. Would your responses alter if you knew that this passage was actually a magazine advertisement paid for by the Pulp and Paper Research Institute of Canada (1990)?

We realize how differently we read a passage when we know it is meant primarily to influence rather than inform. Similarly, we adopt a different stance when we listen to a speech made by a politician than we do when we listen to an informed and dispassionate commentator on the same issue. Readers make such decisions automatically; it is as if the very appearance of a **text** triggers off a certain reaction. Consider the following text:

The forecast calls for mostly cloudy skies with patches of rain in the morning, sunny breaks in the afternoon, and clearing skies this evening.

If you saw these lines in the weather section of the morning newspaper, you would probably worry a bit about the outdoor demonstration you planned to attend that morning, but you would look forward to the bicycle ride you usually take in the evening. You might, at some other time, come across the following text in the book review section of the same newspaper:

The forecast
calls for
mostly cloudy
skies with patches
of rain in the morning
sunny
breaks
in the afternoon
and clearing skies
this evening.

You might decide that what is being forecast here is quite likely someone's emotional state through a certain day. Others may disagree with you, but most will concede that these lines are certainly not just about the weather. The arrangement of the words and their location in the book review section have alerted readers that they shouldn't take these lines literally. Readers know from past experience that certain arrangements of words and lines signal a poem, and that poems are to be read in certain ways.

So it is more than the context in which the text appears and the situation in which it is read that influences how a text is read and understood. The text itself signals to the reader how it might be read and the attitudes a reader might adopt toward it: "I had better read this carefully," or "I can just relax and get involved in this story," or "This is highly technical stuff; I am not supposed to understand it anyway." But whether those signals are picked up or not depends on the reader's own past experiences, specific expertise, prior reading and knowledge, and reasons for reading the text. All these factors will also determine what that reader will experience or take away from the text.

Meaning can be particularly elusive in literary works, such as poems or novels, because literary authors invite the reader's involvement and rely on it and the full play of the reader's imagination to "complete" the work. Still, meaning is not a completely malleable entity. Wolfgang Iser (1978) speaks of the literary text as a blueprint that guides the imagination of the reader.

This means that, while a reader is free to interpret a novel in a variety of ways, she or he is not free to interpret it in absolutely any way. The literary reader must attend to the author's words and their arrangement on the page. This attention to the text controls the direction in which the reader can go and constrains the number of interpretations a literary text can have. Of course, attending to the text does not result in a single "correct" meaning. The meaning that each reader derives from a literary work will vary with the reader's background, even though she or he respects the boundaries set by the text. What each reader of literature experiences is determined partly by the author's words and partly by that reader's general life experiences and past reading experiences.

Writers of academic papers and professional reports, on the other hand, don't want the wide array of responses a literary work invites. The rest of this chapter discusses ways in which you can ensure that readers derive the meanings you intend.

Note: You may have discovered through the exercises in the earlier chapters that your writing does not always go the way you intend; that in the process of writing you often realize meanings and directions that diverge from or go beyond the sketchy or even carefully outlined intentions you began with. When we speak of "intended meaning" here and elsewhere, we have in mind the intentions that have evolved in the writing of the text.

Keeping Readers in Mind

We now acknowledge that writing and reading are interdependent processes: successful writing anticipates the cooperation of the reader; successful reading relies on the writer's awareness of the reader. Much of this concern for readers operates automatically when you write in certain situations: you write to your creditors with tact, to your parents with a concerned awareness of their anxieties, to younger readers with some regard for their inexperience. The earlier chapters have prepared you to meet the different needs and concerns of your readers in various ways—for instance, by imposing some order or structure on the arguments you use to make a difficult case or by using analogies to clarify a particularly problematic issue.

You have learned about the needs of your readers in other ways as well. In conversation, for instance, you continually attend to signals from your listener that alert you to possible misunderstandings. You are constantly adjusting what you are saying to clarify, reassure, emphasize, and ensure that your listener understands what you intend. Through your experience as a speaker and listener, you become increasingly able to anticipate the variety of interpretations your statements are likely to receive. You are helped also by your growing knowledge of social conventions—the appropriate things to say in a given situation, and the different personalities and various levels of knowledge and experience you must take into account. It is this experience you call on when you write; for then your listeners/readers are not present to signal whether they are understanding what you intend. In fact, recent research is beginning to confirm that the conversations and discussions that go on in one's community are an important means of acquiring not only the language, social norms, and conventions of that community but also an implicit knowledge of the needs and expectations of readers in that community (Spilka).

In your future writing, you will be called on to write in situations that are *not* familiar to you, where you are not sufficiently aware of your readers' needs to be able to write with the assurance that your meaning will be understood. In your academic and professional lives, such writing demands are fairly common. You may have to write a paper in an area with which you are unfamiliar for a reader who must evaluate your knowledge and performance, or you may have to write an analysis of a problem for the customer of the consulting firm that employs you.

Recognizing that readers bring an assortment of agendas, experiences, and backgrounds to this reading, you need to anticipate and account for the differences among your readers. Even when you are addressing one reader in particular, you can assume that your reader expects your writing to be accessible to other readers as well ("*I* know what you mean, but will others?").

There are two main ways in which you can help readers stay within the bounds of your intended meaning. One is to develop structures that clarify the relationships among ideas and the context within which the text must be understood. The other is to study your readership, so that you can take into account the ways in which your readers will probably respond.

Using Text Structures to Guide Your Reader

Certain words, phrases, structures, and forms can be used to nudge your readers along a path you wish them to follow. A glance through a recipe book, for instance, will show how the writer ensures that readers will follow the same steps in preparing a dish. The following sections describe several of the ways in which you can use text structures and relationships to guide your reader.

Drawing on Shared Contexts

Drawing on shared contexts involves establishing a common set of referents in the text by assuming a bank of information held in common by your readers. People who write letters often do this by referring their readers to an earlier letter or to the details of a particular situation; the reader can then, so to speak, pick up the trail and join in the conversation. The author of the cookbook mentioned above creates a context that assumes some common knowledge on the part of the readers. For example, most readers know the difference between boiling, broiling, and baking, and that ingredients are generally listed in the order in which they are to be used. Sometimes writers give their readers too much credit for what they know; on the other hand, a writer might assume too little knowledge on the part of readers and risk alienating them.

For most school writing, shared contexts are already defined by the academic community in which one writes— by what students hear in lectures and by what they are expected to read and write. A paper from a first-year university student is written and read with a different set of expectations and assumptions than is a paper written by a doctoral student. Consider, for instance, what the author of the following passage assumed his readers knew. The writer is a first-year university political science student. The passage is the first paragraph from an essay on the effectiveness of trade sanctions in dismantling apartheid in South Africa:

> Government statistics on the volume of food produced in South Africa would lead you to believe that there is more than enough food to provide an adequate diet to every man, woman, and child in that country; yet more than a third of South Africa's black children are severely undernourished. When you examine figures on electricity production on the African continent, you discover that South Africa claims more than 60% of that production; yet the large majority of blacks in that country are deprived of electricity in their homes. When the South African government argues that continuing trade sanctions will damage the economy and hurt primarily the blacks, it is hard to believe that their protests arise essentially from a concern for the welfare of black South Africans.

How much is the reader expected to know about the South African situation? Would some readers take exception if the writer went into a detailed explanation of sanctions and provided a short history of apartheid? Writers make such judgments all the time, seemingly without conscious effort. It is all a matter of knowing the several communities you write in, and what shared knowledge you can assume on the part of your readers. Writers fail in this respect when they either underestimate or overestimate what they can assume their readers know or don't know about a topic. When you hear your listener impatiently say, "I know, I know," you have probably underestimated the extent of your listener's knowledge. At this point in your reading, you may wish to try Exercise 1 at the end of this chapter. It is framed as a group exercise but can also be done as an individual activity. It asks you to think about the knowledge about a topic (concepts, terminology) you and your intended readers are likely to have in common.

To some extent, all writing assumes a shared context, drawing readers into a world they hold in common with the writer. Shared contexts are already present when people write for themselves and to those close to them or familiar with the situation in which they normally write. Writers of fiction or poetry generally assume that their readers are familiar with the conventions that apply to these genres, that they are aware of certain basic facts about the human and physical world, and that they share some common reference points in other stories and poems; one can say that their stories or poems largely create and define their own contexts.

Creating Shared Contexts

Readers also bring to their reading a set of attitudes toward the writer and the topic, a set of beliefs and expectations that will colour what they read. As writers, you can anticipate some of these concerns and at least let your readers know you are writing with some awareness of how they feel and think. In other words, you can create shared contexts: think about the expectations your readers are likely to bring to your text, and if need be, reorient them in the direction of the goals you have in mind for your text.

Creating shared contexts is often a matter of presenting yourself and your topic in ways that do not set up expectations your text is unlikely to meet. For instance, if you are writing a short paper on the role of women in Thomas Hardy's novels, you need at once to allay your reader's concern that you have taken on too large a topic for the length of that paper. You could state, for instance, that you wish to argue largely from your reading of two key novels (you might then wish to revise your title). If you are writing a report to your employer to justify the purchase of new computer equipment, you might make clear at once that you are aware of the company's low profit margins over the last several months, before you describe how outdated the present equipment is and explain how the purchase will save money in the long term.

Creating shared contexts by acknowledging the expectations or concerns of your readers is a useful strategy for ensuring that you receive a sympathetic reading. If you are writing to convince someone of the validity of your position on a particular issue, you might remember that in any discussion or argument, you listen best when you believe the speaker is a reasonable person and has some understanding of your position. Your readers therefore are more likely to attend to your argument if you begin by acknowledging the reasonableness of their positions. Exercise 2 at the end of this chapter explores how you might create appropriate contexts for some typical situations you are likely to write in. Do the exercise in your writing group or by yourself.

Making Texts Coherent

Cohesion is the term used to describe how a group of sentences are linked together into an integrated text. M.A.K. Halliday and R. Hasan in their book, *Cohesion in English*, have described a wide variety of means by which sentences in a text hold together. You could look at any text in English and notice how one sentence is linked to another sentence that either precedes or follows it:

> As far as the average citizen of any large city is concerned, the growth of cities is not a process that is orderly and planned. City planners, however, look at cities through a different set of eyes. Take the Montreal city-planning team, for instance.

Notice how words and word meanings are repeated or referred to within a sentence and from one sentence to the next; how certain words and phrases like "and" "however," "that," and "for instance" relate sentences and parts of sentences to one another. The topic of cohesion is far too complex and technical to be dealt with briefly; we bring it up because coherence in writing indicates your control over your material and an awareness of your readers.

You make text coherent not solely by applying a set of rules or using a set of devices. You produce coherent text when you make explicit the links between one idea and another. Maintaining coherence involves exercising control over the direction and flow of your ideas; it means keeping the reader's needs in mind. To lose coherence is to lose track, to force your readers to define their own paths through your writing. As you saw in Chapter Six, maintaining coherence is often a matter of creating an arrangement and signalling that arrangement with words or phrases such as "first," "second," "third," or "on the one hand ... on the other hand," or "as a result." You may wish to look back now at Exercise 6 in that chapter, to consider how cohesive devices may have indicated to you how those jumbled sentences might be rearranged into a coherent paragraph.

It is often argued that the reader is responsible for making the text coherent—that coherence is actually in the mind of the beholder. Although knowledgeable and experienced readers may overcome the difficulties of a text that seems incoherent at first reading, less knowledgeable and experienced readers may simply give up. A writer errs in assuming that all readers will recognize connections that are apparent only to those who know enough about the topic and can bridge the gaps that less knowledgeable readers stumble into.

Below you will find the opening paragraphs of an essay on scientific writing by Charles Bazerman. Read the passage, noting the various ways in which the text is held together. If you can do so, get together in a small group and prepare a joint list to be discussed with other groups. You will be surprised to realize how much you already know about cohesion.

> It is generally recognized that writing is a social act—a communication between individuals and within groups; moreover, implicit in every writer's concern for audience is the realization that skilled writing relies on knowledge of the social context and intended social consequences

of the writing. Yet sociological thought and knowledge have rarely been used to aid the study of writing, except for the politically important sociolinguistic studies of the difficulties particular dialect groups have in mastering the standard literate code ...

Scientific and technical writing particularly lend themselves to sociological study because they serve limited functions within distinct communities. The discipline of sociology of science has, furthermore, done much to map out the structure of the scientific community and its activities. This essay will review the literature in the sociology of science to explore what light it may shed on scientific and technical writing and to see what questions it may raise for further study. (156)

Other Guides for the Reader

As a reader, you have likely noticed other ways in which writers guide readers. Tables of contents, headings, introductions, previews, conclusions, summaries, and lists—all these highlight for the reader the topics the writer is addressing or the several steps or threads in the writer's argument. Look through journal articles or textbooks (this book, for instance) to note how chapter introductions give a preview of the chapter's contents or how headings are used to highlight how the content is organized or what the key steps in an argument are.

You need to be judicious about how you use these tools: they are not always necessary, and overusing them can irritate readers who do not like to be led by the nose. There are many examples of good writing that do not rely on headings and subheadings or introductory previews to help their readers. The means you use to organize your writing do not always have to be obvious. Above all, do not be trapped in simplistic formulas that are often presented as organizational cure-alls. For example, the advice, "Say what you are going to say, say it, and then say what you said," may be useful in situations where you need to ensure that your readers or listeners understand and retain the main points of your text; in other situations such a strategy may alienate them.

Studying Your Readers

If you stop to think about how you read, you may realize that you bring particular expectations and ways of reading to the texts you read. You may also realize that the way you feel about certain topics will influence how you respond to those topics. As a writer then, it will help you to know about the expectations and attitudes of your readers. People who write often do not normally prepare a formal analysis of their readers; they have, over time, become familiar with the needs of these readers and have usually received sufficient feedback from them in the past to be able to write with a great deal of knowledge about them. In what follows we discuss some ways of finding out about your readers and how you might put such information to good use.

Even though most of your present writing may be school related, you should not think of teachers as your only readers. Whether the teacher is your primary reader or whether you see yourself writing for a broader audience which includes the teacher, you should take some time to understand (analyze) your readers' perspectives and attitudes to your topics. Consider the following suggestions for analyzing your readers:

1. Make a list of questions that explore your reader's interests and responsibilities, background knowledge, expectations, and information needs. Here is a typical list of such questions:

   - Who will read your writing? Will more than one person read it?

   - Why will your reader read your writing: to acquire information? to make a decision? for pleasure? (Teachers, for instance, may read to evaluate your knowledge of a subject and/or your writing abilities.)

   - Is your reader expecting this writing? (Term papers are usually expected by teachers, but letters of complaint or memos and reports at work may be a surprise to readers.)

   - What does your reader already know about your subject?

- Will your reader understand the concepts and terminology used in your writing?
- Is your reader interested in your subject or your recommendation? Does your reader have an opinion on the subject?
- Will your reader have time to read your writing? Will your reader scan part of the text or read all of it closely?
- What are your reader's responsibilities? How will your reader be helped by what you write?
- What does your reader need to know about you?

You may choose to organize information about your reader in a chart under headings such as Reader's responsibilities and needs, Reader's knowledge of the writer, Reader's knowledge of the subject, and Reader's attitude toward the writer and subject. Then brainstorm as many ideas as possible for each section of your chart. Keep these ideas in mind as you revise your writing.

2. Think of your writing as part of a conversation in which the reader interrupts with comments such as: "So what?" "Who says?" "Who cares?" "How come?" Talk to your readers whenever you can. If your intended readers are not available, talk to a colleague or to your writing group.

3. John Mathes and Dwight Stevenson advise writers to consider the place of the reader: Is the reader part of the writer's work group? a member of another group in the same department or another department? a reader outside the company? They also suggest that writers classify their readers according to the purposes these readers may have for reading this particular piece of writing. Thus the *primary reader* will use the writing to make a decision; the *secondary reader* will need to read those sections that will allow him or her to implement the decision. *Immediate readers* are those close to the writer; their primary purpose is usually to determine who else should read the document. Of course, roles can overlap: an individual could read in all three roles. A supervisor, for example, may make a decision based on the document, implement

that decision, and pass the report on to other readers. The point is that you can design your text to help your readers quickly identify which sections they might want to read with particular attention. You might also consider whether such sections need to be self-contained so they can be read without extensive reference to the rest of your text.

Collaborating with Your Readers

Besides studying your readers in order to write from an understanding of their expectations and attitudes, you can involve readers more directly in helping you draft and revise. Readers can assist you in a number of ways.

Document cycling

Recent studies of writing in various nonacademic settings describe an interesting pattern of writing and revision known as **document cycling**. Although there are many variations on the pattern, the basic principle is the same: the writer passes a draft version of a document to a reader; the reader comments on the draft document, makes suggestions for revision, and passes the document back to the writer. This exchange may happen many times before a final draft is produced. There are some good reasons for this form of collaborative writing:

1. It ensures that the writing meets the norms of the group. Often the reader is the writer's supervisor and the document is meant eventually for someone higher up in the organization.
2. Since the document often goes to more than one reader, people outside the immediate circle of the writer can also contribute to the writing. They can add information the writer was unaware of, or bring a specialist's perspective to certain sections of the writing. Thus many documents in a company are often referred to the company's legal department before they become public.
3. Such a process is an excellent way to introduce new members of the company to the conventions and styles used in the company's documents. Such beginners

receive immediate pointers from more experienced members of the group on what is or is not appropriate for these documents.

Document cycling can easily be adapted for use with any group of people learning to write.

Peer Review

Like document cycling, this method of collaborating with your readers has many variations. In its most formal usage, **peer review** is the method that determines which manuscripts get published as books or articles and which do not; at its least formal, peer review is simply the exchange of a piece of writing between colleagues. Most large disciplines, or *discourse communities*, produce professional publications that undergo a peer review process. In a field like medicine, thousands of different journals and books are published every year. All of these manuscripts are reviewed before publication—sometimes by a single editor, at other times by editorial boards, and often by a process that might be called "anonymous peer review." In this procedure, a manuscript is stripped of the author's identification and sent by the editor to a number of readers, generally considered experts in their field. These reviewers, who remain anonymous, return the manuscripts with their comments and suggestions for revision. If the manuscript is acceptable, the writer is expected to revise it in the light of the editor's comments and the suggestions of the anonymous reviewers. This book, for instance, went through an extensive process of review and revision. Part of this process included reviews by co-authors and colleagues as well as by the instructors and students who used this book in its draft version.

In a wide variety of contexts, peer review is a fact of writing life. Whenever a person passes a draft to a colleague in the next office or asks a friend or relative to read the rough draft of a letter, some form of peer review is taking place. Like document cycling, it is a process worth adapting for use in writing classes. You will find one such adaptation for classroom use in Chapter Nine.

Taped Reader Feedback

One of the advantages of writing in groups such as class-rooms is the immediate availability of readers for your writing. We have suggested throughout this text that you take advantage of this resource. A procedure that has worked well is the use of **taped reader feedback**. Make sure you have a portable audio-cassette recorder available, and when you have completed your next-to-final draft, ask a friend, classmate, or teacher to read and respond aloud to your writing. The reader is expected to read into the tape recorder every word of your text, responding as any reader would: expressing surprise, pleasure, puzzlement, asking what a certain sentence means, what has been left out, what works particularly well. The reader should respond naturally, pausing to reread a section that isn't clear or is particularly impressive for some reason. The reader should not look for flaws or evaluate the writing as a grader would. As readers and writers get used to the process and a procedure for exchanging tapes and drafts is set up, readers can choose to make suggestions for change and offer counterarguments to the ones offered by the writer.

You will find it useful just to hear another voice reading your writing. You can note the stumbling points, the hesitations, and the questions, the places where the text flows.

We have aimed throughout this chapter to show the close interdependency between the acts of writing and reading. As we have pointed out, much of the writer's concern for readers operates automatically when we talk and write in familiar situations. Our knowledge of our readers and our sensitivity to their concerns derives from our growing social knowledge—knowledge that is embedded in our conversations, discussions, the films and TV shows we watch, the books we read, and the jobs we perform. For several reasons, we seem to block out such knowledge when we move from speaking to writing in formal situations, probably because we have for too long viewed writing as a solitary, individual act. This chapter is designed to help you recover and use that knowledge consciously when you write in new situations and unfamiliar genres, which would include most academic situations. To begin that exploration, try Exercise 3 at the end of this chapter.

EXERCISES

Exercise 1: Anticipate Readers' Knowledge

Decide on a topic you and your group believe you know fairly well. Consider topics that are particular to your field of study or employment, such as *Acid rain, Interest rates and the value of the Canadian dollar, The novels of Margaret Laurence, The genetic code, or Computer-chip technology.* Decide on a particular group of readers you might have to write for on the chosen topic, such as a class of twelve-year-olds or first-year university students in a certain field. Now prepare, individually, a list of ten to fifteen terms or phrases that are specific to your topic and that you can assume your readers will be familiar with. For example, if you chose "word processing" as your topic and first-year arts students as your readers, your list would most likely include *software programs, commands, disks and disk-drives, bytes, saving, function keys,* and the like. Your list would probably not contain less familiar items such as *managing hard disks, printer drivers,* and *macros.* Compare lists, noting areas of agreement and disagreement. Talk about how we know what knowledge we can expect our readers to have in common with us.

Exercise 2: Plan to Meet Readers' Concerns

Choose one or more of the following situations. For each of them, decide what particular concerns your readers are likely to have and how you might acknowledge these concerns. In each of these situations, you need to consider how your request is likely to be perceived. Draw on your own experience of how you and people you know have responded to similar requests in the past.

1. As you look forward to leaving for a long-planned mid-winter vacation, you are also concerned that your teacher will be upset that you will be returning a week after your course resumes. Write a letter to your instructor, informing him or her of your delayed return to classes. Your intention is to reduce as much as possible any negative reaction your teacher might have.

In your group, decide on the kinds of concerns that will be uppermost in your reader's mind and how you might ensure a sympathetic reading of your letter.

2. Think of a situation in which you request an extension of the due date of a loan repayment. You might write to the manager of the loans department in your bank or to the administrator of student-aid loans in your institution. Avoid sob stories; think primarily of the legitimate concerns your reader is likely to have and how you might acknowledge and deal with these concerns.

3. As part of a major assignment at school or a project at work, you need to administer a long questionnaire to the members of a particular group, who are likely to be unreceptive to your inquiries and the demands on their time. Decide on the particular group and the purposes of your questionnaire. Discuss the likely reasons they might resist your survey and how your letter requesting participation might overcome their resistance.

Exercise 3: Write an Expert's Paper

1. Think of a number of topics on which you have specialized knowledge and that would likely be of interest to one or more members of your writing class. The topic might be related to your field of work or study, and should be narrow enough that you could explain it in five minutes or less to someone who is relatively uninformed in the area of your expertise. For instance, you might use such topics as black holes, supply-side economics, or Heisenberg's uncertainty principle.

Include your topic on a list to be circulated in your class. Once that list has been filled, someone will read out the topics and ask each student which topic she or he would be interested in hearing about. For this activity each of you will function once as expert informant and once as uninformed listener. As you present your explanation, try to anticipate your listener's questions. After your explanation, discuss with your listener what worked and didn't work. What are the advantages and disadvantages of speaking on a topic on which you are knowledgeable to someone who is not well informed on the topic?

Since the exercise is repeated with people switching roles, it would be useful to apply what has been discussed to the subsequent presentation. Following the second presentation, discuss some of the difficulties associated with this task. What assumptions do we make about our listeners? Are they well founded? What signals do we look for in our listener's attitude and response, and how do we act on them?

2. Part 1 was a preparation for the following task. It is described as a group task but may also be undertaken as an individual assignment.

Although you may not often think about your achievements, you have gained an "expert" knowledge of many activities or skills that you once found difficult. Sports, hobbies, or practical life skills are many areas of expertise you share with those who have undergone similar experiences. List your achievements and find two or three people who share your knowledge. Together you will develop a piece of writing that allows you to share your special insights with a group of readers. There is just one limitation: the group of readers you want to reach are younger than you. (You may specify the age of your readers.)

Use a realistic, appropriate format to produce an article for a children's magazine, a pamphlet to be handed out at school, or a booklet for a very specific group of young people. Think carefully about your readers—about their language skills and their level of comprehension, their concerns and interests. Make sure you engage their interest so they will want to read to the end.

The length of your text should be a group decision, based on your goals and intended readers. Remember to show your readers that you understand the difficulties of the activity or skill as well as ways of overcoming these difficulties. See the situation from your readers' point of view. Submit a group log that shows how you went about producing the paper.

Optional Activity: As in Part 1 of this exercise, you may wish to use the members of your class as readers. In this case, think of topics based on your expertise that would be of some interest to members of your class. Consider topics such as Small-time investing in the stock market; Desktop publishing; Purchasing a new computer; Running a summer camp in the city; Coaching minor hockey, baseball, ringette, or soccer; Short-order cooking; Going vegetarian. As in the first activity, find someone who is interested in your topic so that you can try out a first run-through of this topic. Be prepared to function as a listener for someone else in your class as well. Keep a log of the processes you went through and the decisions you made in developing this piece.

References and Further Reading

Bazerman, Charles. "Scientific Writing as a Social Act: A Review of the Literature of the Sociology of Science." In P.V. Anderson, R.J. Brockmann, and C.R. Miller, eds. *New Essays in Technical and Scientific Communication: Research, Theory, Practice*. 156–84. Farmingdale, N.Y.: Baywood Publishing, 1983.

Halliday, M.A.K., and R. Hasan. *Cohesion in English*. London: Longman, 1976.

Iser, Wolfgang. *The Act of Reading: A Theory of Aesthetic Response.* Baltimore: Johns Hopkins University Press, 1978.

Mathes, John, and Dwight Stevenson. *Designing Technical Reports: Writing for Audiences in Organizations.* Indianapolis: Bobbs-Merrill, 1976.

Pulp and Paper Research Institute of Canada. "Recycling: An Environmental Idea that Makes Good Business Sense." From *Inside Guide* (Toronto) 4, no. 3 (Summer 1990): 22.

Smith, Frank. "A Metaphor for Literacy: Creating Worlds or Shunting Information?" In D. R. Olson, N. Torrance, and A. Hildyard, eds. *Literacy, Language, and Learning: The Nature and Consequences of Reading and Writing.* 195–213. Cambridge: Cambridge University Press, 1985.

Spilka, Rachel. "Orality and Literacy in the Workplace: Process- and Text-based Strategies for Multiple-audience Adaptation." *Journal of Business and Technical Communication* 4, no. 1 (1990): 44–67.

Chapter Eight

Looking at Language

🌿

The spoken or the written word
Should be as clean as is a bone,
As clear as is the light,
As firm as is a stone.
Two words will never serve
As well as one alone.

ANONYMOUS

Language is the basis of human community. With it we inform, persuade, challenge, support, and entertain each other. So instinctive is our use of language that we take it for granted, at least in speech and in spontaneous writing. When we write expressive pieces for ourselves, we use whatever words and phrases come to mind in whatever order they occur. We toss into our sentences words that add nothing to the meaning, merely to keep up the flow of thought. We seldom stop to criticize or cut out these redundancies. If we censored words the moment they issued forth, we would hardly be able to finish a sentence. When we write for others, however, we need to weigh our words more carefully. We have to rework our first drafts, to trim and polish them.

Chapter Five discussed a number of strategies we can use to revise or rewrite a text, including Donald Murray's suggestion that we read it three times: first for meaning, second for order, and finally for language. This chapter focuses on the final reading, on language itself, and the choices we make about words as we edit a text.

The first part, Editing Techniques, looks at editing strategies that many of us have found valuable. The second part, Characteristics of English Today, examines some features of present-day English that are important for writers and editors as they polish their texts. And finally, Contemporary Concerns in Language-Use looks at some larger issues which can have serious consequences for our writing.

Editing Techniques

Many of us have already learned to be good copy editors—technicians who can spot faulty grammatical constructions or misplaced commas. However, there is much more to the complex process of editing. We do not need a grammar book to help us locate our failures of expression but rather an ability to judge how well our words achieve our intentions. As Gabrielle Rico says:

> "Getting the words right" does not mean mere correction … but refers to the *relationship* the words have to one another and to the overall meaning a writer strives for; it refers to a qualitative fitting together, to the aesthetic totality a writer has fashioned. (238)

Perhaps the major problem most of us face as we sit down to edit is breaking the hold the text has on us. As we read our draft, we often hear what we meant to say rather than what we actually said. To break this hold, we have to distance ourselves from our work. One way to gain objectivity is to let some time go by, to follow the example of the poet Archibald MacLeish:

> I formed the habit long ago of putting new poems into a desk drawer and letting them lie there to ripen (or the opposite) like apples. I suppose everyone else

does the same thing. I learned early and by sad experience never to publish a green poem. (Plimpton 131)

Of course, we may not have the luxury of waiting a long time, but a day or even a few hours can help us see our words more objectively than we would if we plunged into editing as soon as we finished our first draft. Another way to gain objectivity is to ask a colleague to play the part of our reader. As suggested in Chapter Four, editing is, at its best, a communal effort. To develop this notion, we now offer you strategies that, while they can be applied to a writer working alone, probably work best in a writing group where editors help each other rethink the conscious and unconscious decisions they made in the first exuberant draft of a text.

Directing Response

We remind you that the quality of feedback you receive from your peers is determined in large part by the way you solicit their responses to your writing. First you need to be receptive to their suggestions, to realize that they are not lying in wait with sharp red pens to attack your writing, slash your words, or embarrass you by pointing out mistakes. Then you need to guide them toward the areas where you need their help. It is frustrating to have a peer-editor do no more than proofread for minor mechanical errors or say little more than "Sounds great." To get your editor to engage with the language of your draft, write a specific set of directions at the top of the page. Point the editor's attention to areas with which you are not satisfied: "I feel the second paragraph is wordy, but I can't see how to tighten it up"; "My opening sentence is way too long, but where should I break it?"; "The conclusion seems clichéd. Can you suggest a way to change it?" You are likely to get much more focused and helpful commentary as a result.

Avoiding Defensiveness

Almost all writers, at any stage of development, feel sensitive about their writing. It is often tempting to jump into the discussion of your draft in a peer group and try to explain, justify, and defend what you said. This not only interrupts the discussion, it also tends to distract you, the writer, from the points being made and even hardens your resistance to making changes. Instead of leaping in with defensive comments, wait quietly and note down all the points your readers make. At the end of the discussion, you can feel free to explain some perspective the group did not grasp, or analyze what led you to write the draft as you did. Holding back requires self-discipline, but brings great rewards if you can do it.

By directing your editors to problem areas, listening carefully to their responses, and avoiding defensiveness, you lay the groundwork for a lively discussion. In a recent writing class, one group spent a productive few minutes arguing vehemently about the word "smart." Would readers think it meant "well-dressed" or "intelligent" when used to describe someone? Dictionaries appeared, other writers in class were consulted, everyone got involved. Beyond being informative, such debates promote a habit of attention to words and an appreciation of them. These debates go beyond details of meaning; they make us responsive to the characteristics of the language, and to larger issues as well: questions of style, "voice," and the impact of language on the reader.

Here is a commentary on the peer-editing process in the log of one of our students:

> The next day ... we were given the opportunity to read our peers' letters and give each other advice. It was good to see where other students are in their assignments, because some of them were making the same mistakes I was making and we were able to figure out some solutions. What I mean is that I can look at another person's writing objectively. By doing so, I can point out certain errors and make suggestions on how to improve them. When I go back to read my own paper, I notice similar errors that I was blinded to before. Now I can even help myself better. The student I was working with gave me encouragement but also some very constructive criticism. She advised me to

change some words, and she pointed out phrases that needed to be expanded, and words that needed to be explained.

Although this student speaks in terms of "mistakes," editing technique is certainly not designed to catch us out in front of other writers. On the contrary, editing in a group fosters a positive, creative approach to language. The participants find themselves discussing words in fresh and intriguing ways, and, indeed, teach each other continually as they do so.

Editing for Key Words

Few writers can produce a first draft that says exactly what they mean in exactly the way they wish to say it. Lively, direct, elegant words that hold a reader's attention come only after the deadwood has been pruned—needless repetitions removed, key ideas emphasized, and precise words found. A useful approach to reworking a first draft is **editing for key words.** As its name implies, this technique helps you to focus on the core of meaning—the "key" ideas—of your text. By doing this, you will see more clearly which parts of the text are not essential or are poorly expressed. Making your key words stand in key places in your sentences is one of the easiest and most effective ways to strengthen your writing. Asking a reader to locate and circle your key words also allows you to verify whether or not you are using language accurately.

Editing for key words involves five stages:

1. First, break up the flow of the text into manageable segments: sentences or sentence parts.
2. In each segment, circle the key words—the ones that seem to carry and focus most of the meaning.
3. Look at the words around the key words. What role do they play? Are they all necessary?
4. Remove redundancies and inaccuracies. Find more precise and concrete words where possible.

5. Rework the remaining words until the key ideas are in key places (for instance, at the beginning of the sentence, in the subject and verb, in the first clause rather than the second). This reworking must, of course, remain true to the overall coherence and flow of your text. You may need new connecting words, but use them as economically as possible.

Here is a draft of a paragraph before it was edited. The author is writing a letter of application for a job in advertising. Economy is of the greatest importance because the letter can be only one page long:

> I am fascinated by all aspects involved in the creation of advertisements, be it in the business, research or creative sectors and would be willing to work in any of these areas. I have the business background but I also have some knowledge and ability to perform in the creative sector. I have taken two years of studio art in high school and CEGEP[*] and (am) therefore quite able to work on lay-outs. I also have a portfolio of my art work. (82 words)

> Now let us underline the key words in the paragraph:
> I am fascinated by all aspects involved in the <u>creation</u> of <u>advertisements,</u> be it in the <u>business,</u> <u>research</u> or <u>creative</u> sectors and would be willing to <u>work</u> in any of these areas. I have the <u>business background</u> but I also have some <u>knowledge</u> and <u>ability</u> to perform in the <u>creative</u> sector. I have taken two years of <u>studio art</u> in high school and CEGEP and (am) therefore quite able to work on <u>lay-outs</u>. I also have a <u>portfolio</u> of my art work.

It is now possible to move directly from this stage to the "new" version, by simply reading the key words and reformulating the text to connect them more economically and precisely. Alternatively, the editor could mentally go through a set of decisions one by one: "I need to highlight the subject of the first sentence better—I'll switch around 'I'

---

[*]. CEGEPs are "Collèges d'enseignement générals et professionels" (Colleges of General and Professional Education) in Quebec.

and the idea about the advertising sectors. It'll be useful too because I don't want to start every sentence with 'I'—too egocentric. I can economize by turning the 'creation of advertisements' into advertising—that will do just as well. The second half of that sentence is long-winded; I'll cut it down with a new phrase ..." The result might look like this:

> The business, research, and creative sectors of advertising all fascinate me as working environments. As well as business experience I have a background in studio arts, including lay-outs. I also have a portfolio of my own work. (37 words)

Eighty-two words have been reduced to thirty-seven. Although the process sounds laborious when described in detail, an experienced key-word editor can make it happen very fast indeed. Highlighting key words brings into focus all the unnecessary words and sloppy thinking in the sentence or paragraph.

Key word editing has many advantages, especially when you are working with an editing group. It allows writers and peer-readers to test the structure and the language of a sentence or paragraph. It promotes clarity and economy and helps create stronger, more emphatic writing. It is an excellent method for spotting technical errors, such as misuse of words. For instance, in another application letter, one student wrote:

> I am very interested in reviewing my résumé concerning the advertisement you had in the paper.

Not only is this a weak opening sentence, but it also misuses the word "reviewing." The writer probably meant to write "I am very interested in *your* reviewing..." With the help of a peer-editor, the writer was able to catch the problem before it moved onto a further draft.

Experimenting with Different Sentence Versions

To prevent monotony in their writing, writers often try to create variety in the type and length of sentences they use. It is useful to be able to discuss the different effects of simple, compound, and complex sentences as you edit, especially when working in a group.

The *simple sentence* has only one central statement: "This is a simple sentence." The *compound sentence* allows the addition of a second central statement, whose status is equal with the first: "This is a compound sentence and it has two parts." In the third type—the *complex sentence*—partial statements (clauses) are imbedded within, before, or after a central statement and are dependent on the main statement; they cannot stand alone: "This complex sentence, which contains an embedded clause, differs from the two examples above." Much of the character and variety of your writing will arise from the interplay between these three kinds of sentences. Embedding especially is a subtle technique that can create many shades of emphasis you might not otherwise discover.

A sense of these different possibilities and an element of playfulness can often help you edit a particularly difficult sentence. If you are working on your own, write out the original version of the troublesome sentence on a piece of paper. Then rewrite it twice, varying the placement of words, their impact, and the structure of the sentence parts. Leave it for a few moments or longer (remember that "incubation" of ideas during a rest period often improves our ability to see the problem clearly and to find solutions). Then choose the best alternative out of the three. If you are working in a group, ask two other people to rewrite the sentence for you. Compare their versions and choose the best.

Here are the revisions that led to the first sentence of the paragraph above:

1. Often, when a sentence is causing particular difficulty, a sense of these possibilities and an element of playfulness are needed in your editing.

2. When editing a particularly difficult sentence, you often need to remember these different possibilities and be able to play with the words.

3. A sense of these different possibilities and an element of playfulness can often help you edit a particularly difficult sentence.

Obviously you are free to alter words and phrases, but your aim is to arrive at more or less the same meaning. What differences of emphasis result from the versions given here?

This set of general editing techniques provides a basis for improving the impact of your writing. It does, of course, demand some effort and ability to rethink phrases and sentences that you may have been quite proud of. Here is the opinion of one of the teachers and writers in our group, speaking from long experience:

> Writers need to learn that sometimes—*often*—the best policy is to abandon the original version and start fresh. They seem to believe that once words are on paper, they can be altered on the surface but not dramatically changed. They will exchange words, cut out a phrase, or change the tense; but they retain the basic sentence structure. Once they realize that they can perform radical surgery on their sentences, they stand a better chance of producing a healthy, vigorous text.

We will now look at other aspects of language that help to produce a "healthy, vigorous text." The analogy of the body and healing is appropriate. "Vigour" and "liveliness" play as essential a part in writing as they do in the experience of all human beings, since energy is essential to survival. Directing response, resisting defensiveness, editing key words, and experimenting with different sentence versions are all good ways to increase the energy—and survival chances—of your work.

Characteristics of English Today

Contemporary English is an incredibly rich and complex language. It is used in so many different communities and countries, for so many different purposes, that no one can even calculate accurately how many words it contains.

> Today, English is used by at least 750 million people, and barely half of those speak it as a mother tongue. Some estimates put that figure closer to one billion.

Whatever the total, English at the end of the twentieth
century is more widely scattered, more widely spoken
and written, than any other language has ever been.
(McCrum, Cran, and MacNeil 19)

The many speakers of the language and its corresponding
wealth of words result from accidents of historical change
and expansion, not from any innate superiority. English has
simply become the *lingua franca*, or shared speech, of a
large proportion of the human race. To write, therefore, we
draw on our own specific cultural context and on thousands
of unconscious choices of meaning, emphasis, and **style**.
Your ability to recognize and discuss those choices may
help your writing, and will certainly be useful to you in
peer-group editing sessions.

In this section we will look at five main topics. We will
consider the language of special communities and other
kinds of "code language." We will also examine three of the
most basic aspects of language, that influence the impact of
your finished piece of writing: **syntax,** vocabulary, and
spelling. Your editing will improve as you become more
aware of the language's range of possibilities.

The Language of Special Communities

Because of the flexibility of modern English, and because it
is used every day in vastly different social and professional
contexts, it has developed many specialized uses. A particular community—a religious group, a company, a village, a
school, a sports team—will unconsciously begin to adopt a
set of special words and phrases or attach new meanings to
words, in the practice of whatever activities bring that group
together. (See Chapter Six for more on discourse communities.) If you are writing primarily for readers in a special
community, you will need to ask your peer-editors to examine your language carefully for unnecessary *code words*,
and, of course, do so yourself when you reread a draft you
have written.

If you are writing as a member of a special group to
other members of the same group, it is tempting to argue
that the code word or phrase is both familiar and unavoid-

able and that your intended reader will have no problem understanding you. For instance, a problem-solving report, written for and within a company, may contain many references that no outsider could grasp but that insiders immediately understand.

Yet there are at least two objections to this argument. First, your piece of writing may be read by someone you never intended as a reader—a board of directors, for example, or an outside consultant. A newcomer to the special group may pick it up and be both baffled and annoyed because of the unfamiliar language. Furthermore, you, as the writer, can often gain a great deal from the extra mental effort involved in articulating the special term, phrase, or idea clearly enough on its first appearance so that a nonspecialist reader can grasp its meaning too. Your articulation of the "code" can help even the most knowledgeable readers gain a stronger sense of *your* use of the term, which may not, in fact, correspond to their use of the term.

In some cases, you may have found yourself using a specialized vocabulary that, in professional and academic contexts, is often called **jargon.** Most people use the word "jargon" in a negative way. "Oh, that article is just pure jargon," someone might say, meaning that the article uses special words for effect and has little real value. But the strict linguistic definition of the word "jargon" is neutral. Some jargon is not only accurate; it is inevitable. Here, for example, is a piece of writing many of us will find baffling:

• ballet leg to small walk-out

• return eggbeater—small boosts

• reverse propeller to deep join

This set of instructions, found on a chalkboard at the McGill University swimming pool, tells the university's synchronized swim team what sequence to follow in their practice that day. The message is obscure to outsiders, but clear to those who need it. Indeed, for them, no other words would do. Like the language of other special communities, it is remarkably inventive and highly metaphorical, seizing in the language whatever word will adapt to the precise special meaning needed.

Such jargon only becomes a problem when it is directed to a reader outside of the specialized community. Therefore, if the coach of the synchronized swim team were to transfer this sequence of words to any kind of formal writing, such as a report on the team's progress, she might very well have to explain the terms the first time she used them.

One writer, whose text was an introduction to the guitar, used the word "fret," forgetting that this was a technical word that nonspecialist readers, especially younger ones, might not have met. The job of an editor is to point out such words and help the writer to avoid excluding the nonspecialist reader.

Other Kinds of Code Language

As well as jargon, there are two other types of code language that you need to examine, and both are the result of a similar problem: your draft has not yet considered what aspects of meaning are special to you but as yet unavailable to a reader. One kind is the code language that comes from using the wrong level of **abstraction**.

Language and Abstraction

In the kind of mental shorthand that we all use when writing a draft, it is easy to use a **general**, more abstract, term to stand in for a **specific** one. *We* know what we mean, but the reader may not. Is such an abstract word necessary? Is it appropriate in a general statement near the beginning or end of your text, but not elsewhere? To better understand the concept of abstraction, examine the following figure:

High abstraction (general term)
- knowledge
- information
- written communication
- book
- textbook
- writing textbook
- *Writing for Ourselves/ Writing for Others*

Low abstraction (specific term)

We learn to move up and down the **abstraction ladder** according to our needs. A writer who claims that "*textbooks* are under-revised" will not make the mistake of using the far more general term "book." To claim that all *books* are under-revised would have a completely different meaning. An important part of editing vocabulary may involve getting the degree of abstraction right, and making sure that you are not neglecting the reader by using the wrong level.

To discover inappropriate abstraction levels, read your draft or someone else's and circle any word that seems too vast, too vague, or too remote. If your writing is too abstract, it often means you have not yet got close enough to your subject; the focus and range of reference is still too large. It can also mean that your thinking on the subject is not yet deep enough. You have used an abstract, "large," term because it requires less careful thinking. In one paper, for example, a student described how to become a professional cyclist: "The best gains will be made by those who have the best natural potential." His group at once asked him, "What does 'natural potential' mean? How can your readers know whether they have it or not?" After some struggle, the writer was able to look more closely at the physical, psychological, and social elements that seem to make up the typical profile of the competitive cyclist. When you expand a code word or code phrase that is the result of abstraction or vague thinking, you are actually doing a great deal more than "just" editing words: you are advancing your own understanding of the subject, as well as your reader's.

Private Code Language

A third kind of code language can result from the different emotional connotations that people attach to certain words. For instance, you might use an apparently concrete term like "cabin," and mean nothing more than a charming holiday home on a rural lake—a place full of pleasant associations for you. However, "cabin" could also be a grim and ramshackle hut in a neighbouring piece of woodland where your reader feared to go as a small child. Once again, your own personal experience shapes your language in a way your reader may not be able to share. This kind of code language may be hard to spot until you and your readers discuss the overall impact of a sentence, paragraph, or text and discover that the different associations of a specific word may be blocking comprehension.

These three kinds of code language—jargon, over-abstract words, and words with strong private connotations—may obscure your text's meaning and hence spoil your relationship with your reader. Check for all of them by having several people respond to your draft and by paying close attention to your words and their effect.

Syntax

Syntax—the ordering together of words to make meaning—is the most elusive and extraordinary part of language, and one that linguists, psychologists, and neurologists are still struggling to understand. How do we unconsciously use grammatical and contextual rules with such amazing speed to produce well-formed, meaningful, and yet *new* sentences all the time? Noam Chomsky pointed out the existence of all these hidden rules when he made up his famous sentence: "Colourless green ideas sleep furiously" (14). The sentence is grammatically perfect, but makes no sense except, perhaps, as a line of a nonsense poem. Similarly, why did a computer-translation program, struggling hard to equal the verbal ability of even a young child, translate the old proverb "out of sight, out of mind" into "blind insanity?" We know we do better than this computer—whether or not we have spoken the language from birth, and whether or not we have studied grammar books.

Our knowledge is partly genetic (in that humans appear to have an innately "grammatical" brain) and partly environmental, based on language use within a particular community. We need to grow up in a human speech community in order to learn a language. The phenomenon of "wild" children, brought up by animals, proves this to be true: these children learn to imitate their animal hosts, and if they were discovered too late, rarely gain normal human speech.

Control of syntax in any language is a fascinating part of human accomplishment. In English—a language with an enormous number of words and a strong dependence on word order—the possibilities for stylistic variations and subtle shifts of meaning fascinate writers of poetic texts. In transactional writing there are important choices to be made to ensure that word order will best support the exact meaning and effect on the reader that the writer wishes to achieve.

As editors, therefore, we are always, in a sense, working in the dark. There may be a better way of writing a particular sentence or passage; we may or may not find it. That element of the unknown is for many professional writers one of the most exciting aspects of the job. It can also be unsettling and infuriating when we want to arrive at a finished form and to feel that we have ordered our words together in the best possible way but still fall short of our ideal.

Experimenting with word order and exploring ways to create rhythm, precision, and energy in your writing and editing are just two areas of syntactic choice you can investigate.

Word order

Unlike some languages—Latin or German, for instance—English relies heavily on word order rather than on word endings to show the relationship of words in a sentence. This was not always the case, however. In its earliest form—Old English, or Anglo-Saxon—the language depended on "inflections"—the endings of words, or changes in the form of words—to show shifts of function and meaning.

As England was invaded by other cultures, its language was influenced by the languages of its invaders (most notably Old Norse and French). Old English went through a series of changes and eventually lost most of its inflected word endings; meaning was now created mainly by word order. Because English was the language of the common people, it was able to change with relative freedom—a tendency it has maintained to this day, at least in oral forms.

Editing successfully in English therefore demands close attention to word-order as the vehicle of meaning. We can easily tell "who does what to whom" simply by looking at the position of the words: "The dog chased the child" is definitely *not* the same as "The child chased the dog." But it can be much harder to explain how word order completely alters the function and meaning of the word "still" in the following sentences:

Still, I'm sure he meant it.

I'm still hoping to come.

She was standing quite still at the bus stop.

It is hardly surprising that new speakers of English are often baffled when they listen to words they thought they knew suddenly behaving in unexpected ways, or moving to unexpected places in the sentence.

As you edit, therefore, you will gradually develop a greater expertise in shifting particular words around (especially adverbs like "still" in the example above) and assessing the new effects you can achieve. Practise by using the techniques discussed in the first part of this chapter. If English is not your first language, your discussions with more experienced speakers will be enormously helpful.

Rhythm, Precision, and Energy

The **rhythm** of sentences, which is often seen as a kind of fingerprint of a writer's style in poetic writing, is an elusive concept that has been studied for centuries. Whether you are editing poetry, fictional or nonfictional prose, a drama script, or any other kind of writing, you will probably base some of your editorial decisions about rhythm on an intuitive sense of how this kind of writing "ought to sound" to your ear. This intuition is the result of extensive reading in the kind of writing you are working with: over many experiences of similar writing you will have developed a "feel" for what sounds right. Frequent rereading, reading aloud, reading into a tape-recorder, and reading to a new listener will all help you develop a sensitivity to the rhythm of writing. Your increasing experience as a writer and editor will help even more, along with the discussions you hold in your writing community.

There are also, however, some simple and practical ways in which you can improve the energy and flow of your sentences: You can use active rather than passive constructions, balance the number of nouns and verbs, reduce the use of the "be" verb, and change negative expressions to positive expressions.

1. Use the active rather than the passive voice

"My friend planted the oak tree" is an active construction. "The oak tree was planted by my friend" is a passive construction. The passive construction often obscures the "agent"—the acting force—in the sentence, putting the emphasis on what happened. Inexperienced writers use the passive voice in the belief that it sounds more professional or business-like: "The office-reorganization was carried out last week." Usually, however, telling your reader who *did* what, by making the agent the subject of the sentence, improves the directness and accuracy of what you are saying: "Staff members reorganized the office last week." Passives are sometimes valuable and can be used deliberately when you know they fulfil a particular purpose:

- if the "agent" is not known: "The house was set on fire deliberately."
- if the result of the action is more important than who did it.

For example, in a section of a pamphlet dealing with student orientation, the writer chose to keep a passive construction even after his peer-editor had pointed it out to him: "Orientation is strongly encouraged by the Students' Society. It has been a very helpful program in letting members of the University know ..."

In scientific writing the passive voice is often appropriate: "The test tube was heated to 40°C." Here the action, not the agent, is of interest.

Passives are also used, sometimes evasively, to conceal responsibility for an unpleasant action: "A decision has been made in your case. Your appeal has been rejected."

In general, look for passives in your text, and increase the energy and precision of your writing by changing them to active constructions, unless they serve a specific purpose.

2. Balance nouns and verbs

We can improve the flow and energy of our syntax during editing if we pay special attention to the number of nouns the writer uses. If it is much higher than the number of verbs, the sentence is likely to be very static, slow-moving, "weighed down." Increasing the number of verbs and reducing the number of nouns makes the sentence move more briskly; the reader will have less sense of wading through molasses, and more a sense of flowing with an easy stream of thought.

Compare:

The deliberations of the drug-trade investigation committee were concerned with the presentation of the media specialists and earlier government discussions of the issues.

and:

The committee set up to investigate the drug trade deliberated on the issues that the media specialists had presented and that the government had discussed earlier.

It is still quite a difficult sentence, but at least there is a closer balance between nouns and verbs: only one verb in the first version, but four in the second.

3. Limit the use of the "be" verb

The first version of the quotation above has just one verb: "were." When working on our first draft, we tend to rely heavily on forms of the verb "to be." "Am," "is," "are," "was," and "were" are some of the most common words we use. As the example showed, when you try to reduce the number of nouns and increase the number of verbs, you often move from a "be" verb sentence to a sentence with a variety of verbs; each of these verbs conveys some of the meaning that previously was denoted by nouns, noun phrases, or other parts of the sentence. Since verbs carry the action or energy of the sentence, it makes good sense to let them work as hard as they can: "His dance performance is one of passion, ingenuity and flair" can easily be reformulated as "He dances with passion, ingenuity, and flair."

4. Change negative into positive constructions
Like passive constructions, negative expressions slow down the reader's response to the text. Double negatives are especially likely to do this: "The team was not successful in its attempt to undo the damage of the defeats which it had already suffered" could, if you were editing really drastically, become: "The team lost yet again!"

You will have to decide which, if any, features of the negative expression had value in the context. Sometimes an emphasis may be lost, but, in general, your work will gain from the change to a more declarative (and economical) positive expression.

Vocabulary

We have already mentioned the history behind the English language's emphasis on word order rather than on inflected endings. That same history, of repeated linguistic "invasion," also helps to account for the enormous number of words in the language and, in particular, for the wealth of synonyms: words of identical, or nearly identical, meaning.

Old English, the speech of the Angles, Saxons, and Jutes who reached the shores of England in about 450, was characterized by a relatively simple vocabulary that derived from natural objects and common experiences. This language was enriched by Latin, a new source of philosophical terms and words for new objects brought by Christian missionaries in the year 597. Then Norse invaders added their store of words as did the Normans, whose French language was itself enriched from many sources.

In the Middle Ages and the Renaissance, a new wealth of words arrived with the rediscovery of Latin and Greek texts. Waves of colonial expansion into the "New World," the Indian sub-continent, Africa, and the Pacific led to a vast new store of words, such as "teepee," "pyjamas," "igloo," "orangutan," "banana," "kangaroo," and "bungalow." All were added to the word-hoard of the language rather than replacing existing words.

Finally, in more recent times, science, culture, and technology have brought many new words into English, either borrowed, invented, or adapted in meaning. All of these developments exemplify the English language's relentless process of expansion.

Among the many possible topics a study of English vocabulary allows, we will focus on plain words, synonyms, heavy nouns, neologisms, conversion, compounding, and literal and metaphoric terms. The section closes with a brief discussion of printed resources for the study of vocabulary.

Plain Words

As writers and editors, we can enhance our awareness of the resources and implications of the language if we edit for word type. Short, plain words in English seem to convey simple truths very directly.

> See how you feel when you try to write just with short words, and find that you must now drop a lot of the words you want to use. It keeps you on the path of clear, brief thought but it makes you see, too, how good it is to have a choice of big and small words to draw on.

Writing such passages makes you appreciate the larger words, which play an important role in conveying meaning: the word "syllable," for example, had to be inadequately represented by "short words." This activity can be enjoyable to do in a group where you assign yourselves a particular subject to describe in words of one syllable only. What kinds of creative compromises do you have to make?

When you come to editing real texts, look carefully at the balance and number of short, plain words. Usually, the more of them there are, the clearer, easier, and more accessible your work will be. Some writers fear **the plain style** will make their work sound too simple and unsophisticated.

But it need not. Some of our greatest writers are masters of the plain style. Read the following excerpt from James Joyce's "The Dead":

> A few light taps upon the pane made him turn to the window. It had begun to snow again. He watched sleepily the flakes, silver and dark, falling obliquely against the lamplight. The time had come for him to set out on his journey westward. Yes, the newspapers were right: snow was general all over Ireland. (223)

In these lines, only one word, "obliquely," stands out as obviously classical in origin. The majority of the other words are monosyllabic and come from Old English. Whether in fiction or nonfiction, poetic or transactional writing, the plain style has many advantages. It seems personal, direct, and clear and it allows you to communicate with a much larger readership.

Synonyms
The inheritance of Latin, Greek, French and Germanic vocabulary makes English a language particularly rich in synonyms, words that have the same, or nearly the same, meaning. *The Plumed Serpent,* for example, a novel by D.H. Lawrence, could have been called *The Feathered Snake,* though most experienced speakers of the language would agree that the difference of effect would be considerable. "Plumed" and "serpent" both have a French origin. "Feather" and "snake" come from Old English. The triple English/ French/Latin inheritance results in synonyms that come in three's, which has led to the observation that you can choose to be popular, literary, or scholarly: you can rise, mount, or ascend; ask, question, or interrogate; think, ponder, or cogitate. In transactional writing, you will probably benefit from choosing the simplest of the three; in fiction, poetry, drama, or the personal essay, however, you may want to play with the entire range of choices to gain different literary effects.

Obviously, your choices will depend on your context, readership, and purpose and also on your willingness to find out, if you do not know already, what the differences of effect among them are. To do so, you will often need to refer to a large dictionary, one that gives not only definitions but examples of how the word is used.

Heavy Nouns

The Latinate (sometimes Greek) member of the pair or triplet is an example of the vast scholarly, technical, and specialized vocabulary that has made its way into the English language to describe scientific and philosophical advances in knowledge. These are the words that best fit the term heavy nouns: they sound heavy, and weigh down the text in which they appear. Heavy nouns very often come from verbs and end in *-tion, -ment, -ance,* and *-ism.* They often add prefixes and suffixes to a Latin or Greek root-word. (Supposedly the longest, at least outside scientific formulae, is "antidisestablishmentarianism"!)

Consider the following translation of a French work on philosophy:

> To a purely lexematic analysis, metaphor is just a phenomenon of abstraction. But this points merely to the culmination of a process that involves the dynamics of the entire statement. Indeed, there would not be any metaphor if no deviation were detected between the figurative meaning of a word and the isotopy of the context, that is, in the language of Greimas, the semantic homogeneity of a statement or part of a statement. (Ricoeur 182)

The writer (and translator) are not deliberately aiming to be obscure; they are probably not even conscious of the effect such a level of writing—full of heavy nouns—has on nonspecialist readers. The level of abstract thought is extreme, and the terms used have, here, precise philosophical or linguistic meanings attached to them.

In your own work it is always worthwhile circling the "heavy nouns" to see how many there are and whether some of them can be replaced with simpler words, perhaps words of Old English origin. You may also be able to turn the heavy noun back into a verb (from which it may have been formed) and thus reduce the weightiness and apparent obscurity of your text.

One student, writing a problem-solving report on paper waste in a legal firm, produced this sentence:

Decreased consumption of paper products is another recommendation.

An editor might remove the emphasis on the Latinate nouns, and at the same time, strengthen the verb and make the sentence active:

We recommend the use of fewer paper products (or, less paper).

As with key-word editing, the effect is often not only to clarify the meaning but also to shorten the text considerably.

Neologisms

The great variety of different forms of English around the world exists because words are not only brought in readily from other languages, but are also invented in various ways. *Neologisms* are words that are simply made up, often by an individual speaker. Some become accepted, others do not. In the following passage from a Canadian style book, you will see how new words of special kinds are often noted down "officially," perhaps for the first time, even if they have been used in daily speech, special documents, or media reports for some years. If they make the further step up to a standard dictionary, then they have really arrived.

> An acronym is a pronounceable word formed from the first letter or letters of other words, such as NATO, CUSO or NORAD. (Department of Secretary of State 31)

These kinds of neologisms appear frequently in areas of new technology such as computers and leisure equipment. For instance, the word *scuba* is actually an acronym for *s*elf-contained *u*nderwater *b*reathing *a*pparatus. As well as acronyms, there are many other ways of coining new words. If you use a neologism, be sure it is both acceptable and clear to your reader. Commonly you will give its full form (if it is an acronym) or explain it (if it is another kind of neologism) the first time you use it.

Conversion

Writers sometimes change the function of words in a process called *conversion*. One of the features of great writing is how powerfully some of these conversions can stick. Shakespeare and Chaucer figure prominently in the history and development of the English language because of their remarkable manipulation of words—altering meanings, functions, and contexts for a more powerful effect. The word "channel," for example, which we use both as a noun and as a verb, was, at least according to surviving records, only a noun before Shakespeare decided to convert it. When he wrote, "No more shall trenching Warre channell her fields" (*Henry IV, Part I*) there was much more force than we hear today because of the newness of the verb. Note, however, that we still only use "canal" as a noun: "I'll canal the crowd into the street" would still surprise a reader.

To enhance your editing, play with language in as many ways as possible. Try writing a passage in which all the verbs are nouns you have chosen to turn into verbs: "to bucket," for example, or, as one teacher did recently, "to journal." You may be surprised when you go to the dictionary to find that someone, somewhere, has used the same noun as a verb before; or perhaps you are truly original and have found one that no one ever thought of converting.

Compounding

Another productive source of new words in English is *compounding*—putting two other words together to form a new word with a new meaning. A woodpecker is not just any "pecker" of wood —it is the name of a specific kind of bird. "Heartburn" is not literally a burning heart, but an unfortunate kind of indigestion. Again you can develop amusing sessions for an editing group when you set yourself the task of inventing new compound words. In some kinds of literary texts (a comic essay or a text for young children) such words may add colour and entertainment to your work. You need to be careful, of course, not to use them in a more formal context where innovation may be frowned on.

Using Literal and Metaphorical terms

Another major consideration on the subject of vocabulary is the literal or metaphorical impact that your words carry. A word in itself may denote something quite neutral; but the word may have generally accepted connotations that give it a strong emotional colouring. This can be seen in a phrase such as "A house is not a home." In the example of the "plumed serpent" and the "feathered snake," there is a distinct difference of tone: a plume, in English, is a particularly elegant kind of feather; a serpent is distinctly more mythical, literary, and distant than a snake. The second phrase sounds much more down to earth than the first.

Wide and varied reading is, undoubtedly, the best way to increase your awareness of, and ability to use, various degrees of literal and metaphorical language. As an editor you can make changes to your language along a continuum: from the most literal to the most metaphorical. You can play with the colouring of your words and their emotional effects. In the following passage, the writer could have said: "There are a lot of snowflakes falling. The blizzard is a menace." Or he could have used a simile: "The snowflakes are like an army." He could have used a single metaphor that would leap out of the text on its own: "The snow flakes are an army, coming silently in the night." But in this case, he explored the subject through a personification:

Life as a Flake

I felt unsure, almost queasy as I prepared to jump. It was cold—damn cold—which was one of the reasons why the troops were jumping that night. The authorities figured they could immobilize the enemy more easily in these sub-zero temperatures. I jumped silently with the countless others in my squadron. I was always amazed at how quietly our operations proceeded. Slowly, we drifted down, swinging from side to side randomly as to confuse the enemy. In the pitch darkness of the night, it was nearly impossible to see us.

All literal language was probably, at some time, metaphor that has, through years of use, become cliché or has lost its clear linguistic origins. The word "involve," for example, seems abstract to us, but it once meant, in Latin, to roll something up physically (as in a carpet). In modern English we have lost the sense of the root of the word that would point to the real experience it once represented. Many metaphors are coined by inventive speakers and writers of all kinds (the choreographers of synchronized swimming, mentioned earlier, seem to be especially good at it). Once metaphors are accepted and repeated by other speakers, and then find their way into official documents, their existence in the language is assured.

Vocabulary in the Dictionary, Handbook, and Thesaurus

As an editor, you rely not only on your own reading and sense of language to expand your vocabulary, but also on the wide variety of dictionaries, thesauruses, and writing handbooks that are available today. As always, you must keep a strong sense of your purpose when consulting reference works, since you must know how to find and focus on exactly what you need. Become familiar with a dictionary and handbook that you find easy to use; as time goes on you will gain considerable expertise in referring to them quickly.

Inexperienced users of a thesaurus often think that they will improve their writing by using ornate, complicated, or unfamiliar words. This is almost always a disaster. The thesaurus is useful when the word you're looking for has slipped from your memory; when you want to find an alternative to an often-repeated word in your text; and when you want to look up *antonyms*—words that mean the opposite of the word you have in mind. If you are not sure of the meaning of a word you find in a thesaurus, check its exact meaning in a large dictionary. As you do this, look also for examples of how the word is used in the context of a sentence. Often, if there are several examples, you will have a much clearer idea of whether or not it really is the word you want.

Spelling

English spelling has had a colourful and varied history. In fact, the spelling of the language is one of its most striking features; at times it can be wildly nonphonetic (that is, the written words do not represent sounds consistently). For instance we have at least twelve ways to spell the sound "sh": *shoe, sugar, issue, mansion, mission, nation, suspicion, ocean, conscious, chaperon, schist,* and *fuchsia.*

The problem of correct spelling has existed for only two or three centuries. Before then, spelling was at the whim of the writer. Shakespeare wrote his name in several different ways, for example; and all Elizabethans could spell a word like *clothes* in two ways: *clothes* and *cloathes,* even within one sentence. In the eighteenth century in England, many scholars and dictionary makers lamented this wide variety of spellings and tried to standardize them, but unfortunately the standardization in different dictionaries often captured alternative versions of a single word, or relied on different pronunciation patterns or supposed origins. To make matters worse, the words had come from many different languages, with different spelling conventions, and at different times. Mercifully, most of our spellings and misspellings are sufficiently phonetic most of the time to allow communication to proceed, but the social consequences of habitual misspelling can still be severe: the writer looks poorly educated. Spelling has a curious influence over discussions about language even now, as though expertise in this one area equals expertise in thinking and writing too. As Bill Bryson says:

> Language, never forget, is more fashion than science, and matters of usage, spelling, and pronunciation tend to wander around like hemlines. (98)

Like fashions in clothes, fashions in spelling and pronunciation often assume far more significance than they really deserve. In the long term, it is more important to value the person inside the clothes, and the meaning in the writing. But social impact may be dramatically affected by what is on the surface; polishing the surface of your text until it is totally correct is rather like dressing up for an important meeting. In freewriting, journals, and letters to friends, a concern for correct spelling should not distract you from your meaning.

As a careful editor, you always check laboriously for any word that might be wrongly spelled or, better still, you make up a list of words that have been problems in the past. Also proofread for spelling by reading the text backwards, so that your eye focuses on the word rather than on the meaning. You should also consult the lists of commonly misspelled words and spelling rules in writing handbooks. However, there is really no alternative to the outside reader, who can very often catch a misspelling (or a typing error) that the editor or writer missed.

Computer spell-checkers can be very helpful, but they must be used cautiously and in close connection with the proofreading of a printed out copy. The spell-checker will not catch a switched spelling ("to" and "too" or "their" and "there") because both words exist in the language. It will not remind you of a missed agreement ("the horse neigh," instead of "the horse neighs") or a mistaken pronoun. One interesting side effect of spell-checkers is that they allow you to play with words of similar sounds in ways you never thought possible. In some spell-checkers, for example, you are presented with a list of possible alternatives for your misspelled word. With a little careful selection, you can create some delightful word patterns:

loft, lost, lust, least, laced, lazed, liaised, lasted ...

or:

racer, wreaker, rocker, wrecker ...

A writer who enjoys playing with sound can spend hours exploring a spell-checker in a way it was never intended to be used. Perhaps we should be grateful for the complexities of English spelling after all.

Our discussion of the characteristics of English has attempted to show you the richness and range of the language. The exercises at the end of the chapter will help you continue to explore language both in independent exercises and in the projects you are currently working on. Attention to the language of special communities and other kinds of code language, to variations of word order, to the potential of English vocabulary, and to the oddities of English spelling help writers at any level become more alert to the possibilities of words and the need to use them with care.

Adjusting the words of a text can go on forever, unless the reality of a deadline forces us to halt. But, as the English poet W. H. Auden said, echoing the French poet Verlaine, a piece of writing is never really finished, "only abandoned" (16). It takes its place in the world and comes back to life as readers engage with it, making their own meanings out of the words we chose to use.

Contemporary Concerns in Language Use

English plays an enormous part in the speaking and writing activities of a large part of the modern world. Perhaps because of the tremendous diversity of the spoken language, and an increase in democracy and education, older assumptions about the supposed neutrality of its standard written form are being challenged with increasing frequency. As an editor of your own writing and that of others, you need to be aware that the word choices you make often reflect your political, social, and cultural values. Your wording can have a tremendous positive or negative impact, one you need to consider consciously. In this section, therefore, we invite you to reflect on the social, political, and psychological impact of your word choices on individual readers.

Standard English

All writers in professional fields need a command of standard English. This is the form of English enshrined in the education system; in traditional textbooks, dictionaries, and grammars; and in the daily writing of science, business, and politics. You should not, however, be made to feel that standard English is "better" than your own variety of English or, indeed, than your own use of other languages in the home and local community. Ideally, you should be able to maintain and value your own speech in appropriate contexts, and learn to use the standard where it is useful or even essential for your purpose. Standard English is really just one conventionalized form of English that has gained power because of a set of historical accidents:

> Standard English is no less a dialect than any other variety of the language. It is no better and no worse, no more expressive or flexible or beautiful, than any other English dialect. It simply is the variety of English that found itself in the right place at the right time, the dialect that happened to be used by "the right people," those who came to direct the political, economic, and literary affairs of England and eventually, the United States. (Baron 107)

Today the standard is being forced to adjust. In recent years, there has been increasing pressure on the language to abandon words and conventions that have traditionally stereotyped, excluded, or discriminated against certain groups of people: women, ethnic groups, and all those who have only recently begun to make their collective voices heard.

Like most political and social institutions in the English-speaking world, standard English still tends to "belong" to one group more than others, but people from inside and outside this group are working to bring about a more democratic language. Instead of confirming the status quo—continuing to exclude outsiders—the new form of standard English being developed can help to confirm change. In your own writing you can enhance this process by avoiding terms and assumptions that confirm stereotypes or discriminate against some users of the language.

Gender Bias

One central part of the debate on inclusive language is the question of gender bias. In some ways, English is relatively fortunate in that it has thrown off its ancient system of gendered nouns, leaving most words neutral unless their actual meaning is clearly gender-specific (such as "woman", "father," "girl", "stag," "doe"). However, men's historical dominance in all public spheres of writing—politics, education, the law, religion—has resulted in a language with an overwhelmingly male bias.

Male terms have often been assumed to apply to the entire human race, a phenomenon that has often been aided by the way words can change their meaning through time. The word "man," for instance, meant "person" in Anglo-Saxon England; a princess was described as a "wonderful man." Yet, gradually, and no doubt because men were the most visible "persons" socially, the word "man" took on masculine colouring. Expressions such as "mankind" and "the achievements of man" are still used as if they referred to all people, but experiments show that most people will make male rather than female associations in their minds when they hear these words. Expressions such as "the man in the street" similarly imply that male experience is the norm.

There are also many words that traditionally have designated professions and activities that were once dominated by men ("postman" and "chairman," for instance). And some seem to have positive or negative associations according to gender: think of "master" compared with "mistress." History has often assigned primary focus to the males in any group: "the Pilgrim fathers," for instance. The media have tended to emphasize the role of men over that of women: "Two professors and their wives attended the conference."

Even more problematic is that, in traditional English usage, the third-person possessive pronoun (his, her, its) must specify gender even when the subject of the sentence does not. For instance, what pronoun would you use to complete the following sentence: "The doctor treats ____ patient"? If we say "his," we exclude women; if we use "her," we exclude men.

There are many ways in which you can make your text gender-neutral. Here are some examples; refer to the reading list at the end of the chapter for more detailed discussions.

1. Replace "mankind" with "humanity," "humankind," "human beings," "the human race," "the human species," and so on.

2. Replace words such as "chairman" with "chair," "coordinator," or "director."

3. Replace phrases such as "average working man" with "wage earner," "breadwinner," "worker."

4. Replace "If a man can walk a mile in fifteen minutes" with "If a person/adult/you/someone ..."

5. Replace "Pioneers moved west, taking their wives and children with them" with "Pioneer families moved west ..."

6. Replace "If a beginner practises every day, he can master the game in nine months" with "Beginners who practise every day can master ..." or "If you practise ... you can master ..." or "With daily practice, the game can be mastered..." or "It is possible to master the game ..." (The word "master" is worth another discussion).

7. Replace "The doctor treats his patient" with "Doctors treat their patients" or "The doctor treats the patient."

Alternating between "he" and "she" throughout a text can become clumsy, and should be used sparingly. Alternating masculine with feminine pronouns by paragraph or section is also a possible solution, but seems to confuse some readers. Reworking the sentence itself is almost always the most stylish solution and the one that a reader will appreciate most. It means more work for the writer or editor, but can become a useful part of your other editing strategies and your general "diagnosis" of language problems. As you become more familiar with the possible ways of editing for gender-neutral language, you will probably find yourself avoiding such expressions even in your early drafts.

Racial Bias

Just as women need to be seen as equals in language, so members of various ethnic groups expect standard English to recognize and include them. The history of dominant English speakers' attitudes to other varieties of English has been to ridicule and exclude them. Speakers from minorities have felt that they must mimic the language of dominance if they wish to "move up" in the social hierarchy. The Canadian poet Marlene Nourbese Philip encapsulates the experience of an English speaker from a Caribbean background in her essay "The Absence of Writing." She speaks of "Queenglish and Kinglish—the anguish that is english in colonial societies" (26). She argues that an understanding of the history of the English language, and the way it is used today, will help to empower speakers from minorities who have always felt "anguish" when forced to use it, in its standard form, rather than in their own family's or community's everyday speech.

Educational institutions are now considering the extent to which school children should use, and learn more about, their own variety of English as well as the standard. In the United States, linguists have argued that the differences between black English and standard English are consistent, rule-governed, and extremely widespread even among widely separated communities. In black English, for example, "she say" rather than "she says" is normal. Not being able to use their own variety of English, with which memory, home, and feelings are connected, may alienate its speakers from official education; but using it may limit their social possibilities. The current argument for black English and many other local or ethnic variant forms is that a compromise is necessary. Children need to be in command of both their own familiar patterns of speech and of the internationally recognized forms of English that may, one day, be essential to them as individuals and as a group.

Those who are, by chance, born into standard English need to exercise constant care when writing and thinking about language, in order not to promote a sense of exclusion of certain groups, however unwittingly. All major varieties of the language need to be recognized and explored fully. There may be times when your definition of purpose, context, and readership for your own writing makes you conclude that you do want to draw on non-standard usage, or deliberately include words, phrases, and sentence patterns from your own form of English. Marlene Nourbese

Philip does this in the essay quoted earlier, writing the first few paragraphs as if in Trinidadian popular speech, then switching dramatically to standard English to illustrate her subject.

When you use the standard language, be aware of the value words carry, what their history and present usage imply. As you edit, and discuss the impact of words in your draft or in one you are peer-editing, look carefully for words that exclude, insult, or trivialize the reality of any possible reader.

One student, for example, wrote a paper on international economic trends using stereotypes, including physical characteristics, to describe the people of another country. Not only is this evidence of poor thinking and research; it also fails for a typical North American business audience that almost certainly would include people from that ethnic background.

Here are some practical editing strategies to avoid racial bias:

1. Do not attribute a stereotypical characteristic to *all* members of a nation or ethnic group. Instead of "Italians love to eat pasta," try "Pasta is popular among many Italians."

2. Avoid focusing on a person's race when it is irrelevant, or when there is an implication that all members of the racial group share certain characteristics: "Abbas, a Muslim businessman, shouted at the police officer." (Remove the word "Muslim.")

3. Do not condescend and stereotype: "Aboriginal Indians have a natural bond with the forests ..." Some aboriginal people do; others do not. Be more precise in your research and use of words.

4. Do not discriminate by omission, especially when writing about history, culture, or social change. Until very recently, the activities of white male members of Canadian society tended to dominate the news media to the exclusion of other groups of people. Check your sources critically for such biases.

You will find other strategies for avoiding racial bias in *Editing Canadian English* (1988).

As in so many of the editing strategies suggested in this chapter, you need to be able to anticipate and prepare so that your words will fully serve your purpose, making all possible readers feel comfortable with your text.

Doublespeak

This discussion has assumed that writers actually *want* readers to understand their precise meaning. Unfortunately, a lot of the language we see every day in written form is not intended to be clear—it may be intended to persuade a purchaser, silence criticism, keep away the curious, or prevent the loss of votes at the next election. In Canada and the U.S., the annual Doublespeak Awards (inspired by George Orwell, who used the words "doublethink" and "newspeak" in his novel *1984*) are given to those who have produced the most impressively misleading language in a public context. Military and political leaders are frequent winners: doublespeak is at its worst when it describes the deaths of civilians as "collateral damage." In advertising, there is often a similar, deliberate intention to mislead, and, above all, to stifle critical thought. The word "light" (or "lite") on a food-package, for example, has a multitude of possible meanings: fewer calories, smaller portions, less fat (but more sugar), lighter taste, paler colour, and so on. The only common feature is that these meanings are all intended to persuade the customer to buy the product. A post office announced plans to "streamline" and "enhance" mail collection in Vancouver, by removing one-fifth of the mail boxes to save money.

Writers often fall into habits of doublespeak in early drafts because it is part of the linguistic atmosphere in which we live. When editing, you can watch out for the **clichés**, **euphemisms**, and deliberate lies that are so easy to mistake for truth.

When you find printed examples of doublespeak, try to figure out whether the writer is just negligent or whether there is a real intention to mislead and exclude. This is an important aspect not only of our reading and writing but also of our social responsibility. We need to be able to look critically at the information that influences every part of our lives. As the writer William Lutz warns,

> While some doublespeak is funny, much of it is frightening. We laugh and dismiss doublespeak ... at our own peril, for, as George Orwell saw so clearly, the great weapon of power, exploitation, manipulation, and oppression is language. It is only by being aware of the pervasiveness of doublespeak and its function as a tool of social, economic, and political control that we can begin to fight those who would use language against us. (xiii)

In this chapter, we have looked at editing strategies, common features of the English language, and the significance of your word choices and their impact on your reader. Language consciousness seems to be on the rise; when you edit, you are giving yourself and your peers opportunities to learn about the power of words.

Many institutions such as universities, government agencies, and publishing houses have made policy statements encouraging the use of "inclusive" rather than "exclusive" language. They hope that an adjusted form of standard English can escape the negative legacy of the past, a past in which certain members of society were clearly and explicitly subservient. These institutions are also working toward a language that is clear, readable, and honest rather than deliberately misleading or obscure. Your role as editor makes you part of that enterprise, and it is one that will be relevant to your professional relationship with the written word.

At the same time, it is important not to ignore those who argue that the basis of language is shared convention and that we must be cautious as we try to remake written language in line with contemporary beliefs. Tradition plays an important part in the teaching and learning of written language. Passing laws on language change has usually been a futile exercise, unless these laws reflect, and are supported by, massive changes in social awareness. Such awareness does seem to be developing in the debates over gender and racial bias in language.

As a writer and editor, you have probably found yourself already having to make choices in many areas of vocabulary, phrasing, and syntax. You may need to test out different readers, or put yourself in the role of a reader in order to see whom you may have excluded, alienated, or stereotyped by a particular word or phrase.

As they become more multicultural, our societies are also becoming more "multi-voiced"; it is no longer possible to assume a homogeneous audience for any kind of writing. Excluding or offending a reader through careless choice of words is the surest way to achieve the fate that every writer wishes to avoid: that, however important its message, the writing may be thrown aside unread.

EXERCISES

Exercise 1: Explore Language Associations

1. In Chapter Three you learned about the technique called clustering. Do a cluster now, around the circled word "language." Feel completely free to associate it with anything else that comes to mind.

2. Now look at your cluster, and draw from it some key ideas. Use them as a starting point for freewriting. Write for ten minutes, putting all self-criticism "on hold"—freeing your ideas is what matters most.

3. Form a group of three to four people, and discuss what you have written. If you feel comfortable doing so, read out some of the freewriting.

4. As a group, draw some conclusions about what you have discussed. Were some of your associations with the word "language" surprising? Did you find yourself talking about different languages—ones you speak or are trying to learn? Or did you discuss language barriers and conflicts between languages? Or did you talk about the social uses of language? The possibilities are endless. You may want to return to this subject in your log and journal as you work through the chapter and as your writing activities continue.

Exercise 2: Find Code Words

As we discussed in this chapter, we all attach our own emotional colouring, even our own meanings to words; we use language in a way that reflects our own experience. When we write in code, or in a secret, invented language, we deliberately intend to keep some readers out; children invent special languages to exclude parents, and warring nations develop complex codes for intelligence operations. Yet we often use words in a code-like way when our intention is the exact opposite: we are attaching secret meanings to them, but hope or expect the reader to understand. This is a common problem in early drafts and one that your writing group can help you to solve.

Exchange drafts of a current project within your writing group. Make sure you understand the writer's audience and purpose. Read the draft carefully and circle any word whose meaning you are not sure of, any word that seems to be jargon, any word that seems too abstract, and any word that seems to have a private meaning for the writer. Then re-read the draft, and circle any other words that you think may not be clear to the intended audience. Return the draft to the writer and discuss these words in depth. Ask the writer to clarify as much as possible. Use a dictionary or the writer's own knowledge to tease out the real meaning of the code words used.

It is useful to seek out code words both in your own reading "voice" and in that of your intended audience so that you can catch problems that would confuse *any* reader, and those that would be difficult for a particular group.

Exercise 3: Look at Style

In this chapter, there has been an emphasis on linguistic choices. You almost always have several ways in which you can say something. But how does the approach you choose affect the meaning and the larger impact of your writing? What happens when you write in one way rather than another?

You can investigate this question by buying three different newspapers or magazines that deal with the same cultural or political event. Compare the *actual words* with which the three publications describe the event. How is each article introduced? Is there an obvious "slant" for or against a particular position? How concrete or abstract are most of the words used? How long are the sentences and how difficult are they to understand? What audience is presumed, in terms of knowledge, assumptions, beliefs? What impression do you get of each writer? How literal or metaphorical is the writing?

Here are two accounts from Canadian newspapers of an election in Alberta in which then premier Don Getty lost his seat in the Alberta legislature even though his party was re-elected:

The Tory troops won the battle of Alberta as expected on Monday, but were shocked to find their general wounded on the battlefield.

When the Wickman Wave washed over Alberta Premier Don Getty, it left in its wake a ship without a captain.

A third writer, not so anxious to grab the reader, aims for a more formal and literal approach:

Alberta Premier Donald Getty, defeated in his own constituency while his party won its sixth consecutive election Monday, will meet his cabinet today ...

The first two excerpts were a column and lead story in the (now defunct) Montreal *Daily News*; the third was from *The Globe and Mail*. You will almost certainly find some relevant examples of your own.

Editing Checklist

Note: Some of the checklist questions refer to suggested structuring techniques for paragraphs; these are discussed in Chapters Five, Six, and Seven.

Paragraphs
- Are paragraphs of appropriate length for the context and readership you are concerned with?
- Are they clear and logical?
- Have you eliminated extremely brief paragraphs and reworked those that run over more than one page?
- Are preview and summary paragraphs necessary, useful, and well-positioned?

Sentences
- Are all the sentences necessary? Are there any that do not further your argument?
- Have unnecessary clauses been eliminated?
- Have you edited to put the key words in key places?

- Have you used a variety of sentences (compound/complex/simple; long/short; questions/statements) to maintain interest and rhythm?
- Are **parallel** ideas expressed in parallel form? Are all lists and headings in parallel form?
- Have you avoided "dummy subjects" ("it" and "there" used with the "be" verb)?
- Have you changed passive to active constructions unless the passive serves a specific function?
- Have you changed negative statements to positive statements as far as possible?

Words
Have you used a language level appropriate for your readers?
- Have you eliminated code words: unnecessary jargon, abstract terms, words with private associations?
- Have you used strong, active verbs wherever possible?
- Have you kept the noun-verb ratio low?
- Have you maintained consistent tenses, changing only to show a time shift?
- Have you used strong, concrete nouns as often as possible? Do they help you to create images and metaphors?
- Have you changed heavy nouns (nouns ending in -tion, -ment, -ance, and -ism) into verbs or simpler nouns wherever possible?
- Have you eliminated noun-strings?
- Have you avoided clichés?
- Have you avoided sexist and racist language and other terms or concepts that may offend or exclude readers?
- Have you avoided doublespeak and presented your points as honestly and clearly as possible?

References and Further Reading

Auden, W. H. *Collected Shorter Poems*. London: Faber and Faber, 1966.

Baron, Dennis. *Declining Grammar and Other Essays on the English Vocabulary*. Urbana, Illinois: National Council of Teachers of English, 1989. Copyright 1989 by the National Council of Teachers of English. Reprinted with permission.

Bryson, Bill. *The Mother Tongue: English & How It Got That Way*. New York: Morrow, 1990. Used by permission of William Morrow and Company, Inc. Publishers, New York.

Chomsky, Noam. *Syntactic Structures.* The Hague: Mouton, 1957.

Department of Secretary of State. *The Canadian Style: A Guide to Writing and Editing.* Toronto: Dundurn Press, 1985.

Freelance Editors' Association of Canada. *Editing Canadian English.* Vancouver: Douglas & McIntyre, 1988.

Joyce, James. "The Dead," *Dubliners.* New York: Viking Press, 1967.

Lutz, William. *Doublespeak.* Copyright © 1989 by Blonde Bear, Inc. Used by permission of HarperCollins Publishers.

MacLeish, Archibald. Quoted in George Plimpton, ed. *The Writer's Chapbook.* New York: Viking, 1989. Used by permission of Penguin USA.

McCrum, Robert, William Cran, and Robert MacNeil. *The Story of English.* London: Faber and Faber, 1986.

Miller, Casey, and Kate Swift. *The Handbook of Non-Sexist Writing.* New York: Harper & Row, 1988.

Philip, Marlene (Nourbese). "The Absence of Writing." *Brick: A Literary Journal* 39 (Summer 1990): 26–33. Reprinted with permission of the author.

Rico, Gabrielle. *Writing the Natural Way.* Los Angeles: Tarcher, 1983.

Ricoeur, Paul. *The Rule of Metaphor.* Translated by Robert Czerny. Toronto: University of Toronto Press, 1977.

Chapter Nine

The Reflective Writer

ᔔ

*I said to my mother one time, "How did
you ever permit me to let this be printed?"
And she said, "You didn't ask my advice."*

MARIANNE MOORE

This chapter is intended to help you reflect on the quality
of your writing and your development as a writer, so you
can assume fuller responsibility than you are used to for
assessing and evaluating your writing. Toward that end, you
will need to know more about yourself as a writer; to know
what works best for you and what inhibits you as a writer;
to become more fully aware of the criteria you apply in
judging your writing and the writing of others; and to recognize the criteria that are likely to be applied to your writing. This chapter also contends that you learn much about
writing and about yourself as a writer as you respond to the
writing of others.

This approach is in keeping with what we have said
through the preceding eight chapters, where we have
stressed the link between your development as a writer and
your growing awareness of your writing processes. Taking
more responsibility for assessing your writing is integrally

related to this growing awareness. As you followed the arguments of this book and completed some of the recommended writing exercises, you may have realized that you have in fact given considerable time to assessing and reflecting on your own writing and the writing of others. In what follows you will draw on those experiences and consider in some detail ways in which you can become a reflective writer.

This chapter advocates two particular strategies: (1) keeping a log and (2) developing productive strategies for responding to the writing of others and for using the responses you receive in turn. The final section of this chapter suggests an assessment policy that is consistent with helping you take fuller responsibility for your own assessment and the criteria involved in your evaluation.

Reflecting on Your Writing

By keeping a journal and doing exercises such as the Writing Inventory in Chapter Two, you have become more aware of yourself as a writer: your writing rituals, the strategies you prefer to use, your writing history, your strengths and weaknesses, and so on. Keeping a log is another effective way of increasing your understanding of your writing processes.

Keeping a Log

Whenever you are involved in an activity that requires some degree of skill, you are also involved to some extent in monitoring your performance and progress through that activity. Thus, as a writer, you assess what it is you are doing or accomplishing. As you write, you ask yourself implicitly, and often explicitly: How am I doing? Am I getting there? What do I need to do to get there? Is it worth doing? How does this measure up against what I set out to do? What if I changed direction now? As soon as you stop monitoring your progress through a piece of writing, it is quite likely that you have ceased to care about it.

You can make this monitoring more conscious and deliberate by keeping a log as you work on a writing assignment. You will probably be familiar with a log as the official record of a ship or an aircraft. During a journey, notes are made in the log about the craft's speed and progress, and about any significant events that occur. Logbooks of various sorts are also popular with engineers, social workers, scientists, and teachers who record their professional activities, problems, questions, and progress through a particular inquiry or task. To a certain extent, keeping a log is a process of self-evaluation. Keeping a writer's log is a process of increasing understanding of yourself as a writer and a means of recording the decisions and choices you make while writing. You may recall here the extracts in Chapter Six from Anna's log recording her progress through her writing on the topic of women and science.

There is no single way for a writer to keep a logbook. In its simplest form, your writer's log documents your progress through an assignment. This includes keeping and reflecting on all drafts, all the feedback received from readers, and all revisions. This material is labelled and kept with a running commentary describing your process: the problems you encountered; the strategies you tried; what worked and did not work; the decisions you made and the reasons for those decisions; your readers' suggestions and the changes you made in response to them. Such a record, in time, will help you understand how and why you write what you write. Your log for each assignment should conclude with a self-evaluation of the process, discussing what you have learned, and detailing what you would choose to improve if you had more time. Documenting the time you spent on each phase of your assignment will help you decide whether you need to reconsider how you allot your time. The following example of a log on a major writing assignment (much like the problem-solving project described in Chapter Five) is offered only to illustrate how one writer used the log to reflect on her writing process. It is not a model for imitation, but it does use several of the suggestions offered above. The writer is a first-year university student in management.

Process Log
Final Project (due April 9)

Feb. 12—generating ideas in class—I don't have a good topic yet.

Feb. 24—I've been thinking about it a lot—wrote down some more ideas, but nothing too promising yet. I think it will end up being about scheduling computer time at the residence or at school, or about the school's lab schedule hours. I'm trying to think of something like the examples the teacher gave in class.

Feb. 27—decided to write about computer camp and how poorly organized it was. Still wouldn't mind coming up with a better subject though.

March 10—wrote definition of problem, goal, and purpose of report in class today. I've been thinking about it before this, but nothing written down yet. (I've also been forgetting to write log entries when I do some thinking.) I have to have a letter of proposal in for Tuesday, so that'll force me to start producing results and stop just going over it in my mind.

March 14—thinking about it on the bus and subway this week, and just now while walking the dog (10 minutes). The kids were bored—should have been grouped according to previous experience and age, not language—program of study was poorly thought out and prepared. Should write draft of proposal letter today or tomorrow.

March 16—I wrote a draft, then a good (clearer) copy of my letter of proposal to hand in tomorrow (Tuesday). It doesn't sound very formal, but I've been trying to think about this realistically and I can't imagine just writing a formal letter to this guy, totally out of the blue. I think the friendly approach I took would be more likely accepted. I make clear what I wanted from him and what I hoped to accomplish—I think it's OK (for a draft). Also, I've been thinking about how the report should be organized—I'm not sure yet.

March 19—Peer editing of proposal letter in class. I got some good feedback. Tina suggested I show what was wrong with how camp was run previously. Kam thought of a way I may be able to save some of the first paragraph. (It's kind of lacking a problem statement—should get right to the point—it's very friendly and chatty as it stands now.) First draft of actual report is due next week.

March 21—half an hour of generating ideas about the problems with the camp—didn't get into solutions much, but I think that's pretty clear in my mind, I just haven't written it out yet. I'm still not clear on how the report will be organized, but I'll have to think about that more later.

March 25—IDEA TREES all over the place! After quite a few attempts I came up with a wonderful idea tree (I hope). The one for the problem seems to work well, but the solutions don't fit the same pattern too nicely. Worked for about 1 1/2 hours in all tonight.

March 26—In class today I paired up with Donna, and she played an antagonistic reader of my report (actually, just an oral version of the report). She tells me I should include an example of a complaint someone made to back up my analysis of the problem, which is a really good idea. Didn't get a chance to show my idea tree to the teacher, but I got my letter back and it's pretty much OK. Also, Donna suggests that I include estimates of how much my suggested solutions will cost (= Resource commitment).

March 27—missed class today (I tried—honest) but started work on my draft, about 35 min.

March 31—saw prof about idea tree (it's pretty good so far) and worked on draft—1 hour (just before class)—also fixed up idea tree a bit. Worked on intro in class and took notes on report format (very good to know) and executive summary (sounds difficult)—didn't get much work done on the intro.

Worked on draft 1 1/4 hours in library—got intro done and beginning of problem section. The whole section is quite clear in my mind though because of the very detailed idea tree I've got (WOW). I think the intro took longer to write than it should have, because I wasn't clear on what I wanted to say about the background before I started writing (but hey, I'm learning!) I guess I should have done a mini–idea tree. I may still have to if my peer editors aren't impressed on Thurs.

April 2—did peer editing on draft in class. Decided to put the background in prob. analysis section rather than intro. Also need to get prob. definition in intro. (These suggestions were from Tina)

April 5—started typing draft into word processor (20 minutes or so).

April 7—I've got the whole thing drafted, but I still want to go over it again before typing. I've decided not to use the word processors at school—it's more convenient to work at home. Just fixed up the proposal letter so it's all set to type, now I'll start on the draft.

I just finished typing the proposal letter, and first 4 pages of the report. 1 1/2 hours.

April 8—Finished typing!!! I'm pleased with the results—pretty impressive. (At least I hope it is.)

The writer of this log clearly intends to share her log with her instructor. Reading the draft and final versions of the paper with this log in hand can be instructive to both teacher and student. Just as game films allow a hockey or football team to analyze what worked and what didn't, logs allow you to reflect on what happened, to consider your choices and their consequences. This writer, for instance, clearly values using idea trees and feedback from her peers, but has trouble establishing her topic and getting started. Reading her log, the writer may realize what other strategies she might have tried. The teacher can suggest where appropriate idea-generating strategies would have helped.

You may choose to keep your log in a different format—one that is less like a narrative and more like a sketch or outline of your writing process. Each entry can include notes under the following headings:

Date and Time:
Activity/Strategy:
Observations/Comments:

This format allows you to keep track of the amount of time you spend on various activities such as thinking about the task, planning your argument, finding documentation, writing, procrastinating, rewriting, and editing. Most of us are vaguely aware that we would produce better writing if we managed our time better. The problem is that we don't always know when we are using our time productively and when we aren't. Writing a major paper is a complex process, and we often get so involved in one task that we can't see the bigger picture. A log allows us to look back on the whole process and see how smooth or rough the path was.

Under the second heading, describe what you do in the process of working on a paper. Label your strategies or describe them carefully. You might be developing ideas through discussions in or out of class, interviewing someone, letting some time elapse so you can see the problem from a distance, or just thinking about the paper as you go about your daily routine.

Under the third heading, explain why you chose this particular strategy and how it worked or didn't work Try to evaluate whether you are reaching your goals with what you're doing or whether you need to find some other strategies. Focus on how what you did affected your paper and how it affected you as a writer. If your instructor is also reading your log in order to understand the process you went through and the techniques you used, conclude your entries with your own evaluation that tells him what you think of your finished product and the process you followed to arrive at it. Where are the strengths and weaknesses in your paper? Where are the strengths and weaknesses in your process? What goals do you feel you have achieved with this assignment? What things would you do if you had more time? And finally, what questions do you have for your readers? The instructor can probably give you a better response to your writing if he understands how you arrived at it and what you'd like to know from your reader.

In your log, focus your attention on saying what you mean, not on mechanics or grammar. This is personal, expressive writing; its main purpose is to help you learn, not to impress a reader. Don't worry about spelling or punctuation or complete sentences. Concentrate on creating a picture of yourself as a writer at work, one who reports not only the successes but also the false starts, detours, and blind alleys.

Besides tracking your way through individual assignments, you can use your log to chart your progress through the whole writing class by simply recording your reactions to lectures, readings, discussions, group work, and other aspects of the class. Writing about yourself as a developing writer can help you in several ways: it can help you shape clear goals and measure your progress toward those goals; it can give you a truer picture of what actually happens during the course than memory alone; and it can convince you that writing is an essential ingredient in learning. We often have difficulty determining how much we have learned because we forget where we started. Keeping a log enables us to keep track of the changes in our perceptions, questions, and goals, and the progress we make toward these goals.

As wonderful as they sound, logs do pose one problem: it can be difficult to write and at the same time keep track of the processes you are involved in; so that some of the decisions you make as a writer often escape your notice. One way of overcoming this difficulty hinges on your becoming accustomed to recording your writing processes so that, with habit, the writing becomes less and less of an interference in the process. Designing and using a log format that makes the recording process less of an interruption for you will also help. Here are some variations of log formats that may suit your particular temperament and ways of working.

The Process Log
This is the log format described above. You stop when you have finished a particular task or when you are having difficulty or facing a decision, and you make an entry in your log.

The Taped Log
Using the categories of date, activity, and reflection/observation, you simply record your thoughts on tape. Because it is faster to speak than to write, this method tends to interfere less with the actual writing you are doing. Some writers report that the talk they do aloud on tape often helps them think through problems they face in their writing.

The Annotated Log
After completing a written activity—whether it be a brainstorm list, an idea tree diagram, a section of a draft, or just some freewriting—write in the margin in a different-coloured ink or stick a post-it note on your paper to write a brief reflection that explains what you did here and why and whether you're on the right track. By keeping all your rough work and labelling all your strategies this way, both you and your instructor can trace the path of your thinking/writing.

The Story Log
Recreate your process through the paper as a story. Find a metaphor that might vividly say what a particular episode of writing was like for you. The notion of a journey (long, arduous, short, easy) or an adventure is one that easily comes to mind. Is hunting an elusive prey a metaphor that fits your current situation?

Responding to Writing

> The word in living conversation is directly, blatantly, oriented toward a future answer-word: it provokes an answer, anticipates it and structures itself in the answer's direction

M. BAKHTIN, *DISCOURSE IN THE NOVEL*

If, as Bakhtin argues, what we say is determined by our continuing anticipation of an answering response, we need to acknowledge that the responses we receive to our writing and how we respond to the writing of others (in speech, in writing, and even physically) powerfully determine the shape and content of the texts we compose. Such a notion is entirely consistent with a view of writing as a social act, even when it is done as a private activity. It matters then that you pay considerable attention to how you respond to the writing of others and how you receive their responses to your writing in turn.

Unfortunately, many people view responding to writing as primarily teachers' comments and grades on finished products. Response is equated with editing, correcting, criticism, arbitrary standards, subjective judgment, and a sense of powerlessness on the part of the writer. Several changes need to occur in the attitudes of writers and readers if response is to be a positive force for improvement in writing:

1. Responding to writing needs to be redefined to include *all* readers' responses to writing, both during the process and when the writing has been handed in as a finished product.

2. We need to see such responses as part of an ongoing conversation within a community of writers: a conversation that allows writers to take account of readers and anticipate their needs; a conversation that acknowledges that language and knowledge are socially created (while you may be writing and reading in splendid isolation, the language you create derives from and has its life within a larger social fabric of speakers, readers, and writers).

3. We need to develop a language for responding, a language to describe writing and assess it, a language to replace global comments of approval or disapproval and letter or numerical grades. We also require practice in applying this language, in recognizing and explaining what works and doesn't work and why. Exercise 1 at the end of the chapter is one step toward this goal. In general, discussing your assessment of a piece of writing in a small group and comparing your response with the responses offered by others

in the group will help you not only to discover what it is you value in writing but also to get a sense of what your group of writers value. You will also discover from writers' reactions to your responses what particular kinds of comments help or don't help. You may already have realized what kind of feedback writers would like from their readers in the section "Test a Draft" in Chapter Five and the section "Studying Your Readers" in Chapter Seven. If you are working in small groups, you may wish to try Exercise 2 at the end of this chapter.

4. If the writer has not provided background information you need, you should ask for it. Where you think it might be helpful, you should encourage the writer to ask for opinions from other readers.

5. You can make the process of responding somewhat easier and often much more helpful to writers when you use specially designed forms for peer review or create your own. Such a practice is particularly helpful when you and the teacher set criteria together and do so some time before the final draft is due. A sample peer review form is provided at the end of this chapter. A teacher or group may choose to adapt these forms to correspond with the demands of a particular writing assignment.

6. As a reader, you should differentiate between "higher-level" concerns (ideas, the nature of the argument, form, intended readers' needs, for instance) and "lower-level" ones (syntax and other surface-level editing concerns). You need to know which level of concern the writer wishes feedback on.

7. In responding, do not forget that you need to be both precise and positive in your response. Use language that describes what the writer is doing and saying (see Chapter Five). Respond to positive elements in the text as well as negative ones. Concentrate on the important elements in the text; do not try to respond to every detail unless you have been asked for a close reading.

8. To be useful, response must not come too early (before the writer has become interested in the text and discovered what he or she wants to say) or too late (after the writer has put so much time and effort into the text that he or she does not want to make changes). Writers should be allowed to say when they need their work read and assessed.

9. Not all the responsibility for making productive responses lies with the reader; as a writer, you too must work to make that process effective:

- You need to be seen as committed to the writing you are engaged in; that is, you must be seen as wanting a response.

- You must also consider that your readers will read and rewrite the text from their own points of view, especially if your intentions remain unclear. This is why it is important to guide your readers by explaining the purpose of the text and who your intended reader is; otherwise you may find yourself being criticized for not meeting goals you had no intention of meeting. You may also formulate specific questions you want your readers to answer.

- Unless you are clear about your own goals and intentions, you may find it difficult to resist the arguments of your readers and may all too readily agree to goals and directions that are not your own and do not have your whole-hearted commitment.

- You should know how to listen to what your reader tells you, how to evaluate this information, and how to act on it. Do you trust this person as a reader? Get more than one reader to comment—do other readers agree that your introduction doesn't work? You may not agree with your readers' comments, but you should consider them; if one reader responds a certain way, others may as well. You may also wish to find readers outside the classroom, especially when the text you are writing is intended for such readers.

Being a conscientious and helpful reader of someone else's writing will increase your ability to recognize and deal with problems in your own writing. You will as well be defining for yourself and in community the criteria by which you judge what is or isn't a successful piece of writing.

Assessment Criteria

Since you regularly make judgments about your own writing and the writing of others, it might help to examine the criteria on which you base your judgments and compare these criteria with those of other writers. Exercise 1 at the end of this chapter is designed to help you do so either individually or in a group by having you look at pieces of writing you like and deciding what particular criteria determine their "goodness." If you tried Exercise 1, you may have concluded that there are certain qualities that we can expect of most, if not all, good pieces of writing.

A few years ago, the writers of this book were involved with several other writing instructors in a study of writing done by first-year university students. One of the questions we considered dealt with the criteria we might use to determine what a competent piece of transactional (see Chapter Two) writing at first-year university level might look like. The following criteria emerged as basic attributes of such writing:

- a clear orientation and plan
- a clear sense of what the writing is expected to accomplish, that is, its purpose and goals
- good control of ideas: logical selection, sequence, and presentation of ideas
- "substance"—ample explanation and analysis; the writing contains appropriate details, examples, and generalizations
- good control of syntax and **diction**

Obviously this is a broad set of criteria, and you would need to look at the samples of writing we used to illustrate exactly what we meant. You may wish to compare these criteria with those you arrived at in Exercise 1; however, you must keep in mind that these broadly defined criteria should be considered with some awareness of the particular circumstances in which the writing was done: its purposes and goals, the intended readers, and the time available for the writing. The lists below were compiled by a group of writing instructors, who had to evaluate a set of problem-solving papers using a three-point scale: superior, average, and failing. After reading a number of papers from the set, they selected by general agreement three papers—one for each of the categories—and described their characteristics. Their intention was to identify from these descriptions what particular criteria had determined their decisions. The lists below describe a superior paper and a failing paper.

A superior paper

- clear statement of problem or issue
- purpose of the paper presented clearly
- solution to the problem logical, concrete, and practical
- format helpful to readers: information presented in a mixture of well-developed paragraphs and in point format
- ideas selected and organized carefully and logically
- evidence of real insight into the demands of the task
- writing authoritative and persuasive
- tone shows high level of awareness of the reader's needs and sensibilities

A failing paper

- problem presented, but not one that would interest the reader or that the reader (as addressed in the paper) could solve
- problem framed as though not comprehended from the reader's perspective
- reader's needs not understood
- some grammatical and mechanical errors, but none that interfere with readability
- syntax seemingly simple and immature
- necessary information missing
- ambiguous references

- paper entirely "writer-based," story narrated from the writer's wholly egocentric point of view
- writer attempted to deal with the topic, but failed to comprehend the demands of the task

Our point in reproducing these lists is that a group of people who talk, read, and write together in a particular field of study or work can generally agree on a set of criteria that defines good writing in their area, including criteria that are particular to their area of specialization and do not carry precisely the same meaning for people outside the group. Thus it is common practice for editors of journals to circulate submitted articles to peer reviewers, who work from a common list of criteria—often a checklist—to independently recommend publication, rejection, or resubmission with specific revisions. In most cases there is a high degree of agreement among these reviewers. At the end of this chapter, you will find a form that adapts such a procedure for use in the classroom (Exercise 3). Committees of student reviewers are asked to evaluate proposals for major writing projects. You may choose to use such a form in your group or adapt it to review your own proposals or papers.

It is one thing to agree on a list of criteria, but it is another to decide whether they have been properly applied; that is, can we all agree that a certain piece of writing meets such and such criteria? A list of criteria is not an objective standard or measure that people can bring to writing; and readers, as we discussed in Chapter Seven, do not read in a vacuum. Their expectations, their values, their past experiences of reading and writing, and even their state of mind can colour the judgments they make about a piece of writing. Yet we seldom dismiss these individual responses as subjective and personal.

These responses tell you what works for most readers, what a particular reader prefers, and what you might consider doing the next time you write. As you receive additional responses to your writing, you will begin to recognize what it is you do well and what it is you need to do better. As writers, you need to anticipate your readers' assessments and the criteria by which your writing will be judged. As we discussed in the section Responding to Writing, talking about your writing with your readers is one way of developing a sense of how readers receive your writing and the criteria you might keep in mind as you read and revise.

Assessment, Evaluation, and Grades

While this chapter urges you to actively solicit the responses of others to your writing, we do not mean that you are thereby exempt from any responsibility for assessing your own writing. When you assign responsibility to someone else—usually a teacher—to tell you how well or badly you are doing as a writer, you tend not to exercise your own judgment and not to learn from the consequences of your own decisions. You are likely to act as though teachers hold the perfect version of every written piece you hand over to them, and can tell you how and by how much your writing falls short of those perfect versions. If you continue to hold such attitudes, you are bound to distrust your own judgment and remain constantly dependent on someone else to determine whether you have succeeded or failed as a writer.

In such situations, the primary goal for writing becomes one of getting a good grade: "what the teacher wants" takes precedence over your own goals and intentions. And because expectations seem to vary from one teacher to another, you can hardly be blamed if you consider the whole system of grading writing arbitrary and unpredictable. Many students feel that the grades they are assigned do not often coincide with their own estimates of their writing. If you are unsure about the criteria by which you are being judged, you are bound to feel uncertain about how you might improve your writing.

In fact, in a study on how different schemes for assessing writing affect students' motivation, Australian researcher Brian Johnston found that students who assess their own work are more motivated to improve as writers than are students who regularly receive grades or marks from teachers. This finding is rather unsettling to most people who have gone through school generally convinced that grades provide strong motivation for improvement, especially since educational institutions also seem to be firmly settled into such assumptions. When we reflect on Johnston's findings, however, we may realize that they make considerable sense.

We stated early in this chapter that evaluation has been generally conceived far too narrowly as teachers' comments and grades on finished products. We have suggested throughout this chapter a broader notion to include all readers' responses to one's writing both during its development and when it is finished. We are confirming in this way two of the threads that have run through this book: the social, collaborative nature of language and the development of individual language capabilities through such collaborative exchange. This whole chapter (and in a sense, the book) is intended to help you take full responsibility for evaluating your own writing in terms of criteria you continue to define and revise.

The Teacher's Role

Teachers are experienced readers; they can tell why they believe a particular piece of writing works well or doesn't work at all; they can suggest certain changes that might help. However, teachers also expect that you will weigh their assessments and suggestions against your own judgments and the evaluations of other readers. They hope that as you begin to exercise your own judgments with growing confidence, you will turn less often to other readers for approval and endorsement (though we all need approval now and then) and look to them more often for their detailed responses as readers.

Ultimately, a teacher's role is one of helping you achieve full autonomy as a writer—a degree of autonomy that helps you move from school writing to writing in your business, professional, or academic life. Outside the classroom you write generally not to demonstrate what you know (as is the norm for term papers and examinations) but to inform, persuade, or advise those who really need to know or are in a position to act on what you have written. In such a case, it is you who must decide if your writing will do what it was intended to do. You will learn more about yourself as a writer from the responses you receive from your readers, and even more from the people with whom you write. Our discussion of log keeping and responding to writing illustrates the importance of knowing yourself as a writer and learning from readers and other writers as well.

Teachers, as a rule, have another role, a role they relish least: assigning grades. We have used the terms assessment and evaluation interchangeably; it is important, however, to recall what they separately stress. For us assessment is a matter of describing what is happening to you as a writer and what you are accomplishing as a writer. In speaking of evaluation, we would stress the notion of "value" that is at its root. What do you value in writing? What do you find of value in a particular piece of writing? The term does not prescribe a fixed standard as much as it suggests a flexible one defined by the particular context of the writing that is being evaluated. The value of the writing is set by the circumstances in which it was written: the difficulty of the task, the time allotted to it, the relative maturity or immaturity of the writer, the resources available to the writer. For instance, a personal letter is not valued for the same set of qualities as a business report is. As we have already seen in Chapter Seven, the value is also determined by who the reader is and in what context the writing is being read. That there are no fixed standards may be unsettling to some students at first; they might gain some consolation from recalling the many stories of well-known authors whose rejected efforts turned out to be classics in the hands of more discerning publishers.

Paradoxically, the task of grading—assigning a specific mark relative to the achievement of other writers in a group or with reference to predetermined criteria—is made less difficult where the least grading has been done, where students have assumed increasing responsibility for monitoring their own development as writers. In this case, regular conferences between instructor and students will ensure that they will arrive at a mutually agreed on grade with much less difficulty than they would have if the responsibility for grading had been borne entirely by the instructor. The criteria for determining these grades must be discussed in advance, preferably at the beginning of the course.

One such set of criteria is reproduced below. These criteria were arrived at by a group of writing instructors after considerable discussion and are continually being revised. The criteria list the responsibilities of students and instructors, and provide a five-point scale for arriving at a final grade.

INSTRUCTOR'S RESPONSIBILITIES IN
THE WRITING WORKSHOP

- plan and coordinate the agenda of the workshop section
- introduce and demonstrate a variety of writing strategies
- create opportunities for collaboration
- direct students' attention to effective academic and nonacademic written communication
- respond in writing to the content of students' journals
- help students develop confidence in and responsibility for their own writing
- give feedback (written or taped) on all formal assignments and accompanying processes
- keep a record of students' work and progress as writers
- document fulfilment of students' responsibilities

STUDENTS' RESPONSIBILITIES IN
THE WRITING WORKSHOP

- attend all classes, prepared
- keep a journal and hand it in as required by your instructor
- show written evidence of trying out and applying writing strategies
- work independently and collaboratively
- share your writing with others
- evaluate critically the writing you see around you
- work to improve your writing and increase your understanding of how you write

- develop and submit appropriate, original assignments according to your instructor's specifications
- keep a record of and evaluate your own work and progress as a writer

EVALUATION CRITERIA

C You fulfil your responsibilities as a student and make an honest effort to employ the recommended strategies, but your writing remains weak. Your rough drafts, final drafts, and logs show that you can:

- provide the reader with useful information, even if it is sometimes repetitious or lacking in depth or development;
- establish a focus and an organizational pattern, even if you have difficulty maintaining them;
- demonstrate reasonable control over language, even if your text does contain errors in grammar and/or mechanics that interfere with meaning.

B You fulfil your responsibilities as a student, and are able to write papers that meet the demands of the assignment. Your rough drafts, final drafts, and logs show that you can:

- provide a full explanation and analysis of your topic, giving appropriate details, examples, and proofs;
- maintain a consistent focus and clear pattern of organization;
- control your language so that errors in grammar or mechanics are minor and do not seriously interfere with meaning.

A You satisfy the criteria for a B, and set challenging writing goals that extend and develop your writing abilities. Your rough drafts, logs, and final drafts show that you can.

- show insight into the demands of a variety of writing tasks;
- create written assignments that reflect those insights;

- demonstrate excellent control over language.

F   You fail to fulfil your responsibilities as a student.

D   You fulfil your responsibilities as a student, but fail to achieve an acceptable level of competency in written English. Your papers lack adequate organization or substance. Errors in grammar and mechanics seriously detract from meaning.

Nothing can take the sting out of evaluation. Anything but praise is difficult to accept, especially about one's use of language. Correcting or devaluing another person's language is like saying something negative about his or her appearance or ideas. If you remain aware that people are especially sensitive to criticism of their language, you will find ways for giving and receiving that criticism with a minimum of pain. Those ways are more likely to emerge within the give-and-take of your regular reading and responding to one another's writing.

This book has worked in a variety of ways to help you achieve some degree of autonomy as a writer. However, no successful writer is entirely autonomous: the ideas of others, the language that has evolved in our discussions, and the contributions of newspapers, TV, radio, and books all rattle around in our heads to emerge, if we are fortunate, at the time when we need them.

That developing autonomy, we know, will founder if you give up the habit of writing regularly—not keeping a journal for instance. If you are to go on being a writer (and have already discovered the powerful link between writing and learning), you will find opportunities to reflect, through your writing, on what you read, observe, and hear. Talking with people about what you read is one way of clarifying and coming to terms with new ideas; it is also a way of trying out some novel formulations. It is such talking that helps develop articulateness in writing. Above all, find or hold on to those readers who will read your writing for you and provide honest feedback; be prepared to do the same for them. We said at the beginning of this book that we are continually in the process of becoming writers; we hope that using this book has made that journey less frustrating and even more adventurous .

If you have not done so already, explore the potential of the word processor as a writing tool; give it a good try but don't consider yourself a lesser writer if you fail to establish a working relationship. The following appendix provides an introduction to writing with the word processor. It is full of practical advice, anticipates problems, and suggests how some of the strategies recommended in this book may be used just as well on screen.

Exercises

Exercise 1: Explore Evaluation Criteria

This exercise can be done individually or in a group. Choose a short text that you regard as a good piece of writing, preferably about a page to two pages in length. You may choose something you have written yourself, or look for published material you could easily find yourself writing, be it a letter, a journal entry, an editorial, a section of a magazine or journal article, or some passages from your favourite textbook. Think about why you chose this particular text, and write down a list of its attributes that you particularly value. What do you like about this piece? What features make this a good piece of writing?

If you are working in a group:

In groups of three or four, exchange the pieces of writing you selected, and after reading each one, decide on the characteristics that mark each of these pieces as a good piece of writing. Make a list of characteristics for each piece. Some of the same characteristics might appear on each list; other characteristics may apply to particular pieces only.

Now compare lists in your group and, on the basis of those lists, decide as a group on those qualities that, in general, constitute good writing. Consider in what order of importance you would list those qualities.

You may compare your lists with those drawn up by other groups and decide what qualities, in the opinion of the class, constitute good writing. You may also wish to consider whether other groups—professionals such as lawyers and engineers, or junior high-school students, or teachers—would define good writing in closely similar ways. What attributes of good writing would all groups hold in common?

If you are working alone:

Look in your textbook or your favourite magazine or a professional journal for other pieces of writing that you like. Make a list of the attributes that you particularly value in each of these passages. Compare your lists to arrive at a set of qualities that apply to all of these pieces of writing. If you can, show the passages you selected to other readers in order to confirm whether they share the same criteria you identified for good writing.

Exercise 2: Respond to Student Writing

Read the following texts written by two fifteen-year-old students. Their topic is the gap between their parents' perceptions of teenagers' concerns and lifestyles and the teenagers' own perceptions about how they should conduct their lives. Write a response to each of these texts.

Passage 1

I believe that parents are not aware of many things in teenagers' lives, especially the pressures we live under. They seem to see things only from their own perspectives, as if we are still living in the sixties and this is not the nineties.

When my mother asked me one day just out of curiosity if I liked any girls, I told her all about a girl in my class. Before I could finish speaking, she had begun this lecture about sex and kids and the diseases you can get from sex. The way she spoke made me realize she had no idea I knew a great deal about sex and girls, much more than she did, in fact.

My father is no different. Most parents don't realize how many of their children drink and smoke. My father drinks and smokes, yet he is constantly lecturing me about how stupid it is to drink and smoke at my age. I haven't dared asked him when he started smoking or drinking. It would just make me mad to hear him say that he did not then know how bad cigarettes were for your health and as for drinking, he does not drink just to get drunk as most teenagers do.

What parents don't know is the pressure to be "cool." "Cool" boys get the "cool" girls. Smoking is "cool" and bringing a case of beer to a party is "cool." I know I won't take up smoking and I am not really going to become a teenage alcoholic, but I am not going to say no to a cigarette or a beer. Maybe it would help if my parents understood that I am really going along with the crowd.

Parents always keep speaking of teenage years as being difficult; what they don't realize is that part of the difficulty is their parents are not able to communicate at the teenager's level. My parents are always saying that I am lucky I didn't have to grow up when they did and how they did not have this and that. Teenagers really don't want to hear what happened when their parents were young. They want to know how they can manage their lives today. Parents can help by listening to what their children are really saying rather than judging them by standards from thirty or forty years ago.

Jason L.

Passage 2

What I really want to talk about is the communication gap between parents and teenagers. Parents constantly complain that their children pay no attention to their advice. As a teenager, I would say that parents don't know much about the world of teenagers and speak as though little has changed since they were teenagers. It is hard to take their advice seriously.

Teenagers hate these lectures from their parents and probably do just the opposite to spite their parents. Maybe the parents should try a different approach. They should listen to what their teenager has to say before they make judgments about what they should do or should have done. If parents were more sensitive to their children's feelings, teenagers would probably listen.

Communication would improve if parents organized to find out what was really going on in the world of teenagers. I am sure they could get a group of teenagers to speak to parents to tell them what goes on in a teenager's day, why they don't often have time for homework or housework, why they cannot keep to a regular routine, like getting home on Saturday night at a fixed time. Teenagers could also tell them about their music and why it's not just "a load of junk." If parents really listened to rap music, they would be surprised how good the words are.

Parents should keep an open mind, and remember that teenagerhood is a time of rebellion. Teenagers know that their parents are concerned about them. But parents should also know that part of growing up is finding out for yourself.

Terri B.

In small groups, read each other's comments and discuss the relative value of those comments. Report back to the class on what *kinds* of comments are likely to be most helpful to the writers and why.

Exercise 3: Write a Peer Review

Form peer review committees of four to evaluate proposals for a major writing project such as those in Chapter Five, Exercise 2. The committee will read four proposals from outside the group and prepare an evaluation of each proposal using the following form. You may add or delete criteria to conform to the requirements of the writing project. You may also use this form to review your own proposals or papers.

It is best for each member of the committee to prepare individual reports and then collaborate on writing joint reports for each proposal. If there are major differences of opinion, append a minority report.

EVALUATION OF THE PROPOSAL SUBMITTED BY _____

PEER REVIEW COMMITTEE MEMBERS: _____

CRITERIA

1. Does the title sound interesting and accurate? _____

2. Has the writer found a topic that seems important and worth writing about? Will the paper say something unique and special? _____

3. Has the writer identified a problem within his or her topic—a conflict or key issue that can be defined, analyzed, understood, and solved? _____

4. Has the writer narrowed the scope of the topic to a thesis or problem that can be explored and resolved in ten pages? _____

5. Has the writer chosen an appropriate audience? Will the intended reader find the paper useful? _____

6. Has the writer established a clear and worthwhile goal, a purpose for writing the paper? _____

7. Does the writer have a sensible plan for collecting data? Is the writer seeking appropriate data? _____

8. Is the chosen format appropriate for the topic and the reader _____

9. Look at the writer's timetable and the strategies he or she plans to use. Is this plan realistic? _____

10. Would you like to read the paper the writer is planning? _____

RESPONSE

Expand on any of these points. Answer any questions the writer asked on his or her proposal.

_____

_____

_____

_____

_____

_____

EVALUATION

Select one of the four ratings that follow.

____**1.** Acceptable because _____

_____

_____

____ **2.** Acceptable with the following major modification(s):

_____

_____

_____

_____

____ **3.** Acceptable with the following minor modification(s):

_____

_____

_____

_____

_____ **4.** Reconsider planned paper because _____

_____

_____

_____

_____

References and Further Reading

Bakhtin, M. "Discourse in the Novel." In *The Dialogic Imagination: Four Essays*, edited by M. Holquist, translated by C. Emerson and M. Holquist. Austin, TX: University of Texas Press, 1981, p. 280. By permission of the publisher.

Johnston, Brian. *Assessing English: Helping Students to Reflect on Their Work*. Sydney, Australia: St. Clair Press, 1983; Milton Keynes, England: Open University Press, 1990.

Moore, Marianne. Quoted in George Plimpton, ed. *The Writer's Chapbook*. New York: Viking, 1989. Used by permission of Penguin USA.

White, Edward M. *Teaching and Assessing Writing*. San Francisco: Jossey-Bass. 1985

Writing with the Computer: An Introduction

ও৯

He doesn't help you think but he helps you be-
cause you have to think for him. A totally
spiritual machine. If you write with a goose
quill you scratch the sweaty pages and keep
stopping to dip for ink. Your thoughts go too
fast for your aching wrist. If you type, the let-
ters cluster together, and again you must go
at the poky pace of the mechanism, not the
speed of your synapses. But with him (it? her?)
your fingers dream, your mind brushes the
keyboard, you are borne on golden pinions,
at last you confront the light of critical reason
with the happiness of a first encounter.

UMBERTO ECO, *FOUCAULT'S PENDULUM*

The computer can become a writer's best friend. Like the speaker in the above epigraph, you may feel an exhilaration when you begin to write with this powerful new tool. Computers can be remarkable partners in the adventure of discovering meaning, of representing thought in words. But you, the writer, are in charge. This appendix offers some strategies and activities to help those writers who are new to word processing avoid some common pitfalls.

At its best, word processing will save you time and effort, make revision and editing easier, provide multiple drafts quickly and conveniently, and help you publish a handsome, professional-looking text. It also gives you access to several of the writer's key resources, such as the spell-checker, the thesaurus, and perhaps text-analysis programs or networks. Word processing can be a great help in group writing, allowing you to exchange and revise materials efficiently. Some people find that working on a word processor increases their confidence and sense of achievement.

However, the computer is in some ways a "stupid" machine. It will do only what you tell it to do. Even worse, it can suffer mechanical breakdowns, which can be devastating if you have not remembered to save or print out your writing and have not made a backup copy. The machine will not provide you with better ideas or material to support them (although some prompting programs will encourage you to go in search of these yourself). It won't make you a better writer, and can even lead you down false trails, frustrating and slowing down your process if you let it take over.

As you work on the activities and exercises in this appendix, aim to develop a realistic sense of both the powers and the limitations of the computer, keeping in mind that your main focus is the writing process itself and the goal you are trying to achieve. One goal you may wish to set yourself is to develop a computer technique that allows you to operate effectively and comfortably at all stages of the writing process, both on- and off-screen as appropriate. This appendix outlines some effective computer techniques as well as some dangers to watch out for. "Dangers" may seem a strong word, but anyone who has watched a student in a computer lab raging over a lost paper or a missed deadline will understand why we use it: computers seem to provoke extreme responses.

Exercises at the end of the appendix invite you to try out some basic computer writing activities. You will know best from your own situation where you need to direct your personal efforts. As you work through the activities with your class and group, or individually, keep a special part of your log for comments on your computer writing experience. Exercise 1, at the end of the appendix, will give you an opportunity to articulate the points you find most important for your own word-processing needs. You may wish to do Exercise 1 at this point, as a basis for group discussion.

Getting Started

Although the first few weeks of writing on the computer may seem to distract you from the writing process itself and from the new strategies you are trying out, this situation is only temporary. Once you have gained familiarity with the keyboard and the commands, you will find yourself using the computer more freely. With surprising speed, word processing will begin to seem natural.

You will find that by using the word-processing program for real purposes (for instance, to explore ideas, communicate, publish), you will learn a surprising amount almost incidentally. Just as your ability to spell and to choose words precisely develop best through practical use, so the technical commands of a word-processing program are best learned as you need them, not in empty exercises. Almost certainly you will make mistakes, especially as you become a little more ambitious. Accepting this as part of the necessary learning process, and sharing it with your peers, as well as keeping a sense of humour, will help to make your transition to word processing a happy one.

Effective Techniques

Note: The exercises and activities in this chapter assume that you are working with a teacher, class, or group who can guide you in basic computer skills, if you don't have them already. If you are working alone on a computer at home, it is essential to have some kind of reference manual or other resource (even a more knowledgeable friend on the other end of a telephone).

Once you have completed Exercise 1, you have already experienced computer freewriting. First you wrote, then you discussed your reactions. The points that follow are practical reminders, which you should review until they become a normal part of your computer practice.

Protect Your Work

If you have a "hard disk" in your computer, you may come to rely heavily on the machine's powers of storage. Or you may remain distrustful and want copies of everything on paper. But in either case, especially if you are using "floppies" (soft diskettes), you need to become accustomed to saving and copying your work to guard against its loss.

In most word-processing programs, you will find a relatively simple *Save* command. Use this command frequently—ideally after every ten minutes (some people say every paragraph). This means that, in the event of a mechanical breakdown, a power cut or thunderstorm, you will have lost only a small part of your text.

Equally important is the habit of making a backup copy of important material. At the end of each day's work you should copy the revised version of your text onto a backup diskette, so that you have nothing to fear if the original is in some way lost or damaged. Even a hard disk can "crash," but its loss will be much less devastating if you have backed up everything important on floppy diskettes as well. Experienced computer users learn how important it is to make backups, usually from bitter experience.

Experiment and Learn

Freewriting on the computer is an ideal way to experiment. Anything can be attempted; anything can be changed. Try out different kinds of writing that you have never experienced before: a dialogue, a poem, a shopping list, a "stream-of-consciousness" fiction, a guidebook for your school or workplace, a lab report. The need for special features, such as columns, often comes up only in particular kinds of writing. Find out how to use columns before you need them for an important text with a tight deadline. As Chapter Six illustrates, every kind of writing has its own special forms—verbal, structural, and visual. Your computer freewriting offers you countless opportunities to experiment and make discoveries.

Practise

If you have had little keyboard practice, and have rarely used a typewriter, it is important to freewrite as much as possible in your first few weeks of writing with a computer. Eventually, your brain and muscles will become accustomed to the necessary actions and the positions of the various keys.

You may want to do some or all of your journal entries on screen. Or, at the very least, give yourself some time each week to work freely, and experimentally, until you begin to feel that the computer can be as much a friend as your favourite pen or your old typewriter.

Accept Provisional Writing

Accepting the limitations of the current stage of your writing becomes essential when you are using a word processor. You need to be aware that you can leave some problems for later. First deal with the immediate problems, then gradually work toward a polished final form ("Don't get it right; get it written and *then* get it right"). One of the most inefficient ways to work with a computer is to try to get every level of the writing perfect, even as you put it on screen. Instead, acknowledge the "getting started" stage for what it is: a way of unblocking ideas and creative energy, a chance to experiment, to be open, to gain familiarity with what you are doing, to get yourself in the right gear.

Enjoy the Computer's Potential

One of the most striking and simple features of the word processor—the capacity to change parts of a reusable text—can be useful in many practical ways in your own life. Students often seem to take to the computer better when they can see it as helpful not only for school work but also for other writing needs. Perhaps you have had an important experience that you want to inform several friends about, or you have a set of invitations or flyers to do for a party or performance. In all these cases you can readily benefit from the computer's ability to change parts of a text, such as a heading, while keeping the rest the same. If you are working on a computer system that can do graphics, you will also be able to produce illustrations to accompany your text.

Some Dangers to Watch For

Here are some common traps to avoid if you are just beginning to use word processors:

"Walk before Running"

Although everyone can benefit from a healthy degree of ambition—a desire to go further—the beginning computer user also needs to have a realistic sense of present limits. Some students get into trouble when they set up an overly-ambitious task for their first computer assignment. Others run into trouble because of a sudden need for complicated commands (often formatting) they haven't yet grasped. In both cases, the problem is usually compounded by a lack of time. Computer-assisted writing may allow for better use of your time in the long term, but in the early stages it can sometimes slow you down. As you reflect on your progress in writing, learning, and word processing, you will find ways to minimize this problem.

Use the Word Processor for Appropriate Strategies

It can be frustrating to spend computer time on a writing strategy that is much better done on paper. Idea trees are a perfect example of this: unless your computer has a "mouse" and a line-drawing program, you may find that trying to create something like an idea tree on the computer is awkward if not impossible. Even worse, you may find that your computer's lack of flexibility may force your diagrams into a more rigid outline than you would achieve if you drew them on paper. With your group, you may wish to flip through this book and single out those strategies that are really best done by hand and those that adapt well to the computer.

Don't Use the Computer as a Typewriter

Because the keyboards are similar and both kinds of technology produce typewritten text, novice computer users are sometimes tempted to use the word processor as a typewriter. For instance, they may use the computer only to type a single, final draft. The activities suggested throughout this book and the support of your writing group should minimize this temptation. Always print out a draft to revise on, instead of trying to tinker with text on the screen in front of you. (See the next section, *Drafting and Revising*, for further discussion of this important point.)

Manage Your Time Well

Almost all of us lead busy lives and have many demands on our time. If you are a student, a professional, or a parent, you probably have to do your writing under tight time constraints. The problem with computers is that excessive exhaustion, stress, or panic can lead you to make decisions whose consequences are much more severe than they would be if you used pen and paper or a typewriter. You may have spent an hour formatting a text, only to lose it accidentally. You may have absent-mindedly erased the wrong version of a file. Again, experience helps, and your log can give you a perspective on how you handle the pressures of time so that your computer use is relatively free of trouble.

Learn Commands by Using Them

Beginners sometimes feel they can't start "real" writing on the computer until they have gone through a full tutorial provided with the program. Certainly these exercises can be helpful, but they should not be done at the expense of real on-screen writing tasks, combined with off-screen activities such as clustering, planning, and revising. Most writing students who have mentioned this topic in their computer logs say the same thing: "You learn word processing by doing it" and "The exercises in the manual just confused me; they taught me how to do all kinds of things I didn't need."

Avoid Technical Obsessions

If you have a scientific and logical approach to life in general, you may find computers fascinating in themselves; instead of feeling intimidated, you may take to this new world like metal to a magnet. In a writing course, however, this fascination can bring its own dangers: you may spend hours of what was supposed to be writing time on a voyage of discovery through the machine's technical resources that has little to do with your writing process, and even less to do with an assignment due the next day. The computer can be a magic box of great charm—almost addictive; it is important not to let it take over in the wrong context. In particular, if you are busy becoming a "computer genius," watch out for the tendency of your peers to turn you entirely into technical adviser. Giving a helping hand is admirable and will be appreciated, but it should not be at the expense of your own thinking, writing, and learning.

Drafting And Revising

Effective Techniques

Manage Your Drafts

As mentioned above, revising on hard copy is one of the essential parts of your work in writing with computers. As you gain experience, you will probably develop a personal set of preferred techniques for revision, but you may also find that each writing task makes its own demands. If you give a *date* and a *number* to each draft, you will be able to follow your process more accurately, and find material more quickly. For example, while working on draft 4, you might remember that a paragraph you removed from draft 2 had a valuable quotation in it. You may also want to keep a record of the *readers* who have looked at, and written on, your drafts, so you can go back to a particular reader for clarification of a point or for advice on a useful piece of material.

Become Familiar with Revision Commands

During your early weeks of computer use in your writing group, find out the most important commands for revision in your word-processing program and use them often enough to become comfortable with them. In most programs, the most important commands are *Add* or *Insert, Typeover, Delete, Block* and *Move* commands (the names may vary a little). Once you know how to put in extra words, take words out, block a section of text so you can move it around, copy it, or delete it, you are well on your way to being able to revise successfully. Some revision decisions may also involve changes in formatting, which are discussed below. In some programs, many of the formatting commands are shown in a kind of "shadow" text, which can be called up deliberately, when needed. The regular writing screen is free of all the extra technical codes, thus making it easier for the writer to concentrate on what really matters at this stage: the thinking and the writing.

Discuss Work at the Screen

Although all major revision decisions are best made on paper, there will be times when you want to discuss work as it appears on your screen: the printer may not yet be available, or you may be working on a group project with all members gathered around one machine. If so, there are some practical points to keep in mind:

Scrolling: The typical screen contains only a short segment of your text. You may be tempted to focus on this portion, polishing a word here and a phrase there, forgetting that it is the whole text that matters. Try to make a habit of scrolling up and down regularly, rereading what comes before and after the section of text displayed on the screen. Use the arrow keys, the *Page Up/Page Down* commands, or whatever keys your program offers for this purpose. Read the whole text again from beginning to end before printing out a draft. By doing so you will reduce the risk of making your text jerky or inconsistent. You will also increase your familiarity with the version you are currently working on. If you have produced sections of text in a group, this process can be a temporary help in creating more consistency between the different sections.

Looking: Some programs have a "Look" mode that allows you to see, on screen, exactly how the text will appear on the page when it is printed out. This can be a useful device, even at the revision stage, because it gives you a preliminary idea of the layout and impact of your pages. It becomes even more important when you are designing the final appearance of your text.

Use Symbols to Remind You of Code Words That Need Attention

As you revise, you may realize that something in your draft will need clarification or reworking after you leave the computer with your printout. Some people find it helpful to remind themselves of any code words (explained in Chapter Eight) or other areas that need clarification by inserting into the text one or two symbols, such as ** or ##, that will be easily identified on the printout.

Other Techniques

Other effective techniques include those already mentioned in *Getting Started*. *Time-management* is always important, especially if you are working in an environment where competition for computer terminals and printers is intense. *Log-keeping* is equally important and can be used, among other things, to keep time constraints in focus. If you are working on a group project, your *definition of roles and tasks* will have to include the computer procedures you all agree to use. These could include exchanging and revising drafts; bringing drafts together from several diskettes to one file; using text-analysis, thesaurus, and spell-checking functions; making design and formatting decisions (preferably not left too late, but discussed and included as the final version takes shape).

Some Dangers to Watch For

Some of the principal traps that can await the unwary have already been mentioned, and no doubt you have discovered them for yourself: too little scrolling, dependence on the screen, inadequate "hard-copy" revision. Here are some others:

Don't Get Obsessed with Details

It can be easy to destroy the value of your revision time by getting hooked on a detail and forgetting the need to accept provisional material and move on. For some reason, the computer's enormous capabilities sometimes make people obsessive in their concern for a particular local problem, especially if they are working on screen. One student commented that this was like "fiddling while Rome burns." The point is that fiddling with words can be an evasion of your real responsibility: improving your text.

Remember Your Purpose, Context, and Reader

The seductive graphic capabilities of some word-processing programs can cause some new users to be more concerned with the look of the words on the screen than with the meaning those words should communicate. As always, the best "cure" seems to be to get back to paper, where the more traditional impact often serves to remind the writer that the reader's needs must come first. Some students find it useful in the draft stages to type at the beginning of the text their purpose, context, and reader; the reminder is thus constantly with you, and can help readers of your rough work to give better feedback.

Publishing

Effective Techniques

Exercise 5 gives you the opportunity to use some of the techniques you have learned so far and move toward the latter stages of the publishing process. Many factors must be taken into account if you want your finished text to do justice to the ideas it contains.

Choose a Design

Try out any complicated formatting commands before you need them for an important text. The computer program you are using may be relatively simple, allowing just a small choice of *fonts* (type faces) and sizes. Or it may be full of elaborate features that approach the capabilities of desktop publishing. In many programs, you can use **bold,** or *italics* or ***both***. You can also experiment with different sizes of type or use lines and boxes to display important material. Once you have formatted your text, you can make your document look even better if you have access to a laser printer.

Edit Your Drafts on Hard Copy

During the editing process, use the techniques suggested in other parts of this book, especially Chapter Eight, which contains a handy editing checklist.

Use the Thesaurus and Spell-checker

Always remember that a spell-checker is not an alternative to proofreading; it simply allows you to catch some misspelled words and typing errors by highlighting the problem word in the text and asking you to choose an alternative. Spell-checkers vary enormously in their accuracy and range.

Use the "Look" Mode

This feature allows you to call up on screen an exact representation of the text as it will appear on the page, including spacing, margins, and other special features. Some computers, like the Macintosh, have screens that display your documents in a "what you see is what you get" format; in others, the screen version may be slightly different from the printout.

Create a Design Draft

Discuss with your group whether the design decisions you have made are effective. Most of the detailed procedures for these activities will be specific to your word-processing program. You can complete them most effectively by communicating as much as possible with your group members, learning from them, and getting and giving feedback.

Some Dangers to Watch For

Avoid the Last-minute Rush

It is a mistake to leave formatting decisions too late. Formatting can be very time-consuming. After working so hard on the material, structure, and language of your text, it would be a pity to lose the reader's interest because of an unattractive format.

Don't Overemphasize Design

The visual effect of a nicely formatted and printed text is still not enough to redeem it if the thinking and writing are inadequate or stale. It is important to balance all stages of the writing process, keeping an alert eye on the value of what you are saying as well as the way it will look in the end.

Don't Proofread On Screen

Busy writers may be tempted to run through the text one final time on the computer screen, assume it is perfect, and then print it out. However, errors that a careful proofreading on paper would reveal are often missed on the screen. Even a spell-checker will not tell you if you have used "to" instead of "too," since both are real words; nor will it tell you if a word has been left out or repeated accidentally. So, once again, use a printout.

Watch for "Printer Sabotage"

Like all machines that have hard use, printers can go wrong. The ribbon may be faded, the toner may run out, the paper can jam, or the printer may suddenly begin spitting out gobbledygook. Through a combination of good planning and familiarity with your equipment, you can minimize these problems. If you are using a dot-matrix printer, check the position of the paper on the platen—you don't want your careful formatting to be ruined because the page is wrongly adjusted.

Show Your Work to an External Reader

If you can persuade someone who is not a member of your writing group to read your work, you will have the best chance of receiving truly objective feedback. In the early days of printers, the text often looked less attractive than texts produced on a good typewriter. But that has changed. If you have done the best you can with the facilities you have, you will at least know from this external reader how the text looks to the outside world. If the assignment is a letter applying for a job, or a report you must actually send, this objective feedback can be very important. You can run off your work on a better printer elsewhere if necessary.

Learning to write with a computer is easy for some people, difficult for others. Yet in the early stages what really matters is to keep an open, curious mind and simply explore the possibilities of the machine; let it be part of the writing solution, rather than another problem to solve. In a study of human learning and achievement called *Beyond Boredom and Anxiety*, M. Csikszentmihalyi looks at activities that contain their own rewards, such as chess playing, and dance. People who are most successful at practising these activities are those who can balance the challenges of the activity with their own degree of skill, so that they are neither bored (too much skill, too little challenge) nor anxious (too much challenge, too little skill). A state of "flow" results, in which the practitioner can act skilfully and with enjoyment, learning all the time.

Try to keep this concept in mind as you continue to practise your writing skills on the computer. Perhaps word processing will seem initially frustrating, yet it may dramatically change the way you write and the way you feel about your writing. Your increasing command of this valuable tool will be of great benefit to you, both in your professional and your personal life. By using the approaches suggested in this chapter, and trying out and discussing the exercises, you will have a variety of experiences with the computer to start you off and to encourage your progress.

Exercises

Exercise 1: Freewrite on Screen

Call up a blank writing screen. Put your initials and the date at the top, and the title: "FW1" (for Freewrite 1). Then, using the keyboard in whatever way you find comfortable, freewrite on this topic: "A place I've always loved." As usual in freewriting, don't stop to correct words, phrases, or sentences, and don't hesitate for too long. (Because the writing looks "official" on the screen, you may be more tempted to start editing. Resist the temptation strongly!) If you are blocked, just keep writing anything until the next idea occurs to you. You may find you are going very slowly, or hitting unfamiliar keys from time to time. As far as possible, just keep going, thinking about the subject itself.

After ten minutes, stop. Reread the writing on the screen quickly and allow yourself only a few minutes to make minor changes. Then, follow the instructions in your program for printing out a draft version of your text. Ideally you will have a fast dot-matrix printer (or several, for a class) and this process will not take long. As soon as your printout is ready, form a group of three to four people. Explain, first of all, what you wrote about and why this place was important to you. Read out some or all of your writing and listen to others read theirs. Discuss similarities and differences. Make no criticisms; instead, tell each writer what you enjoyed most or what struck your imagination most strongly.

Now, and *not before*, share your reactions to having written this piece on a computer instead of on paper. Did it seem harder? Did anything go wrong? Did you get frustrated? How does the printout look to you? What would you want to change? How did you feel about reading out and discussing something that *looks* finished, even though it is a very rough freewrite? Would you have written more, or differently, on paper?

As a group, sum up your reactions, and share them in an open discussion. It is important to be able to discuss the writing as writing, even in the perhaps unfamiliar setting of a computer lab, or while sitting beside a machine.

Exercise 2: Create a Log

As mentioned earlier, the log can help you a great deal as you start out with the computer. Organize one section that provides a record of your word-processing experience. Develop a personal list of the dangers you've run up against: habits to avoid, accidents you or your peers have had which you don't want to repeat. Beside these, write a list of the positive computer habits you are trying to develop. This list can help you with Exercise 6. One student enjoyed keeping a record in the form of a spaceship's log, with a great deal of fantasy and humour. He said later that framing his early computer experiences in this way helped him get past his initial anxieties and made him feel he was involved in an adventure.

Exercise 3: Revise a Draft

Return to the printout of the initial freewriting you did in Exercise 1. Bearing in mind the revision techniques suggested in other parts of this book, revise your printed-out draft, using a coloured pen. Consider your specific readership: the group to whom you will be presenting the piece of writing (if possible the same group who read the original piece). Your revisions may consist of structural changes or they may centre on one particular section, sentence, or word. This process shouldn't take too long, as the original text is brief, but you may find yourself wanting to add material.

Now call up the file "FW1" and revise the text on screen using your marked-up copy. Print out the new version, and return to the group. Ask at least two group members to write on the new printout with their suggestions and questions, using different coloured pens. Consider their revisions and discuss them, if time permits. Then return once again to the file on the screen, and incorporate the changes that you agree with.

Now you can print out in your printer's highest-quality mode, and present your piece to the group in its "finished" form. Compare it with the two earlier versions. What direction did the changes take? Is the final version very different from your first freewritten draft? Again you can also discuss the experience of doing this on screen. If the piece were to be published, what further changes might you make? What are the differences you found between this process and the same process done manually?

This exercise may take quite a lot of time, but it can be extremely valuable. As you work through it, you are, in effect, creating a model for the process you will use on a much larger scale for a major assignment. Most important of all, *always* use printed-out drafts for serious revision and reassessment of the work in progress. You will not only learn more and have a much clearer record for your log; you will also guard against some of the major problems of computer writing, including "jerky" drafts and poor proofreading.

Exercise 4: Design a Document

The goal of this exercise is to raise your awareness of the visual impact of different formatting choices, and to help you become familiar with the required commands. You can use any short piece of writing—preferably one that includes different text elements, such as quotations, tables, figures, headings, and subheadings. As with other drafts, add a note at the top reminding you of your audience, context, and purpose. The software and the printer you are using will determine the range of formatting choices you have, but almost certainly you will have a variety of possibilities.

1. Discuss and investigate the choices you can make with the text you have on screen. You may want to work in a small group, or alone, on the text itself. Decide on the following:
   - the use of white space and margins
   - headings and subheadings
   - font type and size
   - the use of bold, italics, and underlining
   - cover page features
   - graphics, charts, and figures

2. Create your text in the chosen form.

3. This time, format the text again, in an entirely different way. Change the margins, and areas of white space; alter the lettering in different sections; change the style for headings. Print out this second version.

4. Exchange the two versions of your text with those of another group. Discuss and write comments. Which text has a more striking visual effect? Which is clearer? Which is more appropriate for its intended audience and purpose? Are there inconsistencies? Do you prefer one font over another?

   This activity, as well as being enjoyable, gives you a chance to familiarize yourself with questions of design that were once only in the hands of specialists. The advent of desktop publishing means that anyone who has the appropriate hardware and software can now produce a professional-looking document. The potential for a writing group is exciting.

Exercise 5: Assemble a Trouble-shooting Booklet

By now your group will have had a variety of experiences, learning the commands and publishing capacity of the program you are using. Almost certainly, though, some of you will have run into some difficulties or some results that continue to puzzle you (especially if you are working with a program that does not show the text on screen as it will appear in the printout). Brainstorm a list of these problem areas, first individually, then in a group (again, files can be merged). Work together to find solutions or further information. The resulting trouble-shooting guide can be kept as a resource for your group, or it can be put together with other material, such as parts of the material generated in Exercises 2 and 3, to make up a manual for writers (Exercise 6).

Exercise 6: Put Together a Manual for Writers

To consolidate your computer writing experience and to create a valuable and practical document, your group might plan a writer's manual for next year's students or a guide to the computer and program you have used. Your logs—especially those parts that describe your experience with the computer—and your trouble-shooting booklet (Exercise 5) can contribute material for this project. The structure and presentation of the manual can be a decision for the whole group to make, with responsibility for different aspects of the work assigned to smaller groups or individuals. After drafts have been produced, revision and editing teams can be set up.

Because you are familiar with the special word-processing needs in your class, you will be able to consider details and examples that will be relevant for future students in your program. Focusing directly on your own environment and special conditions will help both you and the manual's future user.

Exercise 7: Prepare a Pamphlet for Multiple Audiences

An interesting way to explore both the implications of audience analysis and the resources of the computer is to prepare a text that will go to different specified audiences. For example, you might write a pamphlet advertising the opening of a new community centre that offers certain facilities, courses, and personnel. Produce three versions of the pamphlet, each targeting one of the following groups: high-school students, professional adults, or senior citizens. The writing group will decide which information to emphasize and how to present it.

If you can find a real example in your school or community, all the better—testing your pamphlet on real readers will be even more revealing.

Note: You may also vary this assignment by setting up your own group newsletter or producing a similar special-interest publication.

References and Further Reading

Csikzentmihalyi, M. *Beyond Boredom and Anxiety.* San Francisco: Jossey-Bass, 1975.

Eco, Umberto. *Foucault's Pendulum.* ©1988 Gruppo Editoriale Fabbri, Bompiani Sonzogno, Etas SPA—Milano.

Parson, Gail. *Hand in Hand: The Writing Process and the Micro-computer.* Alaska: Alaska Dept. of Education, 1986.

Glossary

ও

abstraction. Words such as "love," "information," "impossibility," and "health" are abstractions. They describe things that we cannot see, taste, touch, smell, or hear, things that do not exist in the form of solid objects or well-defined events. Abstractions allow us to rise above the level of our immediate experience, to categorize and summarize concrete, first-order facts into significant statements about our experience. However, good writers make sure that the steps they take in rising above the level of factual data are orderly and can be traced back to that level.

abstraction ladder. This term describes the gradations of generality between concrete and abstract referents to a particular object.

Example: abstract

- culture
- Western heritage
- a treasure
- a work of art
- a painting
- da Vinci's oil painting of a smiling woman

concrete
- the Mona Lisa

Although the words on this abstraction ladder all refer to the same object, the words at the top of the ladder are high-level abstractions while those at the bottom are concrete words that appeal to the senses.

The exact placement of words on the ladder depends on their degree of **specificity** or **generality.** A word is only specific by contrast with a more general one. Thus, "collie" is specific by contrast with "dog" but general by contrast with "Lassie."

Good writers move up and down the abstraction ladder constantly, using abstract words to create categories, and concrete words to create striking descriptions and to illustrate general points. Using too many abstractions can lead to fuzzy writing that is misunderstood or ignored; using too few abstractions can lead to list-like writing that amounts to little.

analogy. An extended comparison (often expressed as a metaphor or simile) showing that the rule or principle behind one thing holds true for another quite different thing. "The heart is a pump." "My love is like a red, red rose." "Developing a marketing plan for a new hair care product is like riding a roller coaster." Analogies like these can be extended and developed to make an abstract, complex idea clear to the reader by putting it in more familiar, concrete terms.

brainstorming. An idea generation technique based on the premise that the best way to get a good idea is to generate many ideas. The simplest form of brainstorming is listing. Concentrate on a topic and jot down ideas quickly, in whatever order they occur, without stopping to judge the value of those ideas. To keep up the flow, work against time limits; to increase the number of ideas you produce, work in a group.

cliché. In the exuberance of conversation, we all use clichés—words or phrases so familiar that we don't have to think about them: (1) stale comparisons (*busy as a bee, strong as an ox, like a needle in a haystack, like a duck to water*); (2) old sayings (*Too many cooks spoil the broth. It's raining cats and dogs.*); (3) words that we associate with a particular context (*ambience* with a restaurant, *charisma* with a politician); (4) words that are always paired—usually adjective-noun combinations—(*vicious circle, foreseeable future, in-depth analysis, foregone conclusion*). If you can predict the exact word or words that will follow the beginning of a phrase, you probably have a cliché. Such language is acceptable as filler in informal speech, but not in formal prose. Readers expect writers to take the time to replace clichés with fresh, lively words.

clustering. This idea generation technique uses the brain's special knack for connecting images and perceiving patterns. Put your topic in the centre of the page, circle it, and then write down all the images and sensuous words that the topic brings to mind. Circle each image, and draw connecting lines between related images.

After just two or three minutes, stop, scan the entire cluster to find a pattern of meaning revealed in the images, and begin to write. This technique is especially suited to personal and poetic writing.

code words. Words in your writing that you can understand, but that most readers find unclear. To remove such coded language from your public writing, search your paper for highly abstract words, jargon, technical terminology, and words heavily laden with personal associations. Be sure to check your key words—the ones you repeat often and rely upon to carry the meaning of your paper.

collaborative learning. To improve your writing, you need to know how people are likely to respond as they read your words. Therefore, writing workshops use peer tutoring, peer review, co-authoring, taped reader feedback, and other group techniques that allow you to talk with other students and solve problems together. To learn collaboratively, students explore and clarify ideas together, share interpretations and insights, exchange opinions and anecdotes, question each other, and negotiate responses to each other's writing.

conferencing. A teaching strategy used in writing workshops. Your teacher meets with you at various times during the writing process to talk about your paper and again after your paper has been evaluated to consider the results and help you plan for the next paper. Conferences may be brief or long, but they must be individual and they must be oral. Conferencing is an efficient method of using the limited time that teachers have for responding to your writing. Teachers can make far more comments in a brief conference than they can in an equal amount of time spent writing out their reactions to your paper. Moreover, at a conference the teacher has you present to provide information about the paper and to respond to the comments you are receiving.

context. The framework you provide your readers in the introduction to a transactional piece of writing (1) by relating what you are about to say to something they already know and care about, and (2) by setting up expectations that the paper will meet and previewing the paper's argument and its structure. Also used to refer to the setting in which texts are composed and read.

descriptive outlining.   A strategy for checking a reader's view of your draft. (1) Summarize briefly what each paragraph or section of your paper *says* and what it *does*. (2) Compare your outline with one made by a reader to discover where you are not communicating your message.

diction.   Word choice. Effective writers avoid trite, clichéd diction. They select precise, original words that are appropriate for their subject and their readers.

discourse community.   People in all academic and professional areas are expected to speak and write in standard English. Still, people in different fields write in different styles: they use different formats and frame their arguments in different ways. A lawyer does not write like a scientist. A paper for an English course uses language in different ways than one written for a sociology course. Any specialized group of people develops its own common ways of using language. We call these groups discourse communities. As a writer, you need to recognize what community you are writing in and learn how its writing conventions differ from those of other communities.

document cycling.   The growing practice of business and technical writers circulating drafts-in-progress to their colleagues for comments that will help the writer revise the draft to everyone's satisfaction.

editing for key words.   The strategy of clarifying and tightening long, awkward sentences by first identifying the meaning-bearing words and then rephrasing the sentence to leave out all non-essential material.

euphemism.   An abstract or "polite" expression used to describe a harsh or unpleasant reality. Handle euphemisms with care. Some may serve an important social purpose; for example, replacing "crippled" with "physically challenged" may give your readers a more positive view of people who fight handicaps. However, many euphemisms are really doublespeak. They hide or distort the truth in the interest of the writer: calling an embezzler a "white collar criminal" makes serious crime seem less serious; calling rape a "sexual assault" leaves the reader unclear about exactly what happened; and describing the dumping of toxic waste and garbage off the coast of New Jersey as "deep ocean placement" makes it sound like a scientific, sanitary, and sane government policy. To create honest and informative prose, avoid euphemisms that mislead your reader.

format. The general physical appearance of a paper, the way the text is organized on the page and presented to the reader. In designing a format, you consider such things as typeface, spacing, margins, visuals, headings, glosses, boldfacing, and underlining.

guided imagery. An idea generation technique that asks you to explore issues not merely by thinking about them but by imagining them as if they are events taking place in the present. If, for example, you want to write about *learning*, you may begin by thinking of a time you really learned something—a skill, a belief, a fact—whether in or outside of school. By carefully recreating the original situation, replaying it in your mind, recapturing the feelings, ideas, sounds, colours, and words associated with it, you may find concrete details, surprising connections, and sharp insights for your paper.

idea tree. A strategy for organizing ideas by dividing and subdividing a topic or thesis down into its parts. These parts may be subissues, reasons, causes, effects, steps or any other details that can support and develop the topic. The branching design of an idea tree helps writers to visualize the logical relationships between their major and minor points. Besides helping writers *plan* the order in which to present their ideas, these trees can help them *generate ideas* by showing them where their arguments need support or development. Trees can also help writers *revise* their papers. In peer review sessions, writers can test the underlying structure of each other's drafts by pulling out the main points and using them to build a tree. If the reader's tree does not match the writer's tree, revision may be necessary.

jargon. (1) technical or specialized language peculiar to a particular profession or community. (2) a style of writing characterized by wordiness, abstractions, euphemisms, clichés, and the excessive use of the passive voice.

mapping. A nonlinear form of brainstorming. Start with a large sheet of paper. (A scrap sheet of computer printout paper does nicely.) Put your key word in the centre of the page and free associate strings of words outward from that centre. Use lines to connect related words. Do not limit yourself to images and sense words as you do when you are clustering: write down *all* your associations. And do not stop after only two or three minutes: make the strings as long as you can.

operational goal. A planning strategy that focuses on your reader and your purpose for writing. To write an operational goal, ask yourself these questions: (1) Who is my primary reader? (2) What effect do I want to have on this reader? (How do I want the reader to think or act after reading my paper?) (3) How will I achieve this effect?

The answers to your questions may produce a statement such as the one that follows. Note that it is, in effect, a mini-plan for your paper.

> "I want to convince university students that taking the time to develop good fitness and eating habits will pay off, not only in better physical and emotional health, but also in better academic performance. To do this, I will (1) Review fitness and eating habits of typical students (perhaps include some amusing anecdotes); (2) Cite statistics on student health problems (use data from campus medical centre); (3) Explain the connection between fitness and grades; etc."

parallel structure. The principle that a writer should express matching items in the same grammatical form. Parallel structures make clear an essential likeness of meaning or a sharp contrast.

Parallel form: I like swimming, roller skating, and tennis.

Not parallel: I like swimming, to roller skate, and tennis.

Parallel: People are usually willing to give advice but not inclined to take it.

Not Parallel: People like giving advice to others, but to take advice is not something they like.

Use parallel form for (1) items in a series or a list, (2) expressions of comparison or contrast, and (3) words or expressions joined either by co-ordinating conjunctions (*and, but, or, nor, for, yet, so*) or by correlative conjunctions (*either ... or, both ... and, neither ... nor, not only ... but also*).

peer review. The process by which students comment on each other's drafts to help the author revise her or his work.

plagiarism. The theft of ideas or words; passing off someone else's thinking or writing as your own.

the plain style. A style characterized by short words of Anglo-Saxon origin, very few abstractions, direct and economical wording, and forceful, active-voice verbs.

problem analysis. A questioning technique for identifying and exploring problems by (1) discovering the key issue or main conflict, (2) distinguishing subissues, (3) tracing cause-effect patterns, (4) considering alternatives, and (5) devising an effective solution.

reader-based prose. Writing that effectively communicates its meaning to a reader. This prose is characterized by (1) a shared language and shared context (rather than coded language), and (2) an issue-centred structure built on logical and hierarchical relationships between ideas (rather than a replay of the writer's discovery process).

rhythm. Poets often create a regular and harmonious pattern of sounds by arranging their words in a careful sequence (metrical pattern) of measured beats. Writers of English prose do not use such measured units of accented and unaccented syllables, but their words, whether read aloud or silently, reveal their own subtle rhythm or cadence. Simply by repeating and varying the length of phrases, clauses, and sentences, prose writers create rhythmic patterns that heighten the meaning of their words.

strategy. A plan or method for reaching a specific goal. Writers reach their goals and solve complex problems by employing subtle strategies that increase the likelihood of success, not by observing simple rules.

style. The way a writer uses language, including such things as diction, syntax, and the length of sentences and paragraphs.

synergy. The combined action of two or more agents to achieve an effect of which each is individually incapable. Thus, individual writers generate more ideas in group brainstorming sessions than they do alone, not merely because there are more people with ideas, but because each person is stimulated by the ideas that others put forth.

syntax. The rules that govern the way in which words may be put together to form phrases and sentences. English syntax is one of a writer's greatest resources, offering a variety of ways to express any idea.

tagmemics. An idea generation technique that asks you to view a subject from the perspective of a particle (a unit); a wave (a process); and a field (a context). To use this strategy, ask yourself the following questions: (1) What are the features of my subject that make it what it is and not something else? (2) How does my subject change over time or in different settings? How much can it change and not become something else? (3) Is my subject part of some larger system?

taped reader feedback. A revision strategy that combines peer review with oral reading. Ask a colleague to read your draft into a tape recorder and to respond to it in whatever way seems appropriate. When you replay the tape, you should hear the reader stumbling over unclear parts of your text or rereading them several times to comprehend their meaning. You may hear the reader laugh at an amusing line or agree with one of your stronger arguments. This feedback helps you see the strengths and weaknesses in your draft.

text. The actual wording of a written work.

transactional writing. Writing whose primary purpose is to get things done: to inform, advise, persuade, or instruct a reader.

writer-based prose. Writing that intends to communicate meaning effectively to a reader, but fails to do so. Such writing usually fails because (1) the writer is talking in a code that the reader cannot understand (using jargon, fuzzy abstractions, and personal references); and (2) the writer is structuring the text around her or his own discovery process (using a chronological narrative or survey pattern that does not reveal the logical and hierarchical relationships between the ideas in the text).

writer's block. The inability to begin or continue a writing task. The strategy most often recommended for breaking through writer's block is freewriting. Working on the principle of continuity—our natural tendency to link each sentence to the one before it—freewriting helps writers coax out ideas. It relieves them of the stress of worrying about correctness, formats, readers, or any of the other concerns that caused them to be blocked in the first place.

Index

ॐ